Valerie Polakow
1984

Reading, writing and resistance

Critical Social Thought

Series editor: Michael W. Apple
Professor of Curriculum and Instruction and of Educational Policy Studies, University of Wisconsin-Madison

Reading, writing and resistance

Adolescence and labor in a junior high school

Robert B. Everhart

Routledge & Kegan Paul
Boston, London, Melbourne and Henley

First published in 1983
by Routledge & Kegan Paul plc
9 Park Street, Boston, Mass. 02108, USA,
296 Beaconsfield Parade, Middle Park,
Melbourne 3206, Australia,
39 Store Street, London WC1E 7DD, and
Broadway House, Newtown Road,
Henley-on-Thames, Oxon RG9 1EN
Set in Linotron 202 Times, 10 on 12pt by
Rowland Phototypesetting Ltd, Bury St Edmunds, Suffolk
Printed in the United States of America

Library of Congress Cataloging in Publication Data

Everhart, Robert B.

Reading, writing, and resistance.
(Critical social thought)
Includes bibliographical references.
1. School environment – United States. 2. Junior high school students – United States – Conduct of life. 3. Adolescence. 4. Community and school – United States. 5. Education – Economic aspects – United States. I. Title. II. Series.
LC210.5.E94 1983 373.18 82-25068

ISBN 0-7100-9450-7

Contents

Series editor's preface

Within the last decade, the analysis of what schools contribute to the social reproduction of an unequal society has progressed at an exceptional pace. Early work was content to debunk liberal assumptions that schools necessarily led to widespread class, gender, and race mobility. Later investigations attempted to show how our educational system, through its hidden curriculum, 'produced' people who ultimately and relatively unquestioningly fit into the social division of labor outside the school.[1] While establishing an important grounding for our further understanding of the connections between schooling and the larger society, we now know these investigations had a number of conceptual and political problems and were rather mechanistic, assuming that there was a direct correspondence between culture and consciousness, on the one hand, and the inexorable power and needs of capitalism, on the other.[2]

The problems with this research on education and social reproduction actually mirrored a debate that was being carried on in the wider community of people who were concerned with the issue of reproduction. Here the major question was 'What is the relationship "between" base and superstructure?' Could the characteristics, discourse, and activity of people and institutions be easily read off against the needs of an economy? The debate still rages over how one answers these questions and indeed over whether they are the correct questions.[3] One thing that has arisen out of the discussions, however, is the recognition of the utter importance of the *problem* of culture, of the need to understand the 'relative autonomy' of culture – in particular the self-formative cultural production engaged in by classed, raced, and gendered actors.

This is the issue that Everhart focuses on. His book is a study of the contradictions of 'agency,' of how people (here working-class students in a junior high school in the United States) act on the terrain of the school in ways that both support and deny the cultural and economic requirements of capital at one and the same time. As such, it is not only a substantive contribution to the literature on schooling and reproduction, but to the more abstract issue of how we are to interpret the ties between popular culture and our social formation.

In many ways, Everhart's study is like Paul Willis's exemplary volume, *Learning to Labour*.[4] Where Everhart goes further, though, is to enter into the school itself, to describe in detail for us the culture that is produced by the very interaction between the class cultures of these adolescents and the formal curriculum and social organization of the institution.

Yet *Reading, Writing and Resistance* has significance in another way as well, in the problem of how we study what happens in schools in general and what schools we study in particular. The book is a missing link in a number of ways. First, there is little detailed research on education in one's early adolescent years. This is despite the fact that a very large segment of students in, say, the United States spend anywhere from two to four years in middle schools and junior high schools. Second, even when studies of such schools exist, they tend not to focus on student life within the institution, on the lived culture that is so visible to anyone who stops and looks at what happens within the day-to-day lives of students, administrators, and teachers as they interact in the school.

The book actually stands between two poles. There has been rapid acceptance of ethnographic research strategies in education and an accompanying growth in sophistication in how one uses them. Yet, while I would be the first to applaud such work, most ethnographies ignore the fact that schools do not sit isolated from the local and national political economy, from class, race, and gender structures, and from the accumulation and legitimation needs of the state. They tend to study microcosms, but without attempting the necessarily difficult task of theorizing their data. In so doing, their analyses are truncated, divorced from the economic, political, and cultural structures that organize that microcosm.

On the other hand, researchers that have sought to place education within these larger structures have fallen prey to a different problem. They have tended to treat schools as black boxes, measuring input and output and then linking that output to the relations of domination and exploitation in, for instance, the labor market later on. Here, what is missing is something I hinted at earlier, the way outcomes are *produced*, the lived culture of the school. In essence, *Reading, Writing and Resistance* puts these two interests together. It places an investigation of the daily lives of students within an analysis of the connections that exist between these lives and what exists outside the school in an advanced capitalist society. In order to see how it accomplishes this, however, we need to situate the volume itself within that larger debate over reproduction I discussed earlier.

A good deal of the literature on the way our institutions reproduce ideological domination assumes that individuals as classed, raced, and gendered subjects 'take it all in,' so to speak. There are no disjunctures, no contradictions, no active involvement in the reinterpretation and partial transformation of dominant discourses.[5] This is not only inadequate as a theory of class dynamics, but it also radically reduces how ideologies actually operate. It reifies them, making them into 'things' that people do or do not possess. This is wholly unsatisfactory. As Therborn puts it:

> It seems more accurate and fruitful to see ideologies, not as possessions, as ideas possessed, but as *social processes*. That is, to see them as complex social processes of 'interpellation' or address, speaking to us. In these continuous processes ideologies overlap, compete and clash, drown or reinforce each other. The actual operation of ideology in contemporary society is better illustrated by the cacophony of sounds and signs of a big city street than by a text serenely communicating with the solitary reader, or the teacher or TV-personality addressing a quiet, domesticated audience.[6]

However, while ideologies 'speak' to us in a complicated manner, we also do part of the talking. That is, 'ideologies never address (interpellate) a naked subject.' Real individuals like ourselves are 'always already constructed as culturally classed and sexed agents, already have a complexly formed subjectivity.' Thus, there is always a ground upon which ideologies work, the ground of culture.[7] In essence, people are not passive. They resist, mediate, and transform – often in cultural not political ways – the forms of domination and exploitation that they experience.

For example, studies of the labor process, of the complex culture that has developed out of the conditions people experience in their daily work in our offices, shops and factories, document this continuously. As has been argued elsewhere:

> Rather than the labor process being totally controlled by management, rather than hard and fast structures of authority and norms of punctuality and compliance, one sees a complex work culture. This very work culture provides important grounds for worker resistance, collective action, informal control of pacing and skill, and reasserting one's humanity. Men and women workers seem engaged in overt and informal activity that is missed when we only talk in reproductive terms.[8]

These points are quite important, for something becomes quite clear when one examines what actually happens in the labor process itself. The actual lives of men and women in our offices and factories paint a different picture than what one is led to expect from either the literature on ideological domination or on the hidden curriculum where a simple correspondence exists between schools and the economy in some straightforward way. For rather than finding workers at all times being guided by the cash nexus, by authority, productivity, and the logics of capital, they often contradict and transform existing modes of control into opportunities for resistance and for maintaining their own informal norms which guide the labor process. These resistances may have contradictory results. They may even sometimes ultimately enhance the power of management. But they exist and are historically significant attempts to control one's own life on the job. If we approach the work of students in schools as a labor process, as Everhart suggests we should, then these very points should help us understand what happens within the walls of that institution too.

But how are we to examine the ways such cultural forms work, how agents are not totally interpellated and have some agency? Paul Willis's argument that only ethnographic research can respond to the complexity and relative autonomy of lived culture makes this point rather clearly.

> An ethnographic method shouts at us that however persuasive and inclusive some of the theoretical arguments concerning the formation of the subject they can by no means fully account for

> real, solid, warm, moving and acting bodies in actual situations. Ethnographic techniques, however, necessarily expose the 'researcher' to the real tensions and struggles of social situations and are well suited to picking up struggles, resistances, and conflict of a located direct and confrontational style – even where, perhaps, against the grain of theoretical predisposition.[9]

It is exactly this sensitivity to tensions and resistances that Everhart brings to his own research since it should be clear that a similar perspective on how there are no 'naked subjects' being passively interpellated should guide our analyses of education. In fact, other recent ethnographic investigations have demonstrated that rather than being places where ideologies are imposed on students, schools are sites where these social processes are produced, but not in any straightforward manner. Like my previous points about the workplace, the 'labor process' of schooling is filled with cultural forms of resistance, forms that are only visible if one gets inside the lived culture of students.

As Willis, for instance, shows in his study of a group of students from a particular segment of the working class, such 'lads' often expressly reject the world of the school. The formal and hidden curricula considered legitimate by the institution bear little resemblance to the actual world of work, to life on the street, to the facts of generalized labor that these students experience through their parents, acquaintances, and their own part-time jobs. By rejecting the 'legitimate' culture within the school, by affirming manual work and physicality, the students affirm their own class background and subjectivity and at the same time act in a way that constitutes a rather realistic assessment that, as a class, schooling will not enable them to go much further than they already are.

This partial 'penetration' into the role of schooling in cultural and economic reproduction is paradoxical, however. By rejecting school knowledge, the students are in essence rejecting mental labor. They, thus, reproduce in transfigured form the distinction between mental and manual labor. While they are affirming and acting on the strengths of particular aspects of working-class culture, they are caught in a real structural contradiction by hardening one of the principles guiding the social division of labor and by partly reproducing the sexual division of labor as well.[10] What we see here, hence, is the complicated relation between student resistance to school culture and their '*qualified* acceptance of future roles in capitalist production.'[11]

Everhart's volume shows similar things, though again with more attention being paid to the dynamics within the school building itself. The students he examines are primarily from a different segment of the working class, one that is 'higher up' on the occupational ladder than the lads in Willis's work. Like the lads, these junior high school students spend a large amount of their time 'goofing off' and re-creating cultural forms that give them some degree of power in the school setting. While these students do not totally reject the formal curriculum, they give the school only the barest minimum work required and then try to minimize even those requirements. These students, like the lads, resist. They give only what is necessary not to endanger the possible mobility some of them might have. Yet, they 'know' – again on a cultural not on a conscious or political level – that this mobility is only a possibility. It is not guaranteed at all. Most of them will, in fact, probably remain within the economic trajectories of their parents and the class fractions they represent.

These elements of self-selection, of cultural forms and their accompanying resistance, both reproduce and contradict the ideological and economic needs of the larger society. And what is of great import, they also document the relatively autonomous nature of culture.

Everhart makes another contribution, however, one that is a useful counterbalance to some of the theories of economic reproduction. He points to the place that the actual knowledge in the curriculum plays in accounting for what schools do socially. That is, unlike a number of the political economists of education who neglect the formal curriculum, Everhart more clearly recognizes some of the complex interconnections between the hidden curriculum of the school and the form and content of what the school considers important knowledge. It is the *form* such knowledge takes that concerns him the most, though. For the very way the curriculum is organized and its connections to the social relations of the school provide the terrain upon which a student counter-school culture is produced. It is in the tension between, as he calls them, the 'reified knowledge' of the school and the 'regenerative knowledge' of the students that we can see this most clearly. Everhart's interpretation of this tension depends upon and integrates two conceptually similar perspectives: a materialist theory of the labor process drawn from Marx and the connections between labor and symbolic action drawn from Habermas. The very act of attempting to integrate these two related theories is an important step and provides a provocative intellectual framework for Everhart's analysis.

Even if the reader is less concerned with the intricacies of theoretical deliberations about the role of education in reproducing and contradicting dominant class, race, and gender relations and is simply concerned with what goes on in schools, *Reading, Writing and Resistance* deserves to be read. It catches the day-to-day interactions between teachers and students and among the students themselves in ways that show the subtle pressures, the cliques, the vitality, the boredom and the humor that make up the social reality of student life in so many of our schools.

It is the last phenomenon – the humor with which students often approach their assignments, their teachers, and each other – that is so very visible in this volume. The humor may at times be cruel or sexist, but it is often very funny. Yet just as playing elaborate games and joking often serves as a fundamental organizing principle on the shop floor in factories or in offices where labor is so often alienated,[12] so too does the students' humor serve the similar functions of reasserting one's control over the time and space of an environment where they too have little formal control. The actual place of humor and play as cultural forms of resistance needs a good deal more empirical work. Everhart's treatment of them here is certainly a step in that direction. By dealing seriously with topics such as those I have mentioned and others, Everhart has written a book of interest both to practitioners and scholars in education and, just as importantly, to those people in the larger progressive community who are deeply concerned with questions of ideology, culture, and economy.

Michael W. Apple
University of Wisconsin

Author's preface

This is a story of everyday life in a junior high school – a story I wrote from two years of fieldwork in one such school. The study focuses upon 'everyday' life of junior high schools, and is a chronicle of the daily routine of students and, to a much lesser degree, teachers.

The book is written for teachers and administrators in junior (and senior) high schools in the hope that it may help them to understand more completely the environment in which they work. A person immersed in any situation finds it difficult to see the nuances of that particular situation because they are too close to it. By being an outsider of sorts, I was able to call into question many of the activities and perspectives that teachers and pupils took for granted. Just as an outsider may have helped me see my role as a fieldworker in a junior high school in sharper perspective, so I hope this book will help teachers and administrators to view their roles more critically.

The people who facilitated this study are numerous and deserve more credit than can possibly be given. Wayne Doyle, the director of the project under whose auspices the study was done, supported the study and gave unyielding support to it when others doubted its usefulness. The educators of the Jefferson School District gave me more cooperation than I deserved and facilitated my every wish. I came to know many of them as good-willed human beings whose friendship I still treasure. The people of the Jefferson community also were warm and supportive, and afforded me and my family many opportunities to know them well.

I also wish to acknowledge the support of Raymond Coward (now of the University of Vermont) and Norman Gold of the National Institute of Education, the agency that provided financial support for the study. Ray, Norm, and I had many healthy discussions about the direction of the study, and I trust this product justifies their faith in it.

Two small but timely grants from the University of California and the National Institute of Education assisted me to move the manuscript along in its final stages. Michael Apple worked with me to sharpen the focus of the document; his comments and encouragement were most helpful and timely. Special thanks are due also to Rena Atalig, Debi Herbrand, Suzi Hettick, Connie Hoover, Ginny Walters, and Jenel Virden, the project secretaries who so faithfully typed the thousands of pages of field-notes, and typed numerous early drafts. Lorraine Del Duca, Mary Griffin, Susan Mitchell, and Sue and Channing Hillway assisted in typing of subsequent drafts completed at the University of California. My wife, Sarah, served as my sounding board throughout the study, and persevered through the long hours of fieldwork, the anxieties of wondering if anything worthwhile would result from all the work, and was an especially sharp critic and editor. I am most grateful for her perspicacity.

Finally, to the students of Harold Spencer who by now have graduated from high school, and to the staff, I give my deepest and most profound thanks and admiration. For obvious reasons they must go unnamed, but they know who they are. This book belongs to them; I am glad that I could write it, and thank them for letting me be a part of it.

Robert B. Everhart
1983

1 Introduction

> You're too close. Back off and survey the big picture and old mysteries will clear up for you and other mysteries will arrive (*The Last Whole Earth Catalog*).

What are the early adolescent years (12 to 15) about? This is a question adults continually search to answer in our modern society. No doubt early adolescence is an age that evidences many rewards as youngsters reach out toward adulthood, increasingly demonstrating their abilities to cope with the challenges and responsibilities of that status. As these adult traits become more evident, we see those early adolescent years as necessary precursors of emergent maturity. However, the ages of 12 to 15 also demonstrate many frustrations for the youngsters themselves as well as the adults who live and work with them. Such frustrations stem from the difficulty many young people have with the demands of responsibility in the context within which that responsibility is defined, the alternating reversion to childlike behavior that parallels increased maturity, and the problems growing out of an almost fanatical allegiance to one's peers – often to the exclusion of family and adult significant others. Many a parent shudders in anticipation of such behavior, and teachers often cry 'good grief' as they attempt to educate the members of this age group.

The frustrations of young people in this age group have for generations drawn the attention of societal leaders, educators, and psychologists. For example, recognition of some of the above-mentioned characteristics of early adolescence has led to the development, in the twentieth century, of what at one time were unknown organizational arrangements (since implemented) to focus on the specialized needs of young people of this age. Counseling services, youth agencies such as the Scouts, and informal educative agencies such as 4-H are among such arrangements.

Perhaps most significant and pervasive among these new agencies was the development of the junior high school, an institution the purpose of which has been to provide specialized educative services and programs to all youngsters of this age group. Here was an organizational form that arose as an institutionalized response to some of the very same questions and observations we have today about early adolescence, and a brief examination of its original purpose seems in order.

The junior high school

The first three junior high schools in the US were organized in 1909 and 1910 in Berkeley, California, and Columbus, Ohio.[1] Two factors explain the evolution of this new institution: the perceived need for student retention and the growing recognition of adolescence as a separate stage in the life cycle of youth.

Educators in the early twentieth century increasingly were concerned about the holding power of schools during the last years of a student's elementary career. Some studies indicated that student withdrawals were most numerous in the sixth and seventh grade and that this occurred because of a lack of interest in school. Other research revealed that, for every 100 children beginning first grade, only eight remained by the end of eighth grade.[2] Perhaps the most influential studies on student retention were those conducted by Edward Thorndike and later Leonard Ayres. Thorndike estimated that only 25 per cent of the school children remained in school long enough to learn basic English, spell simple terms, or perform the basic arithmetic operations, and that only 10 per cent graduated from high school.[3] Ayres's research confirmed much of what Thorndike said.[4] These and other studies defined the problem in terms of an unrealistic curriculum and the poor organization of most school systems.

The retention studies fit in with the emergent theories of G. Stanley Hall, a psychologist whose work was a second important force in the creation of junior high schools. In his two-volume work entitled *Adolescence*, Hall pictured the child beyond the age of 12 as awakening from a sleep, unsure of the influences that may have affected him while in that sleep. Hall says:

> There are new repulsions felt toward home and school, and truancy and runaways abound. The social instincts awaken. . . . Youth awakens to a new world and understands neither it nor himself. The whole future of life depends on how the new powers now given suddenly and in profusion are husbanded and directed.[5]

Hall and others of the era popularized the distinctiveness of adolescence as a definite part of the life cycle and, owing to his belief in the unique aspects of adolescence, he questioned practices of schooling wherein all students studied the same subjects in the same way, the fact that schools did not recognize the special problems of the adolescent, and the lack of specialists trained to handle the peculiar problems of adolescence. Hall's work had practical implications for the reorganization of schools, for it precipitated the creation of new organizational forms in order to meet the perceived needs of youth in the adolescent stage of development. The junior high school emerged as one of those new organizational forms.

What, then, has and is supposed to make junior high schools different? What justifies their existence as a separate entity between elementary schools and high schools? Those reasons listed below seem most common.[6]

1 It should offer an educational program designed for a particular age group – young adolescents.

2 It should challenge the intellectual abilities and interests of young adolescents by providing a program with more depth than is appropriate for pupils in elementary school.

3 It should continue instruction begun in elementary school in fundamental skills and basic knowledge.

4 It should be concerned with all aspects of growth and development – intellectual, physical, emotional, character, citizenship, social, personal, and cultural.

5 It should prepare young adolescents for more independence, self-responsibility, and leadership as they participate in more complex social groups and in the life of the larger school and civic community.

6 It should provide opportunities for pupils to explore present interests and talents and encourage them to identify new interests and talents which may lead to further education, vocational careers, and cultural, intellectual, and avocational pursuits.

7 It should provide for the guidance and counseling of young adolescents about such problems as achievement, plans for further education, vocational careers, boy–girl relationships, citizenship, and preparations for later adolescence and adulthood.

8 It should provide a diverse educational program, appropriate for a wide variety of backgrounds, interests, attitudes, abilities, and needs.

9 It should provide a general education for all rather than specialized teaching directed toward particular educational and vocational goals.

10 It is a transitional school, taking the pupil from the elementary school with its simple organization and program, and sending him to the senior high with its multiple educational objectives, comprehensive curricula and courses, and complex administrative organization and practices.

But what, in fact, is an educational program designed for young adolescents? How does such a program evidence 'concern for all aspects of growth and development?' How do junior high schools prepare young adolescents for more 'independence, self-responsibility, and leadership' as they participate in the life of the civic community? Perhaps most importantly, in what ways does the junior high school 'guide and counsel' young adolescents about preparations for adulthood? What is the conception of adulthood for which they are being prepared? These are important questions with obvious widespread social as well as educational consequences.

Unfortunately, answers to such questions are largely unavailable because junior high schools have been ignored by individuals who investigate life within the halls and classrooms of our schools. While we have works that document in some detail how both adults and students operate in either elementary schools or senior high schools,[7] there is no study that focuses upon junior high schools for an extensive period of time and attempts to describe what life is like for the participants in such an environment.[8] Likewise, the life of early adolescents either in or outside of schools is neither richly nor comprehensively described in the research literature. In fact, early adolescence is the least studied and understood stage of the life cycle in contemporary industrialized and urbanized societies, a point emphasized by one researcher who has stated that 'adolescence is inadequately represented in our present research efforts, and early adolescence even more so.'[9]

This study and the findings reported in it should serve as a useful corrective to that inadequacy, especially since the literature is so silent on the topic.

Related studies

While there exist no studies pertinent to the congruence between the lives of early adolescents and the manner in which the organizational arrangements of the junior high school does justice to these lives, there do exist some research studies that attempt to answer questions of a similar vein about students before they arrive in the junior high school and after they have left it. Examining some of these select studies helps place the lives of early adolescents in context. We turn first to the student in the elementary grades.

Jackson has spent considerable time in elementary schools and has concluded that life for young children in such organizations is quite overwhelming.[10] In most respects, the effects of school cannot help but be overwhelming when 'aside from sleeping and perhaps playing, there is no other activity that occupies as much of the child's time as that involved in attending school' (p. 5). Jackson notes that the average elementary school student spends about 7,000 hours in school over a six-year period of time, and that therein something must be learned. What is learned is partly conditioned by the organizational context within which knowledge is disseminated, and the presence of such a context raises the importance of a number of issues important in their effect on student life in elementary schools. Among these issues is the simple fact that learning occurs in a somewhat 'crowded' setting.

Crowds are important, for, as Jackson explains, all student learning activities in the school will exist within a group setting. As such, learning activities do not happen spontaneously and immediately, but usually are delayed as the activities of twenty-five or more young people and at least one adult are coordinated. Students thus learn early that the sequence of educational life is conditional in part by how it affects and is affected by other people. Equally important is the related fact that activities that one means to have happen may not, simply because the demands of all people cannot be met within a group context. Someone (usually the teacher) thus must make decisions about which activities will occur, realizing at the same time that it is possible that legitimate 'educational' activities may be precluded in such decisions. A third dimension of crowds concerns the practice of 'interruption,' and the consequent realization by students that learning can and is interrupted by organizational contingencies. Interruptions occur for teachers when they must stop what they are doing and provide assistance to other students or reprimand students; such occur for students as they are engaged in one kind of work then are instructed to turn to another or when a clock or bell tells them it is time for a recess, assembly, or lunch. A final dimension of schooling in the context of crowding concerns the constant presence of social distraction within the classroom. In classrooms (unlike other large collections of people) the same students are present daily and come to know each other quite well. This familiarity provides a basis of social interaction among students, the presence of which may be seen to be distracting to teachers as well as students. Yet the pull to interaction may grow because students share a similar experience in the school, as Jackson states:

> Students are there (in school) whether they want to be or not, and the work on which they are expected to concentrate often is not of their own choosing. Thus the pull to communicate with others is somewhat stronger in the classroom than in other crowded situations (p. 17).[11]

An examination of the consequences of crowds in school thus reveals that student life occurs within certain predictable contextual factors pertinent to schools. Said differently, student life in school occurs within an organizational context wherein students 'learn' the proper context for their own involvement. As they learn this, certain unanticipated consequences arise, and Jackson's comment that 'the pull to communicate is likely somewhat stronger in the classroom than in other crowded situations' looms in importance. For Jackson also goes on to note that this communication results in student inattention to the demands of schooling, and that the amount of attention in schools 'is often less than meets the eye' (p. 10). This minimal attention, in turn, may have its roots 'not only in the content of the lesson nor in the psychological deficiencies within the student but rather in the institutional experience called "going to school"' (p. 111).[12] Indeed, studies in high schools bear this out.

When we turn to studies of the student social structure in schools after junior high schools, two works stand out as contributing to this understanding. These investigations reinforce some of the conclusions reached by Jackson – particularly that 'going to school' leads to unique patterns of student life that become ever more apparent in the secondary school.

The first research we will review is that by Wayne Gordon, conducted in a mid-western high school in the 1950s.[13] In this study, Gordon examined the hypothesis that 'the dominant motivation of the high school student is to maintain a general social status within the organization of the high school' (p. 1). Gordon was interested in testing the premise that the chief motivation of students in high school was that of being liked and accepted by peers, and that such motivation in turn affected important dimensions of student life. Although Gordon conducted the study in one school, he found that the quest for prestige occurred mostly through the 'informal structure' of personal relationships, meaning that the students created their own mechanisms to control the distribution of rewards most important to them. Thus the 'pull for communication' noted by Jackson in the elementary school as a trend in its nascent stages, has become dominant by the time the student reaches high school, for herein the students have created a complex, separate, and well-articulated network in which to carry out that communication.

Gordon then makes some interesting observations about the relationship between the student prestige structure (part of the informal structure of the school) and class requirements, grades, and academic values (aspects of the formal structure of the school). While it is true that students in school demonstrated increasing concern for grades with each level they continued in school, still 'the social position of the student in the school seems least significantly related to grade achievement.' (p. 131). This is not to say that grades were unimportant in social prestige, for it is true that such prestige was determined as the result of a variety of factors. Still, the importance of such grades in and of themselves was not an important factor used by students in ranking student groups and ascertaining where the groups stood in relation to each other. Yet even the fact that grades generally improve as the student stays in school does not necessarily signify the growing importance of grades to students. Gordon maintains that there is a subtle but critical difference between grade achievement and grade attainment. In this sense, grade *achievement* is a valid measure of academic knowledge (at least to the extent that grades measure that knowledge) while grade *attainment* may reflect the ability of students to 'psych out' the grading process and thus to attain higher grades.

A second study in a somewhat similar vein to that of Gordon's is Coleman's *The Adolescent Society* which examined many of the same dimensions of adolescent subcultures as did the work by Gordon, but in more detail and through a greatly expanded sample.[14] Coleman, in his examination of ten schools, found the presence of social groups as had Gordon, and documented most conclusively that informal prestige was most frequently accorded to athletes (for boys), to those who were part of the 'in crowd,' and for those who were leaders in school activities. Among boys, high grades rated fourth (just above having a nice car) among six items ranked as most important for high prestige; for girls, it rated fifth (below having nice clothes).

And how do these friendship prestige patterns fit in with the academic issues that are supposed to be the basis of school life? Certainly, the value of 'getting good grades,' 'intelligence,' and other such virtues is not absent in these ten schools but, as in Gordon's study, their importance is minimized as a critical factor contributing towards one's being 'looked up to.' In fact, Coleman reports that the image of good scholarship as a factor in high school prestige actually diminishes during the first two years of high school while, at the same time, the importance of informal prestige generating mechanisms – such as athletics and clothes – increase during those two years.

What do these two studies tell us about student life in formal organizations called schools? Certainly we now begin to see that any organization such as a school consists of two separate but interrelated dimensions. One we call the 'formal organization' and it pertains to all activities related to the manifest accomplishment of intended outcomes desired by the organization. For the school, this consists of all activities that relate to learning and its attendant activities. A second dimension we call the informal organization, and this is the organizational structure that arises from social interaction within the formal organization, but also a structure that the formal organization does not intend or predict. Student social prestige structures and the consequent social groups of students are examples of these.

Coleman and Gordon have both pointed out that the informal organization of students may not facilitate (and in fact may detract from) the formal goals of the school. This is true to the extent that the school is established primarily toward the collective education of individual students and that attaining this educational level, while it may benefit the individual and increase the status of the school organization, does not necessarily affect directly the status of the informal groups of students within the school. Because of this, academic issues are not particularly important for prestige maintenance for social groups while, on the other hand, athletics, clothes, and being popular are. These latter attributes are skills or characteristics borne by the students themselves and which can be increased or decreased *vis à vis* other groups in the school. Academic qualities, on the other hand, are judged by adult standards and hold to individual students rather than groups of students. It is for these reasons that academic matters, part of the formal structure of the school, often do not correspond with the values of the students as they are part of an informal organizational network.

The studies of secondary schools examined thus far emphasize the formal and informal social prestige structure of student life in school – who associates with whom and on what basis. These studies, however, tell us little about the process by which student life in school is carried out and continued – the ebb and flow of daily life as it has meaning to the participants in the school. Yet this day-to-day living is of the utmost importance for in that process the school is formed, maintained, and re-created. Studies that focus upon the social dynamics of student life, then, will occupy our attention in the remainder of this section.

Investigations of this genre actually go back to 1932 when Waller's classic work was published.[15] In this book, Waller proceeds from the assumption that the school 'is a unity of interacting personalities who meet in the school and who are bound together in an organic relation' (p. 6). Yet the presence of this organic relationship does not necessarily symbolize a smoothly functioning system of mutual contribution. In fact, the very theme of Waller's study is that this organic relation is not necessarily stable but rather is continually threatened by forces from within and external to the school. Thus 'there is a constant interaction between the elements of the authoritative system (of the school); the school is continually threatened because it is autocratic; and it has to be autocratic because it is threatened' (p. 11).

That this constant interaction between authoritative systems exists arises in part from the presence of a set of separate cultures within the school. These cultures (both adult and student) are formed, according to Waller, because one of the school's functions is to pass on the cultural standards and behaviours of the larger society and local community to students who may not always accept or be interested in those standards. Because of this, cultural conflict in schools emanates from two different sources. The first source, as we already have noted, exists as teachers represent a culture of the wider society while students, on the other hand, may owe cultural allegiance to the local community or the community of the family. This is most obvious today in those schools heavily populated by minority teachers, sometimes in rural schools where school–community differences may be more pronounced, and in those communities where the philosophical beliefs of the community may be at variance with those of the educators (such as over issues of sex education, theories of evolution, etc.). Waller notes a second and more pervasive source of cultural conflict in schools – one that arises from differences between the adult and student community: 'teachers are adults and students are not, so that teachers are the bearers of the cultural society of adults, and try to impose that culture upon students, whereas students represent the indigenous culture of the group of children' (p. 104).

The presence of such conflicts is one of the key reasons for the evolution and strength of primary groups among students. Such primary groups, or peer groups, form the structural basis for the student culture and grow out of the manner in which students come to define their role within the school. To the extent then that students place increased emphasis upon primary group associations and peer stratification (as noted by Gordon and Coleman), there accompanies those groups some set(s) of standards or norms that regulates how these groups will exist and their relation to each other. These norms, in turn, will grow out of collective beliefs about the important dimensions of school life. Waller notes that the student culture (as well as that of adults) can be described in terms of how peer groups come to define school reality differentially as a function of their location in the school's social structure.

> From the fact that situations may be defined in different ways and by different groups arises a conflict of definition of situations, and we may see the whole process of personal and group conflict which centers about the school as a conflict of contradictory definitions of situations (p. 297).

Waller's findings have been applied to contemporary schools, and most notably in the work of Philip Cusick.[16] In his study (again a case study of one high school), Cusick attempted to examine high school life by spending six months with a group of high school seniors. Cusick's intentions here were to understand the manner in which students, as active agents within the school, construct their 'social self,' thereby forming a 'perspective' on school life. Following the tradition begun by Waller, Cusick came to see the student perspective formed as a result of a unique cultural setting, noting that 'what he does depends upon how he perceives himself in relation to various features of his environment.'

Cusick's understanding of the basis of the student perspective on schooling begins with his observation that the school as an organization has within it two subsystems. The first he calls the 'production system' and consists of all activities designed to further the manifest purposes of schooling (academic achievement). Such activities would include grades, classes, curriculum, testing, and the like. The second system is what he terms the 'maintenance system,' which consists of all activities supportive of but not part of the productive system. Maintenance activities (among which would be rules and regulations, hall passes, attendance procedures, and administration) are necessary, in part, for the production system to exist but do not contribute directly to it. In analyzing classroom life, Cusick notes that the school's production system is highly dependent upon the maintenance system, so much so that these maintenance activities consume significantly more amounts of time than we might imagine. These activities, involving as they do such activities as passing time between class, lunchtime, time to pass out and collect papers, listening to announcements, and so forth, were such at the school Cusick studied that he concluded 'students spend very little actual time involved in actual interaction with the teachers' (p. 56).

Cusick's work provides an important link between the studies of school structure (Gordon and Coleman) and a greater understanding of the meaning of life to students in school. Particularly relevant in this regard is his point that students in school spend large portions of time in a role of 'spectator,' wherein they watch and wait for something to happen. Remember that this was a point made by Jackson about elementary-age students, but in Cusick's study we begin to understand some of the consequences of this phenomenon and how students have come to adapt to it over their school career. For by the time students reach the secondary school, they have formed a complex social and cultural system representative of their perspective about their place in the school and the meaning derived from it. Thus, social interaction comes to assume the importance it does, so much so that the students in Cusick's book stated repeatedly that they would rather flunk a test than be denied the opportunity to sit by friends in the lunch-room. To this extent, then, the meaning of school for students grows from the organizational role that has been defined for them and which they define themselves.

Two other notable studies of high school students point out the importance of the interaction between high school life and its meaning for students on the one hand and, on the other, the manner in which this meaning and its creation is reflective of similar realities outside the school, most notably in the political sphere and the world of work. In these two studies, adolescent life in schools is examined not only as it exists within the confines of the organization called 'the school,' but also as life within that organization is reflective of patterns within the larger culture.

The first study in this vein, conducted by Paul Willis, is a study of the transition of working-class boys in England to the world of work after leaving school.[17] Willis was particularly interested in investigating the extent to which the cultural patterns of working-class students were perpetuated through school-based activities and ultimately transferred into the world of work. While a 'case study' of a small group of boys in one school and thus somewhat limited as to generalizability, Willis's study is most instructive as to the questions it raises and insights provided.

As in Cusick's study, Willis was to examine the meaning that adolescent boys gave to school life; however, his study goes beyond to examine the consequences of those meaning systems as well. Noting the 'non-conformist' nature of this working-class subculture in the school, Willis focuses upon the group's non-acceptance of the very nature of the school, its teachers, and the values stressed within it. Of particular interest to Willis was how the non-conformist nature of 'the lads'' culture came to take on the characteristics that it did, and what students 'learned' in regenerating that culture.

Of special note was the manner in which working-class students, being 'anti-school' as they were, came to view the 'mental work' the school required as the work of sissies, prudes, and 'ear'oles,' those who did not question the authority structure of the school. To the lads, acceptance of the mental labor in the school was tantamount to the acceptance of the authority structure of bosses (teachers and administrators) and required a passivity of role that the lads were not willing to grant. The lads, on the other hand, viewed themselves as independent and active agents pursuing their own destiny despite the imperatives of an institution whose purposes they found irrelevant. This perspective of action and independence was manifested daily through their conscious refusal to participate in a variety of school activities and the inclusion of themselves as a group in activities that permitted the degree of independence they sought. As Willis notes, this independence was sought 'in the struggle to win symbolic and physical space from the institution and its rules and to defeat its main perceived purpose to make you "work"' (p. 26).

Of course, the presence of such actions and beliefs in school has critical manifestations for that time when these students enter the world of work. Willis found that there never was a question about the kind of work the lads would enter, for manual labor on the shop floor was the only choice ever really considered. Herein, then, the lads already had rejected the intended continuity between work and mental labor built into the formalized dimensions of the school, and have accepted instead a more or less consistent view of what sort of people they wish to work with and what situations permit the greatest expression of the cultural skills developed in the school. Thus the world of manual labor on the shop floor permits what the lads are most accustomed to – toleration of authority but rejection of its incursions, masculine work that sissies cannot survive, and the establishment of group cultures that reinforce the ideal that work is a place where one can be 'open about his desires, his sexual feelings, his liking for booze and his aim to "skive off" as much as is reasonably possible' (p. 96).

Willis's study demonstrates, then, the association between student cultural processes and how those processes relate to a class society. Would such processes be present in American society, and for non-working-class students? A recent study by Larkin indicates that they would.

In his examination of student life in a suburban high school, Ralph Larkin indicates that, indeed, the social structure of Utopia High School (his case study school) is much the same as that student social structure reported by Coleman, Cusick, and Gordon.[18] There are the 'in-groups' and the athletes (jocks), the conformists (intellectuals) and the non-conformists (freaks), as well as the various racial and ethnic groups. Given the patterns of association of students to the groups to which they owe allegiance, high school life then consists of a highly sub-culturalized and fragmentized social system wherein action and meaning are self-generated within the context of the norms of the student-defined school social structure.

Yet throughout all the group identity, Larkin saw most students simply going through the motions in school, minimally involved in any required work and rather blasé about their deviant activities pertaining to sex, drugs, skipping, etc. Involvement in academic issues was at the minimally accepted level, and few students aspired to positions of leadership. Even where there were attempts by the teachers to involve students in school activities, these efforts were seldom successful for, as Larkin concluded, to participate was to accept the premise that the school fostered activities that were worth the student's time in the first place. Thus they 'would rather hang out and tolerate the boredom and meaninglessness of their own existence than participate in an activity presented in the context of an authority structure' (p. 148).

Most then chose the path of least resistance by withdrawing emotionally from school, accepting it as necessary for survival but living for free time together when they could take an active role in expressing themselves as authentic beings.

Larkin concludes that this condition of youth wherein passivity within the formal organizational setting is so common actually results in a minimal involvement in the productive process wherein students are consciously producing conditions toward some desired end. Students thus are minimally involved in creating conditions productive for self-determination in the larger society. Instead, their involvement is largely in the role of consumers – of sex, drugs, music, clothes, and all of the activities that permit them expression of their 'authenticity.' As such, they are consumers, too, of those products of capitalism that are dependent upon the presence of a large social group whose purpose is largely consumptive. The consumer culture perpetuated in the school (although not intentionally) is functional for the larger social structure in that 'the culture of monopoly capitalism is organized around consumption. It is necessary then that the individual psyche be molded to conform to the necessities demanded by an economy driven by expanding consumption' (p. 205).

We have reviewed a number of studies that seem to point in the same direction. In the first place, organizational life in schools, beginning as early as in the elementary grades, is such that the student must adapt to learning in what Jackson termed a 'crowded' environment. Thus, the process of learning involves a variety of conditions all contingent upon students learning to wait, to learn upon signal, and under conditions where social interaction is not only possible but probable as well. Of course, while students must learn in such environments, so teachers must teach in them, and they make commensurate adaptations as well. Moving to the high-school-age student, we now find that student adaptation to the somewhat passive role they occupy in the formal structure of the school is through the formation of peer groups and adherence to the norms generated within. More recent studies have pointed to the generation of meaning to the students in those subcultural categories, and the process by which that meaning transcends the boundaries of the school and has relevance to larger cultural forces in the workplace.

But what of the missing link in these studies, the period between elementary school and the high school? If we take seriously the claim of the founders of junior high schools some seventy years ago, these institutions were established exactly to overcome some of the problems reviewed up to this point. Yet we have no empirical studies to show how the student life in junior high school may contribute to the growing formation of separate cultural groups in the school, and what the consequences of this process are. We really don't know much about the interaction between the organizational arrangement of the typical junior high school and how those arrangements match with the developing social, psychological, and physiological needs of the early adolescent. What is more, we have no firm information to tell us if the junior high school 'receives' in its student body, the beginnings of the development of a separate student culture (as suggested by Jackson) and the extent to which that culture is developed within and expanded by the very organizational arrangement of the junior high itself. Finally, we are not at all knowledgeable about how life in the junior high as experienced by the junior high student is preparatory for the life in high school and thereafter as described in the studies noted above. It seems important to understand this, for certainly the four years from ages 12 to 15 are a critical period in the life of the modern adolescent – a period when many characteristics, perspectives, and routines are well on their way to being firmly established.

Perspective for the book

The total fabric of early adolescent life in schools – that is, the culture of student life in schools – is the specific concern of this study. By culture I mean first, what most anthropologists mean by the term, that sum of shared experiences by a people together with the particular beliefs of those people about those experiences. Included in such a notion of culture are answers to a variety of fundamental questions including, in the case of junior high school students, what they spend their time doing, why they engage in some activities rather than others, with what people they associate and why, the consequences of their actions, how they view their experiences, and the factors that affect why they believe what they do. Finally, we will examine how present experiences are a process of acquisition of skills and dispositions that may be part of preparation for later life; or, to answer a question posed earlier: 'How are adolescents prepared for adulthood?'

A second meaning of the term 'culture,' while not unrelated to the first, adds a different dimension. This second meaning advances the argument that culture, while it is a sum of experiences and beliefs, still is not some abstract construct 'out there,' separate from the people to whom it refers. Rather, it is reflective of an active process of people making themselves in a definite span of history through producing their own means of life. Culture in this frame of reference and in Marx's terms is 'materialist' rather than 'idealist,' meaning that it is a constitutive social process built up as man makes himself, rather than a dependent superstructural realm of mere ideas produced *by* material history.[19] Culture, then, grows out of human action as people create history – it is formed out of and is part of a social process. Because culture is made while human interaction occurs, we must be aware of the complex unity of knowledge, communication, and institutions as they interrelate in composite form. Hence, we must concern ourselves with whatever passes for knowledge and forms of communication (ceremonies, rituals, symbols, etc.), in the settings where this takes place regardless of the absence of some ultimate criterion for validity or invalidity of such knowledge or forms. As Berger and Luckmann state:

> and insofar as human knowledge is developed, transmitted, and maintained in social situations, the sociology of knowledge must seek to understand the processes by which this is done in such a way that a taken for granted 'reality' congeals for the man on the street. In other words, we contend that the sociology of knowledge is concerned with the social construction of reality.[20]

Yet we need to be careful about our premise of people as active agents who create history and therefore construct their own culture. In the process of making history, people also live out a history that has preceded them and that has created certain regularities that affect their actions. These regularities exist, for example, in the form of values passed on from generation to generation, appropriate behaviors expected in a variety of situations, and the institutions that regulate behaviors and help define the appropriateness of behaviors. These regularities, then, are present prior to one's place in history and help define both role and consciousness. In this sense then, while people do act out a history and in the process actively create a culture, it is also true, as Engels once said, that this happens 'under very definite assumptions and conditions.' Since these assumptions and conditions are the result of past and present human actions in a material world, such conditions cannot be said to be external and deterministic of human action. Rather they are a part of the active process into which we are born and which we ourselves, in part, determine. While society and culture is a constitutive process of political, economic, and cultural formations, it is true these formations do become internalized and, in the end, are translated into individual and collective wills.

This materialist perspective also raises an understanding of very definite consequences that influence how social regularities are perpetuated. In any society, with its own peculiar set of regularities created through history, the very regularities that satisfy our 'needs' – and in fact within which our needs are created – are produced and reproduced through what might be called, following Marx, 'productive forces.' These productive forces are those fundamental social processes whereby raw materials are turned into commodities which, in turn, enter the economic system of use or exchange.

These forces are present in different forms within various social-economic systems, and such forms influence the predominate cultural patterns created and re-created by societal members. For example, the primacy of such forces was noted by Marx in *Capital*, when he noted that 'Just as the savage must wrestle with nature to satisfy his wants, to maintain and reproduce life, so must civilized man, and he must do so in all social formations and under all possible modes of production.'[21] The influence of such productive forces in pre-industrial societies has also been recently described in a study by Michael Taussig, who discusses the cultural re-creation by Bolivian tin miners as they moved from a productive system characterized by self-regulation and engaged in for its own use to productive forces dominated by a wage system regulated by the owners of production.[22] In this particular case, the miners adapted to such new productive forces by equating the wage system with the darker elements of their religious belief system, and in so doing transformed an unnatural productive force into the realm of Satan, itself a source of resistance. As Taussig says,

> The interpretation that I wish to elaborate is that the devil beliefs form a dynamic mediation of oppositions. . . . These beliefs can be thought of as mediating two radically distinct ways of apprehending or evaluating the world of persons and things. Following Marx, I call these modes of evaluation use-value and exchange-value (p. 18).

It is important to realize the pervasive influence of material life, for, as Marx noted, such productive forces and their consequence can be examined *any time* human actors attempt to maintain life. In our own society, the same processes can be examined as we look at the way in which the uninitiated (children and young people) are brought into a system of production that attempts to direct them to think and act in conformance with the regularities of those productive forces. Here then we can focus upon the extent to which certain institutions in our society (such as schools), charged as they are to 'make' the young into adults, create and re-create productive forces that help move children into functional roles within the dominant institutions of adult society. Focusing then on schooling in modern societies permits us to understand productive forces and their relation to cultural patterns in the same manner as does the examination of radically different processes of labour in pre-industrial societies, as the type discussed by Taussig.

In any setting, however, we need to be aware of the dialectic between the active elements of a culture and those elements that are part of a productive force. In this sense, it is a mistake to think of productive forces in strict mechanistic fashion, as a factory tool stamping out machine parts. To whatever extent social regularities do exist, they are present not because members of social groups or classes always unquestioningly fit into a social structure that predates their own consciousness. Indeed, recent studies that focus on the manner in which social structures are reproduced in the workplace emphasize the contested nature of social and cultural reproduction.[23] Fundamental to this contestation in modern Western societies is an elementary provision within capitalist economic systems. Herein, the controllers of the capitalist productive systems may purchase from workers the capacity to do work (what Marx called labor power) but not necessarily the work (or labor). It is the latter that the workers, to some considerable extent, decide how much and under what conditions they will provide it. When such decisions become conscious and particularly collective, then those elements of the social structure they are expected to reproduce become contested. The extent of production then grows out of the dynamics within which social life is understood and acted out.

Returning then to the literature on early adolescence reviewed earlier, we can now more specifically locate the present study within the framework of Marx's labor theory of value and some extension of its premises.

My concern in this study is with the process and consequences of how knowledge about relevant dimensions of daily life (as well as relevant forms that are part of daily routines) arise and are maintained, and the consequences of this process for the ultimate relationship between those adolescents and the larger society. To view junior high school life as a process wherein students build their own history is to recognize the active role of students as agents with the ability to interpret the meaning of social situations and to take action based on those meanings. Given this stance, this book is in the tradition of the works by Cusick, Willis, and Larkin, because of its heavy emphasis on the interpretive structure of early adolescent life within the organizational structure of the school. It is located particularly in the context of the latter two books because I believe that the significance of interpretive structures within schools are important not only for what they tell us about school-based activities, but also because focus upon them helps us understand better how interpretive structures are formed by, and affect the culture of, the larger society. I consider, then, this study to be a critical link, because it provides important information about the place of early adolescents and the schools they attend in the context of modern technological capitalistic societies, of which the United States is one.

The posture adopted in this book provides a definite slant to the question of what is the culture of student life in the school and the attendant questions of what students do in school. Answers to such questions require, in the beginning, a 'bottom-up' rather than a 'top-down' perspective. In such an approach, understanding the fabric of junior high school student life is most fruitful if we can come to understand such a life *qua* students, rather than as an adult studying students. We need to understand adolescent life as adolescents live it, as if we were living out the same experiences. This then means that the culture of junior high school students is to be understood as a process in the making rather than as a study of an 'objective' product.

The literature reviewed earlier concluded that students play little active role in the determination of a specific formalized role within the school. Such a general conclusion leads one to believe that students are separated, to various extents, from the control of the formalized productive processes in schools and thus are estranged from their labor. Given this base, the framework used to understand student culture is founded upon, but is also a departure from,

Marx's labor theory of value wherein he posited that (a) workers are separated from the means in which labor is carried on, (b) that they lack the formalized opportunities to dispose freely of their own labor, and (c) that the employment of the worker provides more for the expansion of the capital of the owner, with the worker receiving a disproportionately smaller share of his/her labor.[24] The worker thus is selling his/her labor power for something of exchange-value, to use for 'life-sustaining' goods; the labor itself has 'use' specifically for these purposes rather than the intrinsic value of the labor.

Such a theory is useful, but needs rethinking in those situations where labor is engaged in not for wages, and where the 'owners' do not 'profit' monetarily from the labor of workers. It also bears rethinking in those situations where productive forces are seen as not just the creation of direct surplus value for the powerful, but also are seen to be symbolic goods that are reflective of material commodities and, indeed, may even replace them. Thus, religion, communications, music, and learning would be examples of social areas where the labor of participants does not reap them direct 'wages,' does not produce a 'profit' for the controllers of those areas, and where the productive forces most evident are not those that 'reproduce' directly the structure of society but rather are symbolic of basic productive forces. It is these symbols, then, that may in the end enter into the exchange system of the society. Language, communication patterns, and belief systems would be examples of such symbolic productive forces for they indeed may be patterned as knowledge and may in the end enter into the system of exchange in such a manner so as to reproduce that very labor system from which they emerged. Here, then, the labor theory of value must be extended into the dynamics of everyday life in such a manner that we can understand how the essential relationship of people to the basic means of production in institutions and organizations is creative of symbolically rooted cultural forms (language, beliefs). These forms end up to be productive forces that enter into the system of 'exchange' in American society.

In the case of schools in an advanced technological society, dependent for their survival on the accumulation of capital, the educative process via schooling serves as the basis for those symbolic productive forces. Here, it is not just the formal curriculum of the school that serves as such a productive force, but also the very culture of adolescents itself, of which the formal curriculum is only a small part. For in that culture, existing as it does within the school organization, social processes are created by students based upon their interpretation of the material world. Language, communication patterns and belief systems emerge as symbols. To the extent that such symbolic patterns arise, then these non-formalized aspects of student culture – not in the direct control of school officials – also become part of the productive system of schooling. It is these productive processes that 'make' commodities which, in turn, are later exchanged in the economic system in the form of beliefs and behaviors consonant with that system. Thus, it is not just the school and its formal organization that perpetuates the social and political system of which it is a part, but also the very adolescent subculture itself, born of an interpretive process that in many cases strains against the larger regularities. The degree to which the culture of junior high youth renews, re-creates, defends, or modifies these larger order regularities is a major theme of this work.

The approach used in this study is summarized in Figure 1.1. We will focus on the student culture, which is created within and is defined in the context of, for our purposes, the junior high school. This culture is interpretive in nature, and consists of the sum of shared actions and beliefs actively created by students as they live out and create individual and collective roles within the school. As this culture is created and accumulates, that is as it becomes a

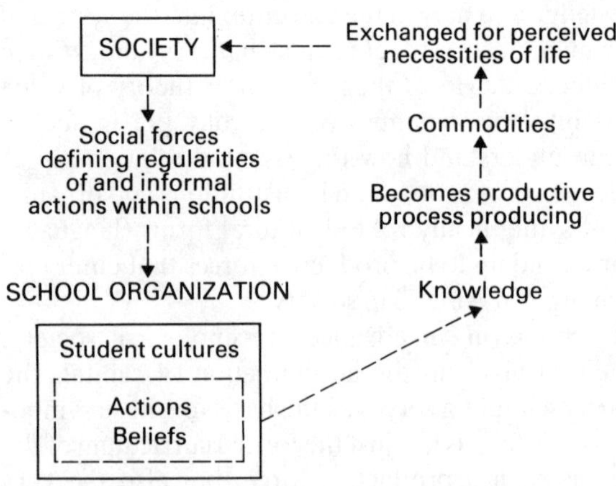

Figure 1.1 The making of student cultures

template by which knowledge and understanding is defined, it then becomes or acts as a productive force, thereby turning informal social processes into 'goods' or commodities – real products that are used in a system of exchange in the larger social structure. As these commodities interact within the social structure, predominate structural forces that remain are sustained or are challenged and in turn relate to the ongoing operation of the school, setting up the 'assumptions and conditions' (Engels) within which a culture is created. As we shall discover in this study, deviations and aberrations are often as contributory toward fulfillment of this general pattern as they are toward its alteration. Over all, then, such a model is useful to the extent it helps provide a framework for interpretation (see Figure 1.1).

Such a perspective implies a methodology that permits total access to the phenomena to be understood, as well as a role wherein one can come to understand events as the participants understand them. The approach I used in this study is that associated with anthropological and sociological fieldwork, sometimes referred to as 'participant observation,' which lends itself best to this access and the role necessary for such an understanding. In this approach, I joined groups of adolescents in a junior high school, first as an outsider but then, as time went by, more as a critical insider when I became socialized into the activities and belief systems of the groups. I tried to be everywhere they were, observe what they did, and talk to them about what they did.[25] Throughout, I recorded information and focused on key issues, letting the data guide me to those issues demanding explanation and refinement. The crucial task remained the explication of reality systems that were those of the participants rather than my own.

Organization of the book

I have sketched the general premises of the study so as to indicate early on in the book the theoretical approach that arose from the fieldwork and which has influenced the eventual organization of this volume. Still, the study is meant to be ethnographic for it is largely descriptive, with analysis of that information largely growing out of that description.

Following this present chapter, I provide a brief description of Jefferson, the community in which I lived while involved in the research of which this study was a part, and of Harold Spencer, the junior high school within which I spent two years conducting this study. In Chapter 3, we gain both an overview of and detailed information about the classes that students at Spencer attended. Having adopted the student role during the two years of fieldwork, and participating in classes in which students participated, I came to understand 'learning' as defined by school officials. I thereby conclude that a central productive force occurring in schools is that of constituting and defining legitimate knowledge. Spencer legitimated what might be termed 'reified' knowledge as the essential definition of the educational process, a knowledge that emphasized and predefined very narrow notions of technical competency for students. Chapter 3, then, deals primarily with the organization of knowledge by the school.

If culture is made as people make their own history, then we need to understand how selected groups of junior high youth create history at Harold Spencer. Two groups of boys and their friends served as the focal point of my two years in the school, and their activities and beliefs are the basis of Chapters 4 and 5. The intricacies of social community formed by these two groups of boys were fascinating and made my time at Spencer a real adventure. More importantly, the stress on community and interpersonal ties pointed out the strength of 'regenerative'-based knowledge for these students, a knowledge system acknowledged but not emphasized by the school. Chapters 4 and 5 do provide, in live panorama, what it is students in school actually do.

Chapter 6 is the first of two chapters that examine forms of student resistance to what is called reified knowledge in Chapter 3. One such form of resistance is 'goofing off,' an activity described in rich detail in Chapter 6. Goofing off is included here not only because I think it is important, but also because the students in the school did. My first and rather naïve approach was to pay little attention to their mention of it until it finally dawned on me that the practice was engaged in because it had the consequence of reaffirming segments of student community. Goofing off, then, was an activity representative of a belief system students had about themselves within the formal structure of the school; it was part of their making their own history through time.

Chapter 7 continues the notion of resistance and the larger topic of students creating their own history by answering the question of how students are able to control their fate in an environment that, quite unabashedly, views them as passive members of the organization. The topics examined in this chapter – among them cheating, smoking, and skipping – are topics familiar to most of us. While options to engage in such activities give students a sense of power, such activities, it turns out, served also to damn students in the end because the very processes of resistance support cultural systems predicated on resistance rather than raising collective understanding of that which is being resisted. Here, then, the productive force of the student culture leaves critical institutional regularities unexamined, thereby sustaining the social structure rather than challenging its premises.

The totality of student culture is analyzed in the final chapter. Here, I re-examine productive forces evident in the process of schooling and the role of students as creators of their own history. I believe my two years at Harold Spencer, and much subsequent thought about those two years, support my contention that schooling has associated with it a certain hegemonic quality that creates, among students in the junior high, a self-identity with knowledge and cultural forms that serve to re-create the patterns of technological capitalism in its present form. I argue, in the end, for teachers to be aware of these patterns, and to emphasize a 'reflexive' knowledge, one based on an understanding of human action as active yet historically limited. This forces us to ask why what is, is, and the forces leading to that condition. For junior high schools, it seems necessary to re-examine the assumptions under which those institutions were created over 70 years ago.

2
The community and the school

> We have to instill in kids good attitudes and work habits. Face it, school is business, not play. Less than half the kids in this district go to college, and those kids have to learn that you can't just take off the job (to go) hunting or turn in any old excuse. We have a responsibility to teach them about being on time and carrying through their responsibilities (Jefferson District Administrator, June 1972).

Most of my time conducting this study was spent in Harold Spencer Junior High School. Yet the school did not exist in a vacuum; it was part of a system of schools located in the Jefferson School District within which a number of people resided, worked, attended churches, and participated in the many and varied leisure-time activities in and around that area. Those people – their life-styles, values, and accustomed patterns of interaction – affected life within the schools and what students brought with them to the school. Before we settle down to our journey into everyday life within the school, it is both necessary and useful to gain a picture of the larger environment within which Harold Spencer existed.

The community

Jefferson is not an organic community, but rather a political entity located immediately to the south of the metropolitan city of Mountainview, an industrial center and seaport with a population of 150000. The western side of the district is the most heavily populated, as it lies closest to an adjacent military base (see Figure 2.1).

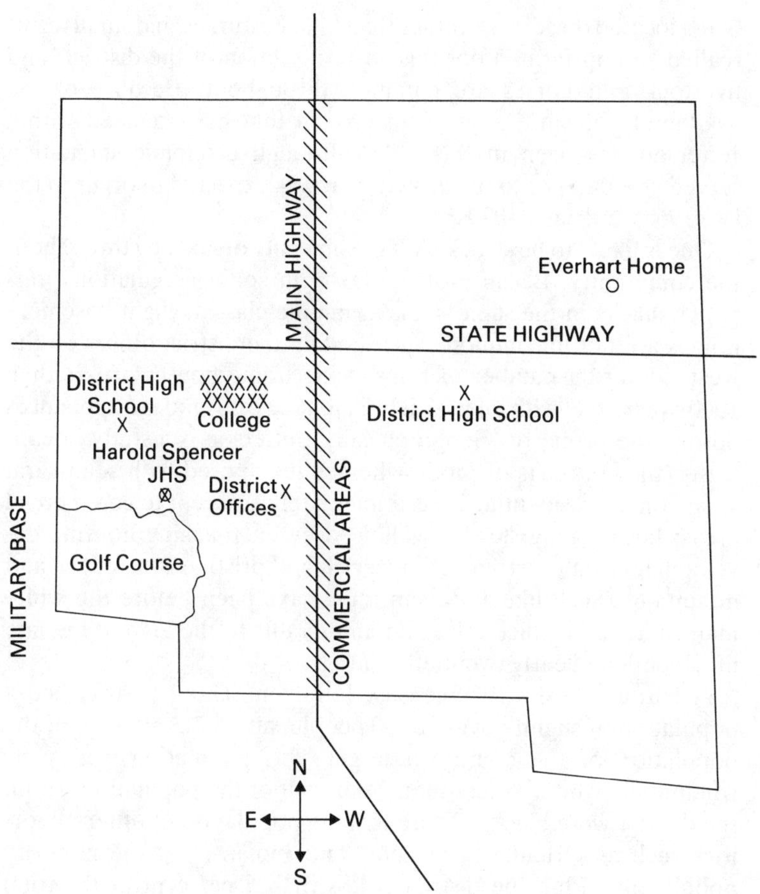

Figure 2.1 Jefferson school district

Here homes tend to be modest, on small lots, and largely ten to twenty years old. Some 63 per cent of the homes in the district were built prior to 1960, and most of these are in the western area of the district. Many of the homes tend to be the one-storey 'ranch'-type home, with the typical available living space being between 1200 and 1600 square feet. To the east of the main highway bisecting the district lies another major residential area with a character somewhat different from the residential areas to the west. The eastern area of Jefferson tends to be semi-rural in nature, with many homes being located on acreage rather than lots. Pasturage and small farms (called 'stump farms') dot this eastern section of the district, and livestock and horses are common throughout. Because of the availability of land, any recent growth that has occurred within Jefferson has been in this area, although economic stagnation served as a damper to the growth that was expected to occur in the late 1960s and early 1970s.

One is likely to be struck with the diversity of housing throughout the community. Because of the laxity in zoning regulations, tar-paper shacks in the same areas as middle-class daylight basement homes are not uncommon. Surrounding the district offices on the west side are a number of ramshackle frame houses of less than 1000 square feet with piles of debris, junked cars, and old appliances dotting the property. Geographically, Jefferson is a study in contrasts: the contrasts of modest homes juxtaposed with semi-rural slum homes; residential areas immediately adjacent to commercial areas; farms being slowly swallowed by encroaching housing developments – all surrounded by a rich and pristine zone of sea and mountain, much like Jefferson must have been before the white man came, and which attracted immigrants to the area in the late nineteenth and early twentieth century.

According to the 1970 census, Jefferson School District had a population of slightly over 30 000 people, about 7.5 per cent of the population of the county at large. This population was overwhelmingly white, as less than 2 per cent of the population within the district were blacks. There is some population of other minorities such as Orientals, chicanos, and Indians, but the minority population within the district is less than 5 per cent of the total population. Occupationally, the district can best be classified as a 'blue-collar' community.

Politically, district voters have never been known to support issues or candidates supporting social change, but rather have steadfastly defeated those motions while voting in favor of more mainstream 'bread and butter' issues such as jobs, defense spending, and support for traditional forms of education. In reviewing some of the major ballot issues of the past five years, district voters failed to approve the 18-year-old voting amendment of 1970, the sex equality rights and responsibilities referendum of 1972, and a community college bond issue submitted during the same year. In contrast, seekers of public office who favored and emphasized the traditional issues of the working person and who favored commercial and industrial growth that would bring jobs to the economically depressed community were usually supported. Generally, the area is thought to be somewhat conservative, although not of the extreme variety (there was an 'American Opinion Bookstore' – sponsored by the John Birch Society near the district office, and rightists often badgered the school board on such issues as sex education, objectionable reading material, and 'liberal' curricula).

The Jefferson district, in this study, will be characterized as 'working class' and the focus of the study will be on 'working-class students.' By that term I refer to class not as a 'thing' that exists as a static category of people defined as working class by sociologists. Rather, following E. P. Thompson, this investigation will support the belief that class is 'made' as a constellation of social relationships as people, through their common experiences, 'feel and articulate the identity of their interests as between themselves and as against other men whose interests are different from (and usually opposed to) theirs.'[1] Yet having said this, we cannot ignore the fact that these 'common experiences' are at least partly determined by those productive relations into which people are born. Such productive relations, then, must be accounted for when discussing class and class relations. In this regard, the productive relations of most Jefferson families placed them in the positions of being laborers whose labor power was bought by either private or public controllers and/or supporters of capital. Now it is true that this more general notion of the structure of the working class differs from its most specific usage by Willis and others in England, wherein the referent is most typically that segment of the labor force within which manual labor is done.[2] Still, whether manual or mental, the basic social relations growing out of an absence of control over the productive process remain the same for the vast majority of Jefferson parents, as does their nascent, if symbolic, cultural/political mobilization. Thus, the structural elements of the term hold, as does the developmental movement of collective grappling toward mobilization.[3]

In using the term 'working class,' then, I am referring to two related dimensions. First, I am arguing that most of the students I associated with were born into families who did not 'have proprietary access to the means of labor, but [who] must sell its labor power to those who do.'[4] Equally important, however, and in keeping again with the notion described above that class is 'made,' is that students at Spencer had minimal control over the tools of capital within the school, and thus were engaged in a process of proletarianization wherein they exchanged their labor for needed commodities. The singular removal of students from control over the productive process, and the reinforcement of that process for the majority within family life, then constitutes the fundamental elements of the term 'working class,' as used in this study.

The Jefferson School District

Jefferson School District, as a political entity, was formed in 1948 when two smaller districts merged into the present unit. The district currently has thirteen schools: 9 elementary, two junior high, and two senior high schools. The total enrollment as of 1975 was 7500 students, compared with 8200 students in 1971. The enrollment of each of the secondary schools ranged from 900 to 1100, while that of the elementary schools ranged from 300 to 500 students. The most recent building, the west side high school, was completed in 1970.

About 300 teachers were employed by the district. The teaching population could best be characterized as being stable and local in origin. Seventy per cent had graduated from a high school within the state and almost half of the teachers had attended a high school in the county or one of the two adjacent counties. Over 50 per cent had attended a college within 50 miles of Jefferson and a full 80 per cent had received their bachelor's degree at an institution within the state itself. The average teacher had been teaching for almost twelve years, and eleven of those had been in Jefferson. Privately, many teachers joked that one had to be a graduate of one of the local church-related institutions in order to obtain a job in Jefferson, and a large proportion of the teachers had in fact attended one of those schools. During the four years I was in Jefferson, over 70 per cent of the new teachers hired had received their degrees from one of the two church-related institutions or one of the three regional state colleges that specialized in teacher training.

The year before I arrived in the district, Jefferson had received a 5-million-dollar grant from the federal government in order to effect a large number of curricular and organizational changes within the school system. The very existence of that grant provided my entry into the system in general and to Spencer in particular, for I was on the staff of a small evaluation team whose responsibility it was to monitor various aspects of the project over the five years of its existence, to assess the progress of the project, and to identify reasons as to its success or lack of success.

It is difficult to state precisely what the grant was to change within the Jefferson system. Briefly, various changes were to be made in order 'to create an appropriate learning environment for each individual student.' Courses and opportunities were to be organized so that every student would 'experience success,' so that students would 'actively participate in the learning process' and 'be given experiences within school which develop real responsibility,' and be involved in 'school sponsored programs which utilize their own interests as vehicles for learning.' These rather vague objectives were to be translated into programs that were 'individualized' and that could occur in a variety of locations and during a variety of times. Ideally students would not be restricted to the school for learning, nor would they be restricted to the standard school day. For the program to proceed as it was proposed, each student would have a course of instruction tailor-made for his own interests and needs, and this program would be arranged so that it could take place year round and for an extensive period of time through the day and into the evenings. Furthermore, instructional programs were to be integrated so that students could pass to each level and continue the next sequence without disruptions or duplication. I will have little occasion in this story to refer to various aspects of this project, but readers should keep in mind as they read this chronicle that Jefferson was attempting to alter its instructional practices.

Harold Spencer Junior High

Harold Spencer opened in 1962. Located on a generous portion of property in the populated west side of the district (see Figure 2.1), it serves all junior high students who live west of the main highway bisecting Jefferson north and south. Harold Spencer is surrounded by athletics fields, a golf course, and borders on the high school property to the west. The grounds surrounding the school are well kept, and the building itself is in excellent condition, considering its age and the number of students who daily run through the halls, slam lockers, flush johns, eat in the cafeteria, and sit (and sometimes draw) on desks within the classrooms.

Figure 2.2 shows the floor plan of the building, which is a single-storey structure with five classroom wings; a wing that houses administrative offices, the library, and a teachers' lounge; a separate cafeteria-auditorium facility ('cafetorium'); and a separate gymnasium. All facilities are functional and somewhat Spartan in appearance. The library, a large group instruction classroom, and the administrative offices are the only facilities that are carpeted. Jefferson had forty-one certified persons on its staff. The principal, Mr James Edwards, had been principal at the school since it opened in 1962, and before that had been an assistant principal at the district's one high school. He attended high school in Mountainview and received his bachelor's and master's degrees from the nearby church-supported college. Edwards had been in teaching and school administration for thirty-four years and had been in Jefferson for twenty-one years.

To understand Spencer one must understand Edwards. Edwards was a very direct and imposing individual whose very demeanor created an air of authority and control that often intimidated student, staff member, and fieldworker alike. More often than not, teachers called him Mr Edwards, perhaps symbolizing the distance that remained between them and him.

Edwards liked to make all major decisions himself, and only reluctantly did he delegate decision-making authority to vice-principal Pall or teachers. He looked disdainfully at the new breed of principals who were 'managers' and who delegated excessive authority to subordinates, saying that a principal had to be on top of everything and know exactly what was going on all the time. He indicated on numerous occasions that too many principals were not 'on top of things' and that many activities often got out of control in a school because the principal had not kept himself completely informed of all major activities.

Edwards stressed the physical maintenance of the building and student discipline as two key indices of a well-run school and an efficient administration. Almost every day he was in the lunchroom, directing students to pick up paper. After school, he was in front of the building, directing the bus loading and general student conduct around the bus-loading area. Faculty meetings (which he

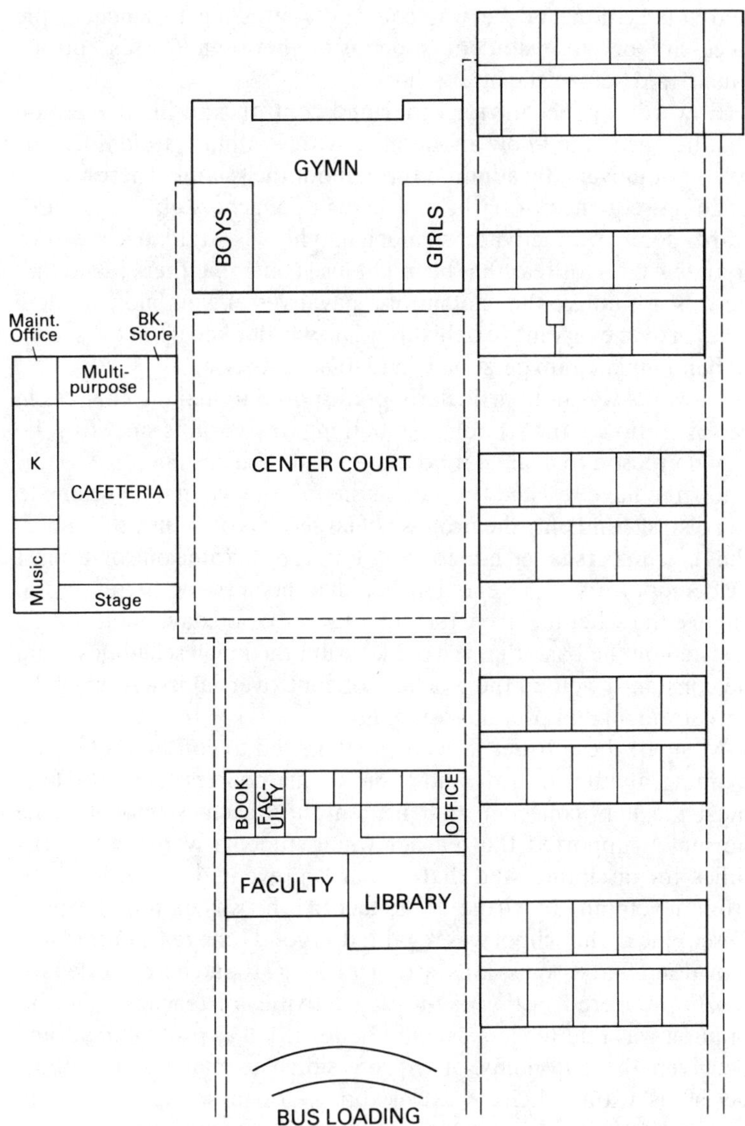

Figure 2.2 Harold Spencer junior high school

usually called) were dominated by discussion of student discipline and supervision and he was constantly stressing to teachers the necessity of close student supervision between classes, during lunch, and before and after school.

Edwards's penchant for order and control, and his perception that he needed to know about all activities within Harold Spencer, were not universally admired throughout the school. There was an ongoing sequence of barbs and jokes by teachers about how Edwards dominated activities so much that he was afraid to leave town for a few days for fear that he might lose control. Others joked that he was not unlike the captain of a naval vessel who had complete control over every move of his crew and who looked upon the school as belonging to him personally and to nobody else.

Edwards was not particularly predisposed to making changes in the operation of the school. If something was working smoothly, he saw no reason to change it no matter what the arguments. He was known to have resisted the idea of the Interim when it first came to the district, and only the promise of large sums of money to support the Interim persuaded him to try it. Later, he became one of its most avid supporters. For years teachers had been trying to get him to change the schedule from a six- to a seven-period day, but he firmly resisted on the basis that it would disrupt the lunch schedules. And he constantly vetoed the teaching of controversial issues which he was afraid might upset the community.

Many of these issues as well as others led to considerable complaining about Edwards and some of his policies. Nevertheless, most teachers conceded that he ran an efficient school, that he normally supported the teacher when students were sent to the office for discipline, and that Edwards prevented many problems from developing by virtue of the fact that he was on top of things. Discipline at the school was regarded as good (one teacher told me, 'you don't find wise-ass kids lasting too long around here'). Edwards rarely interfered in the day-to-day activities of teachers, and his opinion was that teachers should be regarded as professionals and be given the autonomy of a professional to make instructional decisions within their own classrooms. In these respects, then, Edwards was looked upon as a good administrator.

The vice-principal, Tom Pall, attended high school in Mountainview and received his bachelor's and master's degrees from the same school as had Edwards. Pall had spent his entire career in education within Jefferson, first as a teacher, then as a school counselor, and finally as vice-principal, a position that he had held for the past six years.

Pall was different from Edwards in many respects. In the first instance, Pall was much more sociable with teachers and in fact probably knew more about their daily lives than did Edwards, who rarely interacted with teachers unless some problem arose. At the various social events that the faculty as a whole and various smaller groups of faculty members held, Pall was likely to be in attendance whereas Edwards rarely went to any social events, with the exception of the annual faculty dinner.

Second, Pall was more interested in bringing about changes in the manner by which the school operated. He felt that the school (as well as the district as a whole) had not used the money from the federal grant very wisely, and that, for all intents and purposes, life was going on much the same as it had before the grant. He was much more interested in some of the changes that the superintendent had proposed (but which many principals and teachers in the district had not supported) such as variable scheduling and alternative learning environments. There were a number of ideas that he wanted to try, but felt that he would never be able to do them unless he could become a principal at his own school.

Since Pall's main responsibilities were to handle discipline, most students who were sent to the office came in contact with him first, although serious issues were often reviewed by Edwards as well. When it came to discipline, most students knew of Pall but very little of Edwards. In fact, during seventh grade when I asked students to tell me what they thought Edwards and Pall did, most students replied that Edwards did not do anything and Pall disciplined kids. Despite the fact that Pall was the official hatchet man, most students liked him because he was fair. There was no doubt that he was firm, that he expelled kids and, at times, paddled them, but he also gave kids a break when many acknowledged they did not deserve it.

Another vice-principal, James Hopkins (affectionately called 'Hawkeye' by the students), was responsible for scheduling the Winter Interim and a variety of other administrative duties. He had attended high school in a town about 100 miles north of Jefferson and had attended one of the state universities for his bachelor's degree. Hopkins, like Pall, had spent all of his career in education within Jefferson; in fact his first year in teaching was the year that

Spencer opened and he had been there in one capacity or another since that time.

The remainder of the teaching staff fit the same general characteristics of the teaching population mentioned earlier in this chapter; that is, the staff was experienced and had relatively long tenure within the building itself. The average Spencer teacher had been in teaching for eleven years, of which almost ten years had been spent in Spencer itself. That meant that a large number of teachers had come to Jefferson the year it opened and had remained there ever since. Fifty per cent of the staff had attended high school in the three county area around and including Jefferson while the other 50 per cent were equally divided between attendance at high schools outside this area yet still within the state, and high schools outside the state itself. Half of the staff had received their bachelor's degrees either from one of the local privately supported colleges in Mountainview or from one of the state universities. Most of the remainder had attended college at one of the three state colleges specializing in the preparation of teachers.

Pall and Edwards both spoke highly of the faculty as a whole. While granting that many of them were 'traditional teachers,' this was not seen in a negative way and was taken to be the standard mode of operation within the district. The traditional teacher did his job, was willing to spend time with students, maintained an orderly classroom, and would comply when called upon to serve on district-wide curriculum and policy boards.

In the classroom, the teacher was in control of interactions with students and the normal sequence was similar no matter what the class: the teacher gave out certain information via a lecture or by reviewing material in a book or handout, called on students to demonstrate their understanding of the material presented, made an assignment to be completed in class wherein the material was reviewed again, all followed by a teacher presentation of new material and an assignment that reviewed the new material just presented. Any interaction involving students tended to be short, direct, and to the point. Teachers usually structured the interactions so that certain points were elicited and little else.

Such a pattern might seem somewhat strange in a school district that had received large sums of money to 'innovate' its instructional program. When I first came to the school, I expected to find some things being done that were different from the time that I had attended seventh, eighth, and ninth grades; indeed, some activities were different, but by and large I found that the school operated very much like the secondary school I had attended twenty years ago, and the similarities were much more outstanding than were the differences.

This raises the issue of how committed the teachers were to changing the manner in which the school operated and how the operation of the school facilitated or inhibited certain changes in the instructional program. One teacher, within a month of my arrival at Harold Spencer, reflected on the attempts at innovation within the school and the district as a whole. She was describing her reaction to filling out a survey distributed by the district's evaluation team regarding the progress that had been made within the school.

> I just got through filling one of those [surveys] out a few days ago, and I'm really getting tired of doing it. I answer the same questions every time and nothing seems to happen as a result of it, so what sense is there in doing it? Like one of the questions is 'How clear is the experimental effort in your school?' I replied that it is very clear. Now they might construe that as good, but when I marked 'very clear,' I was saying so in a negative aspect. By that I meant that it was very clear that it was not going anywhere and not much was going to happen to anything that was tried. I'm sure that when they get back there they're going to misinterpret that, even though I did write some comments in the margin.

I went on to question the teacher about her reaction to being in an 'innovative' project for two years. Her comments were cryptic and to the point: 'The first year I was pretty excited about it, you know, the possibilities and all that. The second year I was really mad, nothing was happening. This year? – blah.'

Part of the reason for this rather fatalistic feeling about changing the operation of the school was the result, in many teachers' minds, of the fact that Edwards very carefully controlled which changes were to be entertained and which were not. Some teachers had proposed a history and current events class which students might not attend every day and where much of the instruction would be off campus. Edwards did not favor this course because he felt that such a class would disrupt the normal operation of the school with students coming and going at times when regular classes were in session. Other teachers favored extending the school day so that students might attend in the evening rather than all day, but Edwards felt that such a plan would present too many 'supervision' problems. The fact of the matter, then, was that Edwards effectively controlled the changes that were to be attempted within the school, and he tended to be very careful and deliberate about the changes he would support.

Parallel to Edwards's general conservatism, a large portion of the teachers within Harold Spencer were not particularly anxious to make any widespread changes in the operation of the school. Most were subject-matter specialists in their own field, and felt that the teacher's role as a dispenser of knowledge and facts was legitimate and necessary. Even though certain teachers had various confrontations with Edwards and disagreed with some of his 'hold the line' policies, the majority were generally satisfied to continue the operation of the school in the manner in which they had been accustomed to operating for the past years. Remember too that the staff was an experienced staff, many of whom had grown up in the Jefferson area and who themselves had not been exposed to any different form of schooling from that offered by Harold Spencer. A number of teachers referred to the staff as a basically 'traditional' staff and most saw that as a positive approach. In fact, staff members often chuckled when they heard of schools in the area where 'open-space,' 'modular-scheduling,' 'student-choice' experiments had not worked very well or were causing unanticipated problems. As one faculty member said one day in the teachers' lounge, 'Well, everyone's coming back to OUR way of doing things; that shows we've been right all along.'

Thus the majority of teachers saw their job as one of passing out information to students and seeing that the organizational procedures of the school were followed. While most worked hard in doing that which they did, few saw their role as one of continually attempting to assess what the purpose of their particular class was and how that purpose might be more effectively realized. Teaching at Harold Spencer was much like teaching in any other junior high school, and one sensed little or no excitement or spark to indicate that many teachers were intensively pondering what they were doing and proposing some better ways to do it.

Summary

The Jefferson community and the organizational arrangements of Spencer Junior High were important dimensions of the students' total life space and greatly influenced consequent school experiences. First, the school itself was structurally and hierarchically organized so as to facilitate the imperatives of mass education. Patterns were clearly delineated and the lines of authority were well specified, all of which permitted the procession of students *en masse* from one location to another six times a day, for fifty-five-minute intervals. In order to facilitate this orderly flow of students and in the time allotted, teachers relied on passing out information to students, standardizing activities, and on an enforcement of school-wide and classroom regulations.

These and other factors led to a certain separateness between the school as seen and lived in by teachers and that visualized and acted on by students. The sheer number of students and the need to channel them efficiently into classrooms where definable segments of knowledge could be disseminated affected the treatment of students as separate but collective products that could be shaped and treated in an orderly and somewhat predictable fashion. Accordingly, students were expected to pay attention in class, display that they were somehow 'developing' as a result of the time spent in school, and to act in such a manner so as not to disrupt the flow and sequence of maintenance activities and requirements upon which the daily operation of the school was so dependent.

Other indices of separateness between adults and students were common and institutionalized. For instance, there was a separate entrance to the administration wing for 'faculty and guests' and a sign on the door indicated that students were not to use that entrance. Additionally, teachers rarely, if ever, considered sitting in the same lunch area as did students, nor would they normally sit with students on the bus to and from field trips. In the classroom environment, most teachers were careful to avoid direct answers to student questions of a personal nature, such as what a teacher thought about a particular political point of view, a certain social issue, or even an ethical question such as whether Watergate meant that Nixon was a crook.

Instructional life at Spencer continued on the even plane that it did because there were no significant internal or external forces to cause it to operate in any other manner. School administrators throughout the district prided themselves on knowing what the community wanted from its schools. By and large, the message they received was that the community supported orderly and efficiently run schools, free of controversy, unrest, or anything that indicated that the schools had gotten out of hand. Residents of Jefferson rarely demanded that the schools innovate more, and any complaints they had usually were over such issues as better playground facilities or the realignment of the athletic leagues in which the senior highs participated so that the schools would not be participating with schools twice their size. Most parents wanted a basic education for their children; most administrators knew that and gave them what they wanted. Since many of the teachers themselves had lived in or around Jefferson all their lives, and since the assistant superintendent carefully screened applicants for teaching positions so that they were 'safe,' it would be unreasonable to expect any mandate for change from within. I do not necessarily mean this to be a criticism of the teachers, for most of those who were at Jefferson did a good job at what they did. Yet one must realize that the school system, as constituted, presented a number of endemic properties that mitigated against significant change, no matter what the personal motivation of the individual teachers.

Finally, regarding any prospect of a more dynamic educational system, community consensus, as reflected in school policy, supported programs oriented toward providing children of the largely working-class parents a better life within the given corporate/capitalistic society through more training in the 'basics,' emphasis on more 'saleable skills,' more attention to attitudes that prospective employers would deem significant. Schools represented something quite important to the Jefferson community, and certainly the success of students in obtaining well-paid jobs in the local economy or, for the small minority, the chance to go on to one of the local colleges were highly regarded attributes that the school system should create. These attributes were outcomes, and the community was supportive of educational processes they thought would produce these outcomes. Such processes, however, were present not so much in the single-handed rigidity of a highly authoritarian school system. Rather, they were evident in the deep structures representative of rules for knowing – those epistemological rules that oriented the educational process and which, in turn, led to systems of knowledge, or those circumscriptions within which 'knowledge' was based. As we shall see in Chapter 3, the school, in the daily process of instruction, constituted and reinforced a system of knowledge dependent on deep rules that emphasized standardized information and how to manipulate that information in order to increase the probability of 'success' within the given political/economic framework.

3
The classroom world

> 'Then if this is true,' I said, 'our belief about these matters must be this, that the nature of education is not really as some say it is; as you know, they say that there is not understanding in the soul, but they put it in as if they were putting sight into blind eyes.' (Plato, *The Republic*, Book vii).

The typical day begins with the yellow buses rolling up to the breeze-way in front of the school at about 8.10 a.m. By 8.25 – only five minutes before the first class – some students have already filed into their first-period class and are sitting on the desks or standing around in groups talking to each other. Others stand around in the hall outside the classroom, talking to friends who are going to other classes. At 8.30, the shrill electronic pitch of the bell pierces throughout the school, and at that instant those still left in the halls and outside corridors scurry into their first-period class; those in the rooms proceed to their assigned seats. The halls are empty and quiet as doors to the classrooms are shut. It is time for the schoolday to begin 'officially.'

The first-period class starts as students listen to the notices for the day. Following these announcements, the class settles down and students begin the work which the teacher has planned for that period. The bell rings at the end of the fifty-five minute period and students flood into the halls to go to their second-period class. The second period proceeds much as the first with some variations occurring depending on the class, be it shop, PE, art or the typical 'academic' courses such as English, math, social studies or science. In the middle of the day, students go to the cafeteria for one of three thirty-minute lunch periods during which time they eat lunch and talk to each other. More classes follow lunch until 3.00 p.m. when the students who had arrived on the buses pile back on to them for the return trip home while others take to the streets and roads and walk home. Various students remain for athletic practices, club meetings, detention, and other activities of a required or optional nature.

To the casual observer, the student day seems fairly typical and not unlike those schooldays they may have experienced five, ten, maybe thirty years ago. But beneath this rather pallid veneer is a distinctive way of life that students lead: this life reflects their confrontation and interpretation of a given environment and the meaning they draw from it. First, we will examine the environment of the classroom more closely; later in this chapter we'll examine the *meaning* of classroom life for the students at Harold Spencer who lived it.

Time in class[1]

Waiting and getting ready

'Hey Bob, get your math done for today?' Don, a seventh-grade student, poked me on the shoulder as he came into the math room, grabbed his math folder from the large file hanging from the wall, and walked toward his assigned seat.

'Yeah, got it all done,' I replied.

'I'll bet,' he said in disbelief as he sat down.

Just then the bell rang, signaling the beginning of the school day. Mr Glenn (one of the math teachers) went to his office to get a copy of the daily bulletin and then walked to the middle of the large room where students were sitting around tables and at study carrels located along the wall. 'OK, listen up for the announcements.' He paused a moment, waiting for the class to stop talking and then proceeded to read the daily notices: 'The *Spencer* [the weekly school newspaper] arrives first period today. Room representatives should go to room 100 to pick them up. Cost is five cents with a student body card, ten cents without a card. After the announcements, Chris, you and Midget take a count of those who want the paper and collect the money.' He continued: 'OK, there will be a Thespian meeting on Wednesday after school in room 500. Officers will be elected and all new members are encouraged to attend. There will be a Camera Club meeting after school in Mr Jackson's room on Wednesday. Any ninth-grade students who wish to apply for a position on the photography staff at North High next year should turn their applications in to Mr Jackson by the time of the meeting.'

Mr Glenn then looked around and asked if there were any questions. A student shouted from the side of the room, 'The paper, don't forget to collect for the paper.'

'Yeah, that's right. Chris, you and Midget count hands. Raise your hands so they can see and don't take all morning doing this.' Chris and Midget counted the number of hands for the school paper, then left the room to pick them up in the journalism class.

Glenn turned to the class and said, 'OK, you people know what you're supposed to be doing, let's get humming on those math problems. For those of you who have tests to take, get into that test room.' The students slowly opened their math notebooks and began moving around the room to take tests, to get problem books; some raised their hand for help. There was the usual line at the pencil sharpener to fine tune the pencils.

Some of the math classes at Harold Spencer were 'individualized' and the class that I usually attended with Chris, Don, and other seventh-grade boys was one of these classes. At the beginning of the year, students in this class took a placement test, used to designate at what level of math difficulty they should be placed. Once the students were placed, they then used their math notebook in which was outlined the types of problems they had to do at each level. The answers to problems were found in the various 'teacher's editions' of textbooks located on a table at the side of the room. The students could periodically check their answers in these books and, once they had mastered the problems, they were then eligible to take a test over the whole unit. If they passed the test, they then went on to the next level; if they did not pass it they were given a 'prescription' by Mr Glenn or Mr Charles (the other teacher in the room) that outlined the type of work on which they needed additional review.

About ten minutes after they had left, Chris and Midget returned to distribute the papers. 'Papers here, get them while they're hot. "No-no Song" voted number one song at Spencer,' Midget chanted as he walked into the room. Chris started singing in a low voice: 'A lady that I know came from Columbia, she smiled because I did not understand. Then she held out some . . .' Mr Glenn seemed mildly irritated by this interruption. 'All right, let's knock this routine off; get the papers passed out and then get back to work.' As Chris and Midget distributed the papers, Don and Steve began reading them, commenting on the top ten songs at Spencer as listed in the paper.

'God, "Angie Baby" is number two, what a lousy song.'

'There aren't even any Pink Floyd songs on here.'

'Everyone get those papers put away or you'll find out you won't have any,' said Mr Charles, looking at Don and Steve and then the rest of the class, most of whom were also looking at the papers. With that admonition, everyone put the papers away.

Soon a number of students had their hands in the air either wanting help or desiring to be certified to take a test. Carl, a friend of Chris's, was sitting at the table next to me complaining that he had his hand up off and on for twenty minutes in order to get permission to take a test and still he was waiting. Bobby, sitting at the same table and talking to Tony about skiing, replied, 'That's nothing, I've been waiting almost the whole period just to see if I passed the test which I took yesterday.' Finally, Mr Charles walked over to Carl, checked the work that he had done, and told him he could take the post-test – but then noted that the test room was full so he would have to wait until someone left it. Carl then went over to sit with Bobby and entered into the conversation about skiing. Finally, Carl shot into the test room and had been there for about ten minutes when Glenn announced that there were five minutes left in the class and that everyone should put their materials away.

The individualized mathematics class was not representative of all classes, yet it still illustrates that much of the time spent in the classroom situation was time spent waiting – waiting to do something, waiting to begin something, waiting to go on to a new activity. I say individualized math classes were not representative because there was somewhat less waiting there. Waiting was even more pronounced in most of the other classes at Spencer as the class moved along in unison rather than in smaller segments, an activity that happened to some greater degree in the individualized math class.

Waiting abounded and was so pervasive in most classes that it is impossible to enumerate all of its manifestations. Waiting for students to give up books needed by other students, waiting to use filmstrips, reading machines, or other instructional devices, waiting for grades to be recorded or waiting to have papers distributed – all were events that affected large segments of the class at any one time. Individual students had to sit through exercise reviews, oral reading sessions, and class discussions, all of which may have been irrelevent to them at any one point in time. The fact that waiting itself was pervasive is clear, but takes on even more meaning when looked at in the context of the entire school day.

We can safely assume that the announcements, attendance taking, the passing out of school papers and registration forms, head counts on a variety of topics on which the school needed information (like the number of students whose parents worked for the federal government, number planning on coming to open houses) consumed anywhere from five to ten minutes of the first period of every day. Announcements and attendance taking in each of the other five class periods also took at least five minutes from the beginning of each class. It is also safe to eliminate at least the last five minutes of each class for papers to be collected, books to be returned, desks to be lined up, and for other classroom maintenance activities. Thus, at least ten minutes was taken from each class for these procedural activities – time during which students essentially waited around for the class to begin or end. Add to this the five minutes passing time between each class and the thirty minutes for lunch, and the sum of 115 minutes each day were *formally* set aside for the student to move, eat, get ready to do something, or wait for a class to end. If we round this off to 120 minutes, two hours out of a six-and-a-half hour day, or almost one-third of the student's time in school, was formally used for activities necessitated by the fact that certain activities such as passing, attendance taking, and announcements were required, yet this figure of one-third of the time does not even include the time spent *between* the first and last five minutes in any class during which the student was required to adjust to the pace of instruction. Now let us turn to see what students did during instructional activities.

The pacing of instruction

Instructional events for a given student are determined by a number of considerations. One is the time available within any one class period and the pacing of events within the limits of time. In this respect, the constraints on the teacher are set and unyielding – the period begins at a certain time and ends fifty-five minutes later, and within these limits whatever instruction the teacher has planned will and must occur. This simple observation carries considerable weight when used to describe and interpret the students' environment in the school.

Instruction at Spencer was organized so that things 'came out' in such a fashion that the majority of students ended up with the same product at essentially the same time. In Marcy's English class, for example, the group had been writing a business letter in order to learn the proper format, style, and content of such a letter. First, Marcy asked the class to turn to the chapter on business letters in their grammer books and read that section. After five minutes Marcy asked the class, 'How many have not yet finished?' Initially, about one-third of the class raised their hands. Roy, sitting in the rear near where I was sitting, nudged John. John then spoke up, 'I'm not finished.'

'I ain't finished either,' Roy added, smiling. Needless to say, they both had finished; I had seen them close their books a few minutes earlier and then proceed to trade a *Mad* magazine back and forth.

'Well, I'll give you a few more minutes, but hurry up,' said Marcy. Those not finished continued reading while the rest of the class began engaging in different activities: looking out the window, doodling, and pulling pictures from their wallets and looking at them. Roy then pulled a copy of *Cycle* magazine from beneath his desk and began leafing through it. After a few minutes Marcy went to the blackboard and began outlining the structure of the business letter.

'Ok, first thing we do is to place the return address – where, class?'

'On the paper,' said one boy slouched in his chair and tapping his pencil.

'All right, comedian, that's obvious. Where else?'

'On the front side of the paper.'

'Come on class, get serious! Where do you place the return address? Larry?' Marcy obviously was in no mood for students' wisecracks although she was usually tolerant of this constant undertone of comments.

'I don't know . . . on the top?'

'OK, good, now where on the top?' Larry thought for a moment and then Marcy said impatiently, 'Larry come on, you just read it in the book.'

Steve volunteered, 'He can't read.' Someone let out a 'Duh' from the back of the room. A few people snickered, Marcy stared at Steve for an instant, then turned to Larry and asked him to turn to page 236 in his grammar book and look at the example on the page to see where the return address was. Larry looked at it and finally answered, 'In the upper right-hand corner.'

'Right.' She then proceeded through a description and explanation of the form of the business letter. After a discussion lasting between ten and fifteen minutes, she then asked the students to begin thinking about writing their own business letter, an assignment due at the end of the following week (this was Tuesday). First they were to write an initial paragraph for a business letter to anyone they chose and concerning any subject. After about ten minutes of writing, Marcy asked, 'How many are not finished with their paragraph?' About six students raised their hands. 'OK, I'll give you a few minutes to finish up. The rest of you, I want to read your paragraphs to each other because I want you to read them to the class tomorrow and they'd better be clear; if they aren't clear to you now they won't be clear to the class tomorrow.'

One of the students at the back of the room seemed somewhat surprised at this. 'Hey, you didn't say anything about having to read these in front of the class.'

'Yeah, I don't want to read mine in front of the class,' added Phil.

Marcy put her hands on her hips and stated emphatically, 'Now come on, class, you'll all want to do a good job and this will give you a chance to practice and improve your paragraphs before they're submitted for grades. And you all want to get "A's", I'm sure.' There was a chorus of laughs from most of the class and Marcy smiled.

'I don't care,' I heard one girl say under her breath.

'Yeah, I don't care either, just so I get this stupid thing done.'

After saying that, Don turned to Art and said, 'Hey, Art, what you writing your letter on?'

'I am writing the Elephant Rubber Company, telling them that their rubbers were too small.'

'Wow,' Ron replied.

'Don't think I'll write that letter though, Marcy will have a bird.'

'For sure,' Art replied.

The students continued talking to each other, which finally prompted Marcy to get up from her desk and say, 'Class, get busy or some of you will be in after school.'

This incident, typical of classes at Spencer, illustrates how instruction was paced in most of the classes and demonstrates the different uses of time for both teachers and students. For the teacher, instruction was paced in such a manner that the different rates of student progress were 'leveled,' resulting in large blocks of students moving along to approximately the same spot at the same time. However, this pacing provided a different situation both for the individual student and groups of students. The uniform orchestration of instruction provided, for the students, gaps, sometimes small and sometimes large, in the attention they had to pay to the formal requirements of the classroom. When these gaps were present, students filled them readily with their own activities. Thus Don and Steve talked about motor cycles, Karen and Terry talked about going to the store after school, and Larry doodled on his peechie.

Management of time

This incident in Marcy's class points to the perennial problem in the classroom where students serve basically as respondents bounded in time and space by the limitations of legitimate behavior happening within the physical boundaries of the classroom. The problem at Spencer revolved around the teacher having to organize between thirty and thirty-five students within these limits. Since it was physically impossible to fill the allotted time for all these students, the best the teacher could do was to manage activities within a restrictive time frame and, as in the case just explained, to stretch out tasks so that time was filled with relevant activities, all accomplished at about the same pace, and involving something close to a majority of the students at any one time.

This 'staging' procedure had other ramifications in terms of the management of time. Usually, teachers taught multiple sections of the same class. Ideally, the teacher attempted to keep these sections at approximately the same place so as to avoid confusion on his part in ordering films, preparing handouts, grading papers, and preparing lesson plans. But disjuncture was often unavoidable when assemblies, school-wide testing, early dismissals, and field trips cut into one period's time but not the other. While some might question the legitimacy of such time management, innumerable situations made it seemingly unavoidable. This was most pronounced in Creadley's science class wherein he had students involved in laboratory work between 40 and 50 per cent of the time. Preparing labs meant setting up experiments the night before, and having to prepare two different sets of labs the same day with equipment restrictions, space limitations, and the like was difficult. So if, for reasons of schedule changes, the two seventh-grade science sections got out of 'synch' as he used to say, Creadley often let the students do whatever they wanted (which involved anything from playing chess to doing assignments for other classes to the usual talking about sports and after-school activities) until the other class had caught up. Realistically, there was probably little choice in his holding the class up as he too was a victim of time and its limitations.

The management of time also created a situation wherein students who did not relate to a certain pace of classroom instruction and desired to deviate were compelled to adjust to the normal procedure. In reading class, for example, Don and the other students were reading a book called *The Peddler War*, a book that they read out loud in class and individually. Don was mumbling to himself about what a 'chicken shit' way of reading a book this was – 'just like a bunch of candy assed fourth graders,' – so he raised his hand.

'Can we take these books home to read them?'

Mrs McBride said, 'No, hand them in at the end of the period, we have to use them for another class tomorrow.' Hearing that, Don then simply closed his book and, propping his chin on his hand, stared out the window for about five minutes. Finally, McBride said, 'Don, get to work, you can't read staring out of the window.'

Don raised his hand and asked, 'Can I go to my locker, we're not doing anything in here anyhow?'

'No, you'll have to wait until the period ends. Tomorrow, we're going to work right up to the bell instead of having five minutes left over like we do almost everyday.'

Time and its uses were an important regularity of classroom life. In virtually every class and throughout the school year, variations of waiting and getting ready, the manner by which instruction was paced, and the management of time defined a large part of the daily instructional happenings. This phenomenon assumes additional meaning when we look at the timing of any one instructional unit, that is the time taken for and timing of relatively discrete activities required of students. Using the example of writing the business letter in Marcy's class (a particular exercise that took the best part of seven days of classroom time), the subject was first introduced in class, the relevant sections of the grammar book were reviewed by students, discussions on where to place headings and how to write individual paragraphs were reviewed, and the exercises were practiced. It was expected that all of this work be done in class and, as I discussed earlier, carrying out the assignment outside of class was, while not always prohibited, certainly not facilitated by virtue of the barriers put up for students taking books home.

Even when the assignment was due on the Friday following the week the assignment had been introduced, provision was made in class for the relatively minor task of preparing an envelope to be submitted with the letter. At the beginning of the class the day the letters were due, Marcy said they had fifteen minutes to complete anything they had to do with the business letters. 'I haven't told you about envelopes but I want an envelope submitted with your letter. The form is on page 254 and there are some blank envelopes up here on the counter.' The students got the envelopes and began to fill them out, a process that took at most five minutes. But during the fifteen minutes allowed for this activity I noticed a number of students (who had apparently done very little on the assignment thus far with the exception of having paragraphs on white paper stuffed in their peechies) rewrite the entire letter in ink and make out the envelope. In other words, an assignment that had consumed a greater part of over a week of classroom time was virtually written by some of the students in the fifteen minutes ostensibly allowed to 'finish up' the assignment.

Earlier in this chapter I said that almost one-third of the students' time was spent in such organizational maintenance activities as passing between classes, eating lunch, having announcements read in class, and giving out and putting away materials. But this estimate of one-third of the day does not include the more informal and somewhat unpredictable elements of the management instruction just described. That is, it does not include aspects of time built into the process of instruction – things such as the generally slow pace of instruction, staging and proceeding as a group, juggling classes so that all sections were at approximately the same spot, utilizing time in class to complete assignments, and adjusting time so that the majority of students handed in the assignments at the same time. Saying that the student spent a third of his time in what may be considered 'organizational maintenance' activities is a very conservative and incomplete estimate. If we add these *informal* but recurrent elements of pacing of instruction and the management of time to the one-third we said was *formally* allocated to classroom and school maintenance activities, the figure representing time spent in non-instructional affairs comes close to 45 per cent.[2] This, too, may be a conservative estimate in that it does not include time to discipline students, times when individual students may be excused for trips to the office or be legally excused from school for athletic events, band concerts, photograph taking, and the host of other extra-curricular events that occur daily. It also assumes that the individual student is awake and has his mind on the subject-matter being presented, an assumption that, to anyone who has spent any time in a classroom as a student, is highly questionable.

Classroom demands

The fact that the students at Harold Spencer spent such a significant portion of their time governed by the contingencies of time has parallels with what was required while they attended school. The constant reality of waiting, moving with the group, and fitting in with the stream of instructional events as they were arranged by the teacher meant that the student's involvement in 'learning' had to fit into that stream as he was caught by the flow. That the stream bypassed the students or was not flowing for significant portions of their existence in the school speaks to the instructional demands placed on them.

Not all classes were alike, of course, but the social studies taught by Richards and Mr Bruce illustrates some typical requirements placed on students. One day in the Fall I walked into the class with Chris, John, and Don. We took our assigned seats and were talking before the bell rang. As usual, Chris and I were trading Polish jokes. The bell rang and Mr Bruce directed everyone's attention to the side blackboard on which was written the cycle of events for the unit that they were beginning:

Monday: work in large room on summary charts and watch film.

Tuesday: work in small groups reading from text and working on worksheets.

Wednesday: work in large groups correcting worksheets and on maps.

Thursday: work in large room on essay assignments and watch film.

Friday: small groups, reading and worksheets.

Monday: large groups, review of unit.

Tuesday: test on unit.

Bruce said, 'OK, now that you have that [the schedule] you can decide on which days you want to stay home.' He smiled as he looked around the room for responses.

'Far out,' Roger said, 'how about everyday?'

Bruce replied, 'Roger, your mind is home everyday anyhow.'

'What mind?' Carl chimed in a low voice that Bruce could not hear at the front of the room. 'His mind is like a sponge that's been squeezed dry.'

Roger looked over at Carl, smiled drolly, and produced an obscene gesture. Ann, sitting in the seat between them, giggled.

Richards then passed out the worksheets for the summary charts (papers the students kept on salient data such as climate, population, products produced, major landforms and other such 'encyclopedic' information as it pertained to countries being studied). The week began with Richards listing on the overhead projector the information that should be included on the summary sheet. As the period progressed, most of the students in the class dutifully filled in the information as Richards outlined it.

The next day (Tuesday), Richards passed out a worksheet that was to be used in class to answer some questions on the assignment. 'Remember, on these worksheets you should print rather than write. Since many of you people never had writing in grade school, you're going to have to communicate so I can read it. That means PRINT. Next, the answers on the worksheet must be the same as those given in the text – none of your own thought about what you think the answer should be. Just write the answer as it appears in the book. Next, number 12 asks you to underline the correct answer, and this means to underline it, not circle it. Finally, number 13–25, the directions state to circle the correct word and this means the whole word, not just the number in front of the word. Any questions? Get going.'

The students slowly opened their books and began to work at the required material. I was sitting near John, who was soon busily talking to Steve sitting next to him about the intramural touch football game after school tomorrow night. They did this while simultaneously working on the assignment and keeping vaguely aware of Richard's and Bruce's location in the room.

'Which team are you on?' Steve asked. John responded that he was on 'Fillmore's Fighters,' each team being named after its captain.

'God, you guys really got killed last week,' said Steve. 'Hey, what kind of farming do they practice in Switzerland?'

'What do ya mean, "What kind of farming?" How the hell do I know?'

'Well, it's question number seven.'

John ignored the question and went on to recount the horrors of their loss to 'Victor's Victors' last week, and added that they were not at full strength then but they would kill Steve's team. A few minutes later he said rather nonchalantly, 'Oh, here it is.'

'Here's what?'

'The kind of farming they practice in Switzerland; it's called vertical farming.'

They both began copying the answer in but Steve hesitated and looked over at John.

'V-E-R-T-I-C-L-E, is that how you spell vertical?'

'Na ya dummy, it's "al" not "le." Hey, is Runger playing for your team?' And on they went like that for the remainder of the period, talking while paying minimal attention to the work required.

The next day they watched a film on Switzerland and corrected the worksheets that they had completed the previous day. Friday was spent as the previous Wednesday except that Steve and John talked about the game the night before in which 'Fillmore's Fighters' had won by one touch-down in the last minute.

The following Monday was devoted to review for the unit test on Switzerland to be given the following day. Richards was his usual ultra-organized and precise self in providing directions for the review. He asked students to take a piece of paper on which they would write answers to various review questions he would pose.

Bruce turned the overhead projector on and wrote in large block letters on the overlay, 'Review for unit tests.'

John immediately shot his hand in the air. 'Are we supposed to center the title like that, like you have it on the overhead?'

Bruce responded, 'Well, this is for your own use so it's really not crucial at this time.'

Another hand went up toward the back of the room. 'Well, I put my title on the right-hand side and not in the center and besides it's lower than yours. Is that all right?'

John and Steve both snickered as Bruce responded. 'Come on, people, this is for your own use so it's not all that important where you put it now. All right, the first thing we are going to review is the mountain climate region. Now, one of the things that characterizes a mountain climate is that there is a variety in the climate.' Bruce underlined the word 'variety' but in such a manner that the line looked like it had a period at the end. John then raised his hand and asked, 'Should we put a period after variety?' Bruce turned around to look at the overhead, extended the line to the 'y' and then explained that there was no period there. This made little difference as half the class was smiling to themselves over Bruce's penchant for detail.

Characteristic of the demand placed on students was what seemed to be a 'quota' placed on acquired knowledge. The dominant form of instruction was the acquisition of information dispensed by the teacher, a form that resulted in the teacher being unable to provide all students with enough to keep them busy on instructional tasks for the entire period. It also made the teacher tend toward minimizing variety, effectively placing a ceiling upon what was required of the typical student. Mrs Mackle, the instructor in English, told the class one day that they had problems alphabetizing words, and consequently they were going to work on alphabetization during the period. After some initial admonitions regarding behavior, she placed eight words on the board and then asked the class to alphabetize the list. After about ten minutes, she asked students in which order they had placed their words. She then passed out a dittoed list with five groups of words and asked the class to spend the rest of the period arranging them. Janet raised her hand and asked, 'Do I have to do them?'

'No.'

'How come?' asked Melvin.

'Because she and some others got an A on the test and they don't need to do the review.'

'Well, that shouldn't make any difference,' Melvin continued, feeling somewhat cheated.

'It does, so get to work. You people who got A's on the test, I'd like you to either find something to read or come up here and help me staple these papers.' Six people came to the front of the room and Mackle gave them some papers which they took to a corner of the room to staple. Chuck, Gordon, and Jerry went to the corner to look through a stack of magazines and books piled on a table. Soon they were thumbing through a copy of the *Whole Earth Catalog*, and came across some pictures of a woman in a position for natural childbirth. Jerry showed it to Susan, sitting in front of them, and said, 'Hey Susan, here's where you'll be pretty soon.'

Susan replied, 'Hey Fontel, that really turns you on, doesn't it?'

Jerry replied, 'No, but it turns you on doing it.'

For most of the remainder of the period, the students gathered in ones and twos and leafed through magazines while talking about things that interested them. Those who had received A's on the tests spent half the period either helping Mackle staple papers or laughing at the pictures in the *Whole Earth*. This was a typical experience in many classes, for in a classroom organization where everyone must be juggled into approximately the same spot on the continuum, the demands placed on others not at that spot are often minimal. The teacher simply finds it difficult to respond to everyone at once, or everyone with equal effort or time. The assignment is given to keep the majority of the class directed toward some activity for a length of time. Those activities, however, can only apply to a portion of the students. If Mrs Mackle is attending to one group, then Chuck, Gordon, and Jerry are free to leaf through the *Whole Earth* as long as they are not disruptive. If Mackle attends to them, then Janet and her friends stapling papers at the front get further from the assigned task. Work assigned then becomes a quota. Once that level is reached, students are 'on their own' and will be brought back into the instructional mainstream only if their behavior threatens the existence of the quota system.

In many ways we now can begin to see what Jackson was talking about in *Life in Classrooms*. The organizational arrangement of the classroom – be it elementary or junior high – is such that students do learn in 'groups' or crowded settings, all of which regulates to a great extent the processes of learning in the classroom. After all, classroom learning is predicated on the assumption that there is a modal learning style and a modal learning content, otherwise why would between twenty-five and thirty-five students be fitted in, so to speak, one classroom with one teacher? This is, after all, the modal environment of the junior high school: an environment that helps reinforce a standardization of responses as well – what I call 'the right answer.'

The right answer

One day during lunch Chris was saying how he and his father stayed up until 2.00 a.m. the previous night talking about politics and philosophy. 'Really heavy stuff,' he said. That prompted me to ask if he or John (sitting next to him) ever discussed subjects similar to that in class.

Chris volunteered first: 'No, and I think it would really be neat to have a class in philosophy, maybe during Interim.'

'Well,' I said, 'how about just talking about things like that in class, do you guys discuss things in class very much?'

'Naw, not in this place,' Chris responded. 'Every class we have is the same, just straight book work. We never discuss anything, it's just . . .' Just then John interrupted and said, 'Just like in social studies, you know . . .' and he began pointing his finger at Chris and pounding his fist on the desk in an obvious reference to Richards and his behavior. 'We never discuss anything, I think we did more in elementary school than we do here. It's just the same old thing.'

Students rarely expressed an opinion on classes, but a sense of the absence of challenge came through when they did. One reason the instructional demands on students appeared minimal is related to the issue of 'quotas' – that teachers restricted, in essence, student output. Also connected with the tendency toward what appeared to be an implicit ceiling on required learning was what I came to call the 'right answer' syndrome, a factor present in most classes that students at Harold Spencer attended.

In Marcy's English class the object was to elicit from the students what had been preconceived by the teacher as the 'right' or correct answer. In the area of vocabulary, this meant that the students were expected to memorize definitions rather than to understand what a word and its relation to other words meant. The following dialog between Mrs Marcy and the class illustrates the pattern of the teacher asking the students how well they had memorized the definitions:

'To look over carefully or examine in detail is what, class? Roger?'

'I don't know.'

'Dale?'

'Canvass.'

'Right. Mike, to make or utter a chuckling sound?'

'Uh, ch–, chat, chatal or something like that.'

'Close, who can help him? All right, Tina?'

'Chortle.'

'Good, "Alice chortled when she saw his clothes that day." How about the word for modern or not long past? Yes, Philip?'

'Recent.'

'Yes, Tina you have a question?'

'Yeah, how are we going to have these words on the test tomorrow; I mean will you give us the definition and we'll have to fill in the word?'

'Yes, that's the way we've always done it and I don't see any reason to change now. OK, how about the word for concise or pithy?'

Linda immediately raised her hand and volunteered the word 'terse.'

'Good, Linda.' Linda turned to Tina sitting next to her, smiled triumphantly, and said, 'I'll always remember that one because she uses the word "pithy".'

The premium placed on wringing out the correct answer as determined by the teacher was even more pronounced in, of all classes, music class, a class I usually attended daily with Chris. This class, taught by Mr Hackett, emphasized the structure rather than singing of music. A day in November was not unusual as the class discussed the differences between 'phrase' and 'cadence.' Hackett began the class by playing a song on the piano, after which he asked the students to identify the phrases and cadences in the song and whether they were 'consequent' or 'antecedent' phrases, 'complete' or 'incomplete' cadences. He said, 'These are the last songs you are going to hear before the test, so you'd better pay attention to what we are talking about.' As he turned his back to the class to play another song on the piano a few students began to mimic Hackett directing music by waving their hands in the air. Hackett struck up a verse of 'Home on the Range,' after which he turned to the class and said rather sternly, 'Now, I want to know what this is I just played . . .'

'Home on the Range,' David blurted out and then caught himself, realizing Hackett would be mad at him for the less than serious reply. He prepared himself for the response.

'Funnnnny,' replied Hackett staring at David. 'Now, as I WAS saying, I don't want the name of the song, I mean what this is called in music. I want it in one word and one word only. Class?'

'Phrase.'

'No.'

'Cadence.'

'No.'

'Musical sentence.'

'No, you're guessing. They are all parts of it but what is the whole?'

'I think it's called the melody.'

'Yes, there you go, that's the *right* answer.'

Much of the students' day was spent in this type of environment, one in which they were perceived as an empty vessel into which knowledge was poured. The role of the student as someone to whom knowledge was put was an important aspect of the environment that the student faced at Harold Spencer. Most teachers perceived this as a legitimate enterprise and the students accepted this role with little open complaining. After all, most students had been involved in classes of a similar nature for six years in elementary school. To have expected open defiance was unreasonable, especially given the rather conservative nature of the community and the absence of pressure on the schools to do much beyond what they were already doing. Students came to school, did what was expected of them and acted out their life in those interstitial areas where they could. Their role was basically to learn, and to learn meant to show evidence of what was taught by giving the right answer. Yet the school was aware of this problem and had designed procedures to minimize this pattern, to permit an instructional mode matched to the students' needs. Such was the nature of individualized instruction, an approach to reduce boredom and exacerbate excitement.

Demands of individualized instruction

It is difficult to pin down exactly what was or is meant by individualized instruction, but the school district made various claims such as the 'need for students to experience success,' the 'need for every student to actively participate in the learning process and to be given experiences in school which develop real responsibility,' and the 'need for school sponsored programs which utilize the student's own interests as vehicles for learning.' As in all statements of educational goals, these objectives were variously interpreted. It is possible, however, to provide a brief picture of how these objectives were translated into the experiences established for students at Harold Spencer.

The most 'individualized' class at Harold Spencer was the mathematics class to which about half the seventh-grade students were assigned. The class had about sixty students with two regular teachers and usually a few student helpers who came over for one period a day from the nearby high school. While the class was designed to allow students to 'proceed at their own rate' through the mathematics material, the structure of the class did not allow for any diversity on means or ends. By that I mean that students performed the same tasks at one time or another in order to learn a prearranged set of mathematics principles. There was no differentiation on *where* students were heading or *how* they got there; only the time and rate at which they performed the activities differed.

But even variations on time were placed into a series of constraining parameters. Mr Glenn and Mr Charles told students at the beginning of the year that in order to get a 'C' for the course, they had to finish a minimum of seven math activities a quarter, pass the review test for those activities, and receive an average 'effort' grade from the teachers. Thus the student could not 'coast' for one quarter and make up for it the next, as he had to complete the minimum number of activities each and every quarter. Other procedures also leveled the rate. For example, toward the end of the first quarter Mr Glenn told the class: 'I want to let you know that we're not going to be hoodwinked by you guys turning on the steam during the last week or two of the quarter. Don't think that you can fool us by impressing us how hard you've worked just because you have worked hard for a week or two. We sort of keep an eye on you throughout and if we see you getting up and down a lot or doing a lot of talking, that sort of sticks in our minds so we remember that and when it comes time for your effort grade we think to ourselves, "Well, what has that kid done for the quarter?"' The so-called 'effort' grade was then used to enforce a 'floor' on the work done so that students were busy 'working' most of the time and not just when they were motivated. In this respect, then, even variations on rate were regulated.

While individualized classes ostensibly allowed the student to pace himself, significant amounts of time were still spent waiting even when the students decided to work on the materials and talk less to each other. Waiting to take tests or have tests returned and reviewed was one area that I have already mentioned. But often students raised their hands for assistance on a problem, an incident that raised the perennial problem that the teacher could only attend to one detail at a time. As we were sitting in class one day Carl had his hand up for twenty minutes waiting to get help on a problem. 'God, I can't hold my hand up any longer,' he complained.

'Does this happen very often?' I asked.

'Enough,' he replied. 'That's why I always bring a science fiction book to class but then old "Snap-Snap" [the aide who worked in the class] comes out and takes it away from me for reading in math class so I have to be careful.'

One day Mr Glenn told me after class, 'You know, the superintendent thinks these individualized classes are great because you can handle more kids with a fewer number of teachers. Well, that's bullshit. Like this morning, I spent about ten minutes with Janice, God knows she never does anything anyhow so when she does you have to seize the time. But I really felt guilty about it because I knew while I was spending time with her there were thirty to forty others with whom I wasn't spending time. And there's nothing I can do about it, but I really feel guilty.' He was right, for even in the individualized classes such as math, which were certainly better in this regard than some of the other classes, the teacher simply could not attend to all demands at one time. Students had to wait and learned to live with this situation. And because of these demands, some students simply went unattended for long periods of time. Even in individualized classes, then, the individual student had to face many of the same problems seemingly inimical to life in classrooms.

Other classes at Harold Spencer were not as totally 'individualized' as was the math lab, but a few classes had segments that could be classified as using an 'individualized approach,' that is, with significant segments of the classroom instruction arranged to allow students to proceed at their own pace.

For example, in reading, students had some choice as to what to read, but were still constrained by the structure of the classroom setting on when to read and how to read.[3] There are times to read and these factors are determined by the fact that children attend school in groups and the groups are moved along in batches from one subject to the next.

I remember a number of vivid portrayals of this fact, one of which occurred in the spring of the seventh grade. The class was reading a novel called *Light in the Forest* in class. Students were first told that they were to read Chapter 3 only for the period. 'When you are finished with that, just review the chapter. Don't go ahead because we are going to discuss Chapter 3 tomorrow and you might get confused if you go ahead.' Here was the quota system I have discussed before, a ceiling placed on how far students could go. Since the teacher had to deal with the whole class on a particular focused subject, she felt that it would be confusing if new material were introduced in the discussion. Two of the boys, Paul and Danny, were soon talking about baseball games when McBride told them to start reading.

'Can't we take these books home to read them? I don't feel like reading right now,' Paul asked.

'No, the books have to stay here. I think you could get done if you didn't visit so much. Why don't you try to work a little harder and not do so much visiting this week, then you won't have to take the books home, okay?'

Thus far I have described some of the important regularities about classroom life and what it is that students experience in them. These regularities focus upon the use of time in the classroom situations and the demands placed on students in the context of instruction. First, I stated that almost a third of the students' time in school was spent in non-instructional activities, necessary because learning took place in an organizational setting, thus requiring the switching of classes, the passing out and collecting of materials, and other time-consuming tasks. When aspects of instructional pacing and the management of time were considered, about 45 per cent of the students' time was consumed in non-instructional activities. I also stated that instruction itself, by virtue of it occurring in an organizational setting where students were batched and moved along as a unit, was paced rather slowly in order to facilitate the management of the instructional process. With the premium placed on managing instruction, most of the work done in the class was at the teachers' direction, allowing for relatively little teacher–student interaction.

A second and related point has to do with what students were expected to do during the instructional process. Because most instruction was conceived as a process of providing students with knowledge that was parceled out in doses throughout the year, the demands placed on students usually did not go beyond 'knowing' the material that had been dispensed for a certain period of time. Such 'knowledge' placed a great priority on knowing the right answer in order to pass the course successfully. All of these factors were true to a great degree, even those classes that had been 'individualized' – an aim of the school district as a whole.

Finally, I have questioned how 'individualized' individualized classes really were, and from my two years in the school I found that assertion largely questionable. There was variation on rate in some subjects, but the bulk of the student's day was spent moving along at the pace decided by the teacher.

Yet certainly there were exceptions. Mrs Paul was a young and very energetic teacher, well liked by the students, and one who encouraged students to think, debate, and devise schemes to learn centered around some of their own interests. Chris, a good student to begin with, took advantage of this situation and did a great many things on his own – a paper on the Kennedys, a simulation game of the Civil War with a student from another class, and various other papers and projects that he wrote on his own. Toward the end of the eighth grade, when the class was studying world famine, he even phoned in a $10 pledge to a national telethon and then gave an impassioned speech on how the class should raise the money.

But the significance of this event is more in the contingencies under which it occurred. One day while I was sitting in the teachers' lounge Mrs Paul came in and said, 'You people wouldn't believe Chris, that kid is amazing.' Knowing that I spent a lot of time with him and that I had been in the school infrequently during the last month, she said, 'Bob, you have to listen to this too.' She described how Chris had watched the telethon, called in the pledge, and had even called Mrs Paul at home in the evening to tell her what he had done. In an animated way, she went on to say, 'That kid is amazing, he does all these things on his own and doesn't even care if it's extra credit or not. Why, a few weeks ago, we had a unit on the "twenties" and he brought in records, old books, the whole works. I thought to myself, "Why am I teaching this class? He's doing a better job than I am. He should be teaching it."'

The importance of this particular event is surrounded by two basic and overshadowing facts. First, Mrs Paul's history class was only one of Chris's six periods a day and certainly there were few other classes in the eighth grade where the teacher pushed so hard to allow students such diversity. And the class was small (about twenty-three students) and operated for a semester for two consecutive periods, a fact that mitigated to some extent some of the time constraints present for most of the other classes. Second and most importantly, Chris was an exceptional student in terms of self-initiative. Mrs Paul could afford to work out many different approaches for him because only a few of the other students in the class were as demanding and, as she admitted, fun to teach. What if *all* students in her class, small as it was by comparison, had shown as much interest in the topics of the class? Mrs Paul would have been overwhelmed and unable to handle the input. While she enjoyed Chris and he made the class interesting, there seems to be no doubt that, contrary to how much teachers crave students like Chris, they could not handle a class full of Chris's given the limitations of one teacher, a crowd of thirty-five students, and the constraints of space and time. Thus, for the vast majority of the students and for the vast majority of the time spent in class by any one student, Chris included, classroom life was still notable by the heavy presence of standardized instructional pacing and management and the relative absence of demanding activities.

Thus, while some of the classes (social studies and Von Hoffman's English classes in particular) were seen as 'stupid,' it frequently surprised and even puzzled me that there was as little complaining about the content of classes as there was. But classes and the content of classes was not usually a subject discussed among the groups of students. Besides, most seemed to understand that, despite the routine, classes were 'easy' anyway, so what sense was there in complaining? Just adapt and provide the right answer when required. This is not to say, however, that students did not have a rather clear image of classroom life or that such an image did not influence their activities. The manner in which students viewed classes was reflected in the meaning which they attached to the activities and the teachers who organized them. This subject, together with a discussion of what students were doing during much of their time in class, constitutes the next main section of this chapter.

Students and classroom life

Thus far I have discussed some regularities of classroom life that clarify the role of students in the school. We now begin to see that organizational forces within Harold Spencer create, in part, an environment that defines students' lives in particular ways. First, students are massed in the learning process in such a manner that relatively little differentiation occurs among them. Given this approach, academic involvement does not require much of the students' energy – so little in fact that students often are at a loss for something to do. Finally, because of the standardization of treatment, standardized outcomes (answers) tend to be what is expected.

If this is the organizational life that students experience, then we would expect them to form some relatively consistent set of beliefs about those experiences. In turn we would expect these beliefs to influence subsequent actions. Since classroom life is pregnant with attempts by teachers to create these academic products – these constellations of right answers – we need to understand how students come to interpret this process.

Work

As a result of structured interviews with students I was able to construct a composite map of what students said they did in school. When I asked this question of them a typical response was 'we work.'*

*For a more complete listing of what students say they do in school, see Chapter 6.

I became intrigued with the notion of work for two reasons. First, in my two years within the school I was somewhat puzzled by the relative infrequency with which it was discussed by students among themselves. Quite simply, the subject of schoolwork rarely was entertained during student chatter, and I wondered why. Second, when it was mentioned, I noticed what appeared to be subtle distinctions between activities assigned to the notion of 'work' and those that were discussed as 'non-work.' As I explored more fully how students saw work in the school, I began to understand their perspectives within the ongoing regularities of the classroom environment.

Toward the end of the seventh grade, I asked Don and Steve, Chris, Bill, and John and a number of other students what type of activities constituted work. From what they told me, the list reflected in Table 3.1 was generated.

The students, by their categorization, were telling me that work was something that characteristically came from teachers. Of course, not all things that teachers did in class constituted work, but then most of what came to be seen as work emanated from the teacher. This distinction became clear after I talked to three girls, Sharon, Susan and Anna, about work in school. I asked them what activities constituted work.

'Assignments.'

'You know, sentences, stupid stuff.'

'Yeah, I forgot to do mine today too,' Sharon replied.

I asked them if work was the same in all classes or if it differed from class to class. 'Like how about social studies, what kind of work do you do in social studies?'

'Write down different stuff about a story . . . watching a film.'

'Is watching a film work?' I asked.

'It's boring, it's not work.'

'Where does work come from?' I asked.

'Teachers,' replied Anna.

I continued in a somewhat different vein. 'But what if you write a story yourself; for example I noticed you were writing a story about your horse the other day in Creadley's class. Was that work?'

'Oh no,' Anna replied emphatically. 'That was extra credit. I was doing that for English class. You get extra credit on your grade for doing that.'

Thus for these girls (and for most of the students to whom I

Table 3.1 Work and non-work activities

Work	Writing. Having to write on paper. Read so many pages in so much time. Do assignments. Things teachers make you do. Films if there is a quiz or notes to take. Piling it on. Doing questions at the end of the chapter. Graded assignments. Doing the same thing over and over. Memorizing. Something you have to do alone. Do exercises.
Non-work	Experiments. Listening. Extra credit. Art. Science. Going at your own speed. Things where you can get away with doing other things. Things assigned I never do. Watching films. Easy work ----- Just reading stuff you already know. / Assignments with lots of time. Chorus.

talked) 'work' or 'doing work' did not depend so much on the type of activity being done as much as on whether or not the person in authority required it be done. Anna made this clear by emphasizing that writing things down about a story was considered work because it was *required* in Richards's class, but writing a story in English class was not envisioned as work because Anna herself had *initiated* the writing of the story. Without the imperative of the teacher standing over her telling her she had to do it, she saw what was essentially the same activity in a different light.

The notion of requirements – having to do something stated by the teacher – helps to distinguish analytically between what were considered 'work' and 'non-work' activities. In this respect, a film could be perceived as 'work' or 'non-work,' depending upon whether the students needed to pay attention in order to fulfill the expectations of the teacher. Thus, a film might be considered work if students had to watch it to pass a test, but be considered non-work if they could ignore it.

Another criterion, already alluded to, that made work distasteful and which tended to be a definer of work was that it was something you did alone. The preponderance of activities listed under work were those where the students had to sit at their seats, pay attention to the lesson that the teacher had arranged for them, and do what was required by themselves. On the other hand, most of the activities classified as 'non-work' were those in which some semblance of social interaction could go on while the activity was being performed. Science and art were the two classes where students could usually do what was required of them and discuss personal subjects at the same time, and these two classes appeared most frequently on the 'non-work' list; no other specific classes appeared with any regularity on the 'work' list.

The perception of work as a required activity coming from someone in a position of authority and an activity the product of which had an exchange-value (usually by the submission of a paper indicating the satisfactory completion of the work) made sense in the world of the student at Harold Spencer. Work itself was something done not so much because of its intrinsic interest or value, but rather as it was commensurate with the student role that demanded students selling labor power (or the physical and mental capabilities of a person used through labor) in exchange for some symbolic reward. Such a role helps explain the location in Table 3.1 of such activities as 'doing exercises,' 'memorizing,' 'doing the same thing over and over again,' 'doing questions at the end of the chapter' and similar activities listed under the rubric of work. These activities all were congruent with the position of the student as a recipient of knowledge – as one who not so much created knowledge as consumed it. Classrooms were dominated by the teacher. These mandatory activities were subsequently evaluated by the teacher and a grade assigned to them. Such activities were not 'individualized' but were required of the entire class to be done at approximately the same time. Work then developed a negative connotation because work, rather than something emanating from within students themselves, was something that controlled them.

Students' views of my role further illustrate their over-all perspective on work. To them, I was not working most of the time I was in the school. 'You get paid for this?' was a comment. I replied that I did, and their response was to ask who was crazy enough to pay someone to sit around in a school all day with junior high students. But what made my role one of non-work was the students' perceptions of my liberties to come and go as I pleased and to decide for myself what needed attention. Since I was in the school almost every day of the first year, my infrequent absences were noticeable and many wondered how I could work and still 'skip' from the location of my work – the school. The fact that I could choose which classes to attend, which lunch to go to, which students to hang around – all were conditions simply not connected with work. To the students, work meant having to do something, being regulated, the presence of tight parameters and the like. They had come to see work as the absence of control over the conditions of their own labor.

Teachers and teaching

Parallel with students' perspective on work were the visions they carried with them on teachers and what teachers did. I should note here that, like the subject of work, characteristics of teachers were not frequently discussed either. As students filed from classes, they immediately began or continued their conversations relating to their personal interests with few comments on either how interesting or how boring the class had been. Minimal discussion does not mean that students did not construct certain perspectives on teachers and the teaching process, for they obviously did. Yet these perspectives must be placed in context, for other activities were far more important and occupied a much more pre-eminent space in the student's cognitive framework than did any discussion of work or the teachers who parceled out the work.

Table 3.2 is an arrangement of the comments made regarding teachers throughout the year, gathered mostly by my being with the students when the subject was raised but also during formal interviews which I held with a number of students near the end of the seventh grade. Generally, students believed that teachers could be

Table 3.2 Kinds of teachers

Teachers with negative attributes	Strict. Those with favorites. Those that hate the whole class. Bastards. Screwy. Fairies. Femmies. Busters. Mean. Those who don't communicate. Worse teachers. Narcs. Hard to get along with teachers. Fish. Pick n'flicks. Those that think they're funny. Those that do the same thing over and over. Slave drivers. Crabs. Snappers.
Teachers with positive attributes	Nice------- They respect us. They trust us. They listen to us. Those that let you chew gum. Neat teachers. Cool teachers.

divided into two groups, those labeled 'teachers with negative attributes' and 'teachers with positive attributes.' It is interesting to note the distinction that the students made between the two groups.

Two conditions characterized teachers with negative attributes. The first centered around *physical or personal characteristics* and included such characterizations as 'bastards,' 'screwy,' 'weirdo,' 'fairies,' 'hard to get along with teachers,' 'fish,' 'those that think they're funny,' 'crabs,' or 'snappers.' There was not uniform agreement on what every one of these terms meant as distinguished from the other, but it was obvious that certain ones were reserved for specific people. The term 'bastard,' for example, was usually reserved for teachers who carried on in ways that were seen as unfair or demeaning. Don and Steve, for example, thought Richards was a bastard because 'he's always yelling, standing up there getting red in the face, making a fool out of himself.' 'Treating us like kids,' was another of Richards's attributes.

Terms like 'screwy,' 'weirdo,' 'fairies,' 'fish,' 'pick and flick' related to personal habits such as voice inflections, mannerisms of walking and other movements, and dress. Discussions frequently occurred over whether Mr Bruce really was 'queer' simply because he had a high voice, dressed fairly well, and bounced a little while he walked. A few students even debated the same issue about Mr Charles simply because he called people 'honey' or 'sweetheart,' and because often he put his arm on a student's shoulder while helping him with a math problem.

Personal appearance, too, often served as a basis for students' discriminations among teachers. Mrs Ansel was considered 'weird' because she wore what students considered to be mismatched clothing. Students usually picked on Mr Von Hoffman because of his short haircut, a butch cut from the 1950s. Mr Franks was considered 'screwy' because he wore old ties and was reputed to pick the wax out of his ears and flick it across the room while talking, an act that I never personally observed although Steve and others swore a hunk of wax once landed on their science book. Mr Hackett, who often had bloodshot eyes, was suspected of being a heavy drinker; the students never placed much credence in the fact that he wore contact lenses and held down a part-time job in the evenings, a combination that, I imagined, would give anyone bloodshot eyes.

The *specific actions* of teachers in the classroom was a second criterion used to assign negative attributes to teachers. Such attributes as 'strictness,' 'those with favorites,' 'those that hate the whole class,' 'those that think they're funny,' 'those that do the same things over and over,' and 'slave drivers' were included. These conditions often overlapped and many were assigned to the same teacher as an over-all negative indictment.

Negative attributes connected with specific actions usually were connected with the notion of 'teachers who don't communicate.' Chris described this during a discussion about Von Hoffman. 'I don't think he communicates with kids. Like he's giving a spelling test and the word is supposed to be "entered," like "He entered the door quickly." He pronounced it "innard" so I said out loud, "You mean entered." He just says, "Look buddy, you have a detention slip." He's one of the most self-conscious persons I have ever met, he's always worried about another person looking at him . . . you see him talking to himself a lot and doing things like pointing and hitting his fist and maybe frowning and hitting the table and you think "What's going through that guy's mind?"'

The characterization of 'hard to get along with teachers' was another category that included a variety of descriptors and that reflected the over-all flexibility of the teacher in the school. I once asked Chris and John what a hard-to-get-along-with teacher was.

'They're the ones who have been at Harold Spencer since the first year . . . they've seen year after year of kids come through here and I think it just gives them the impression when a new group of students comes in that "Oh man, here comes another group of those brats," and they think that they have to push their thumb on someone completely and if they let half their thumb off the class is going to go wild.' To many students, these teachers were inflexible and students had to meet them on their terms, which meant 'doing the same thing over and over.' Barry and John, both good students, commented that their English teacher was hard to get along with because they did the same thing in class over and over again: 'prepositional phrases, prepositional phrases, just do it over everyday, do assignments three and four times, and it gets so boring, you just sit there. Everyday I hate to go to that class because I know we are going to do the same things again.'

Hard-to-get-along-with teachers, in other words, were like bad bosses – they extracted the most from the students and viewed work as an exchange process that operated on the basis of the controllers of production having authority over the means of production.

To understand characteristics about teachers that students did not like is also to understand the characteristics of the teachers they viewed positively. I found surprisingly little disagreement among the students when they specified what it was about a teacher that made them, in their terms, 'nice,' 'neat,' or 'cool.' John said that most of the kids thought Mr Creadley was the best teacher in the school. 'He just says, "Okay, we have some work to do, let's do it and keep the talking down." He gives you work and he expects you to have it done. It's not that it's that hard, he just gives you a little incentive.'

Chris added, 'He's the only teacher I know who gives you an opportunity to go ahead and do other things. Like with Mr Franks, he just wants you to answer the questions and then you sit around waiting for everyone else to finish but Mr Creadley encourages you to do things other than just answer the questions.'

While John and Chris mentioned some ways in which Creadley ran his class, it was Creadley's style and personality rather than what they learned in class that appealed most to them. Most of the other students liked him because he treated the students 'fairly,' was not 'uptight,' did not 'yell a lot,' and so on. When most students talked about 'cool' or 'neat' teachers, these seemed to be the attributes to which they were referring.

Also common were comments such as 'they respect us,' or 'they listen to us.' In their more reflective moments, many of the students could tell what they saw in teachers they valued positively, and usually this had little to do with how or what they taught, but rather how they interacted with the students as people. One boy who spent considerable time in the office for minor discipline problems told me he thought the vice-principal, Mr Pall, was really quite fair and that 'at least he usually listens to you.' He could not speak as highly of his other teachers for, as he saw them, 'they don't look at you as an individual, they look at you as a group like they want you to be. In fact a lotta times the only time a teacher remembers your name is if you're always getting into trouble or if you're especially good, but if you're just sort of average they don't notice you.'

Most teachers fell between what students perceived to be completely positive and negative attributes when they did talk about teachers, but I never felt that this signified a real resentment against most of the teachers.

What teachers did in the school appeared, at least on the surface, in conflict with what the students thought was best or desirable, as shown in Table 3.3, wherein I have presented the students' belief about what the teachers did. This list dramatizes that students saw themselves as passive and the adults as the active member of the relationship. In the area of what I have called 'interaction with students' students portrayed a picture of themselves as being less than or below adults. Students saw many adults in terms of authority hierarchies where the adults interacted with students on the basis of the authority vested in their office. Thus, when teachers interacted with students, the students perceived they were underestimated and treated 'like third-graders' through a simplification of work and assignments. Students also thought they were talked down to and that little allowance was made for their input as individuals.

The tendency of the teachers to give out work and the students to do it is clear in Table 3.3. Teachers 'pile it [work] on' and then turn around and 'write,' 'sit at their desk,' 'correct papers,' and 'grade us.' If there were problems with the class, teachers 'scream,' 'watch people,' and 'be strict.' From the student point of view, there was little else involved in what teachers did in the classroom other than

that represented in this simple 'factory model' of learning; that is, the teachers pouring in the facts and the students pouring them back in the form of papers and tests. Students had little, if any, conception of teachers planning lessons, debating alternatives of what to teach, agonizing over grading, the treatment of a student, wondering if their teaching had an effect, or anything like that. The student picture of teachers provided little room for emotion, with the exception of that associated with student violation of school standards. The teacher's world, in the student's eyes, was straightforward and linear, hardly complex at all.

Such viewpoints on teachers – their characteristics and what they do, confirms the presence of a separate student culture – one poised at odds with the adult culture in the school.[4] First, students saw their academic activities consisting mostly of 'work' and it was the teacher who so defined their task, thereby providing students with little formal control over their own labor. Second, upon examining student-held beliefs about teachers, we see that teachers were viewed negatively owing to the extent to which they maintained tight control over student activities in the classroom; teachers who were viewed more positively were those who provided some greater degree of self-determination, although this did not necessarily mean that these teachers might be less demanding. Finally, students' beliefs about what teachers 'did' was remarkably congruous to their own conception of what they, as students, did. Accordingly, the student-generated belief system held that the teacher's job consisted mostly of handing out work and enforcing the standards by which work was done. Most social interaction with students by

Table 3.3 Things teachers do

Interaction with students	Simplify things like third-graders. Don't treat us as individuals. Don't listen to us. Not congratulate you. Embarrass us. Take for granted you know what to do. Try to build a reputation with students. Sit around and expect you to learn by yourself.	
Duties	Run projector. Sit. Talk – – – – – – – – – – – – Pile it on. Read papers. Correct papers. Sit at desk. Give work. Tap pencils. Grade us. Write. Read stories. Give detention.	to us. to each other.
Discipline	Catch people smoking. Scream. Argue. Eye you. Stare at the girls. Cuss. Give hacks. Throw people out.	Study people's jaws. Watch people. Tell us to stop talking. Be strict. Send us to the office. Nag. Give sentences.
Actions	Be self-conscious. Act like commandos. Try to be cool– – – – –	Dumb jokes to us. Dirty jokes to each other. Don't take things seriously.

teachers existed from a position of authority, making even sharper the divisions between the adult and student way of understanding the junior high school.

The social basis of classroom life

Up to this point, I have stated that the student spends a significant portion of time as an observer and a sometime participant in instructional events, playing a passive role in the many organizational maintenance activities; parallel to this I described the relatively undemanding pace of instruction and the concern about exhibiting readily accessible answers rather than a process of thought and inquiry. I continued by outlining the students' perspective on the important instructionally related activities: work, the differentiation students made among teachers, and what teachers did. This information reveals that classroom demands and the instructional process affected students and their life in school to a lesser degree than we might normally expect (or even hope for). Thus it is relevant to ask what students were doing to occupy so much of their time in the six and a half hours they were in school. Furthermore, if the topics of 'work' and the actions of teachers, be they viewed positively or negatively, were subjects that were not discussed with much frequency or force, then what subjects were discussed?

Social aspects of instruction. On Monday mornings in the Fall I usually walked to math class first period with John and Chris. Mondays were rather special because John, Tom, and a few others interested in sports always compared the predictions they had made the previous Friday on who would win designated collegiate and professional football games over the week-end. The local paper printed a coupon that listed twenty teams (fifteen college teams and five pro teams) and John and his friends cut the coupon out and put in twenty-five cents a person, winner takes all. As I arrived at class a few minutes before the bell rang, they were comparing their scores.

'How many?' asked Tom.

'Only fourteen right,' said John glumly. 'I really blew a few of them, like that USC-Notre Dame game. God, Notre Dame was ahead like twenty-five points at half time and they lost the game by twice that.'

'Yeah, I missed that one too,' said Bill who had won the pot with seventeen correct out of twenty.

Mr Glenn then read the announcements while Chris and Phil collected money that the students had raised selling magazines for the student body treasury. While that was all going on, Tom and John continued their analysis of the games. As soon as the announcements were over, Glenn told the class to get busy on their math, but Tom and John launched into a discussion of the upcoming Monday night game between Pittsburgh and Washington. This continued for twenty minutes.

When possible, being with their friends and talking about items of mutual interest occupied students during much of class time. In the case of John, Tom and sometimes Chris it was sports, although Chris was not interested in football but rather hockey, which he talked about whenever he could during the winter months. For other students the subjects could vary, but activities before and after school, at week-ends, television programs, motor cycles, and other people were all popular subjects.

I was always amazed not only by the fact that students carried on so much of their personal agenda during the day but especially by the way they did it, fulfilling the academic requirements but seemingly unconcerned by the omnipresent adults in the school. One afternoon I had gone to the library with some students from McBride's class for the weekly library period, during which time we were supposed to 'read,' that is, check out a book to make a book report, two of which were due each quarter. As I sat down at a table, Don, Chuck, and two girls (Patty and Sandy) joined us. The period had not officially begun before Chuck asked Patty, 'What did you think of the party at Jimmy's Saturday?'

'Wow, heavy, I think I was gettin' smashed.'

By this time the bell had rung for class to begin and Patty got up, took a magazine from the magazine stand, brought it back to the table and began leafing through it while talking about the party. McBride made Don sit at another table and it did not look as if much work was being accomplished. Don sat in the corner near Steve and Chuck continued to chat about the party. Between five and ten minutes later, McBride approached the table. Chuck, who like the rest of the people at the table (myself included) had a book or magazine open while talking about the party, saw her approach. He simply said, 'Hey,' quite softly, nodded, and buried his head in his book. The others did likewise. McBride approached the table and said something about people getting to work. She was no more than 5 to 10 feet away when Chuck started almost where he had left off.

'And those sounds, I just DIG Alice Cooper.'

'Who brought that Osmond Brothers Album?' asked Patty.

'I don't know, I think it was Betty Crane.'

'Figures, how come she came anyhow . . .?'

And on it went through most of the period. It did not make that much difference whether McBride was around or not. They continued their conversation as soon as she was out of hearing range and preoccupied with other things. Students usually gave the impression of looking busy and seldom were loud or disruptive in their conversations, for as long as they, like John and Tom in the earlier incident, could keep up their communications without being disruptive and could finish their work in reasonable order, then teachers like McBride and others had little reason to break up sessions like this. After all, they had to be concerned with between thirty and thirty-five students every period, and there were students who did little of anything who needed to be watched much more closely.

To the reader who has not been in a school for some period of time, and who might attribute all of this to poor teaching or somewhat of an uninspiring faculty, let me say that I suspect that this is not the case, at least it is not the sole reason why students filled up so much of their time talking to each other about non-academic-related subjects. Two of the most popular classes in the school, art and science, found students interacting frequently even though the students thought the teachers were good. Mr Creadley, the science teacher, presented the material well, set up interesting experiments for the students, and had a knack for making science more than just learning to use the scientific method. The art teacher, Mr Dennis, allowed the students to design their own projects and was very facilitative in helping them. Yet the general situation was not that much different in either of these two classes. Even when they were doing experiments that they enjoyed, Don and Chris were able to write up their lab work while simultaneously discussing a range of personal topics. In the classroom setting, where the use of time left so much empty space and where the students had been taught, throughout the years, that learning in school meant doing by and large what you had been told to do and when you were told to do it, there were a great many voids that the students could fill with their own interests.

The overwhelming frequency of discussions centering on students' personal interactions rather than the specific content of the class prompted me to wonder what daily events stood out in the students' mind. So one day I asked Gordon, sitting across from me, to name the five most important things he did yesterday. Of course, he looked at me somewhat skeptically as he asked why I wanted to know that. Finally, after thinking for a moment, he said, 'Let's see . . . I worried about a test, that's one thing; I wondered about what we were going to do in PE, that's another thing for sure . . .'

'Anything else?'

'I was thinking about wrestling after school today. I think I'm a pound overweight,' he said as he stuffed the last half of his cinnamon roll in his mouth. 'And then I wondered what was for lunch yesterday. When I found out it was corn dogs I didn't eat. That's why I'm really porking today.'

I then proceeded to ask Don the same question. He replied, 'I got bawled out, I got bawled out, I got bawled out, I got bawled out, and I got bawled out.'

Thereafter I made it a point throughout the year to ask a number of students to tell me the five most important things they remembered about the previous day. I asked this question of all types of students, students who were doing extremely well in school and those not doing well at all, those who spent a lot of time in the office and those who spent very little, boys and girls, athletes and motor cycle enthusiasts and the like. The list as follows was typical:

Got on the bus.
Went to my locker.
Talked in math class.
Kicked my brother out of the house cause he's always late for school.
Figured how much money I'll need for skiing.
Talked to you at lunch.
I was so bored so I wrote on my peechie all day.
Kept thinking about working on 'reverses' in wrestling.

My dog stole my clothes this morning.
Had a cigarette after lunch.
Can't think of anything else.

Got up.
Didn't want to go to school.
Smoked a cigarette before school.
When I was at school I thought about going home.
Smoked a cigarette after school.
Got a 'poor work slip.'
Played cards with some guys.
Smoked a joint.
Fed my dog.
Hurt my hand in PE.
Finished my math.
Got wiped out in medicine ball in PE.
Wrote a lot in geography.
Got in trouble in band cause I stole some kid's mouthpiece.
Didn't get hit with food at lunch even though I sat near the garbage can.
Got a 100 on a reading test today.
Didn't do any work in reading today.

These lists confirmed the fact that even though students spent six-and-a-half hours in the school, ostensibly for instructional purposes, instruction did not remain uppermost in their minds on a day-to-day basis. Only a few students made any reference to activities associated with learning, and then it concerned rather mechanistic activities such as finishing an assignment or taking a test. In some instances students talked about the *absence* of doing any work such as not doing anything at all or getting out of work. For most students, then, daily instructional activities, while most did them, were not something of prime importance. What was of greater significance was the time spent in social interaction among groups of friends.

This point took on added importance when I asked students what it was that they did spend most of their time doing while they were at school. One particular time, while sitting at lunch with John, Chris, Bud, and a few other students (all, by the way, excellent students academically and not the type that frequented the office for discipline problems), I said, 'Doesn't it seem strange that all the time you spend in school hardly anyone talks about classes or what goes on in classes?'

John replied, 'Are you kidding?'

'Who wants to?' Chris asked.

'That's not where it's at anyway,' John continued.

I was genuinely puzzled by this time. 'Well, where is it at then?'

'Well I don't know; I guess it's the things we do all the time.'

'What do you mean, what kind of things are those?'

'You know, the things we told you about when you asked us what kids do. That's where it's at.' Sharon, a girl I knew fairly well, once asked me what kinds of things I was going to write in my study. I answered her rather ambiguously by saying simply, 'All the things that kids do in school.' Her reply to me was, 'It should be more than just showing that kids do work and that kind of stuff; that's not what we do anyhow; it's what teachers think we do.'

Because doing things with other people means so much to the typical junior high student at Harold Spencer, it was important to have a reasonably close set of acquaintances with whom to interact. Students at the junior high did not seem to be undifferentiated, as Coleman suggests in his study of the adolescent society, nor were there tight friendship cliques as found by Cusick in his study of senior high students.[5] Rather there appeared to be large blocks of students with similar interests but with fairly frequent crossovers among groups for relatively short periods of time.

Some students, however, had few friends and life did not appear particularly pleasant for these 'weirdos' (as they were called) because they were, in various ways, excluded from the ongoing social interaction that consumed so much of the student's day. They usually sat by themselves in the library, ate alone at lunch, and tended to be ridiculed in class despite what the teacher was able to do to prevent such ridicule, which often was not much.

To illustrate what 'weirdos' experienced let's look at a boy named Donnie in the early part of the seventh grade, when he was obviously attempting to be accepted by some group of students and in the process subjected himself to ridicule. On this occasion, I was eating lunch with Don, Roger, Steve, and Gordon when Donnie sat down at the end of our table to eat his lunch. He had never participated in our discussions much, but Don and Gordon found good reason to exploit Donnie's wanting to please as he readily returned their empty food trays, brought them milk shakes when they asked him, and performed other tasks on request. He became a rather handy 'coolie' and they tolerated him – for a while.

But the group soon tired of this and began to ridicule him one day at lunch. 'God, Marin [Donnie's last name], what shitty clothes, looks like you puked in them this morning.'

'Yeah, real neat,' said Gordon as he fingered his shirt. 'The thing stinks like puke too.'

'How often do you take a bath, Marin, once a year? I see mold growing behind your ears. God, it's ALIVE,' Steve shrieked as he moved away from him to the other end of the bench. Marin stoically tried to ignore all these taunts but returned the next day.

Marin again returned the food trays, but after a few days the group tired of his presence. This time their low toleration seemed prompted by Chuck, the only seventh-grader playing in the varsity basketball team, who was taunting Don and the others: 'Hey, Don, when did you start sitting with weirdos at lunch?' Roy, sitting at the same table, said, 'Yeah, how can you stand the smell?' That seemed to do it. The next day Gordon started harassing Donnie by messing over his lunch.

'Want your pudding, Marin?' said Gordon as he took his vanilla pudding with artificial whipped cream topping and ate it. A few minutes later Steve took Donnie's cherry 'jello' and turned the plate upside down on top of his mashed potatoes. Everyone laughed, but Marin tried as best he could to ignore it. Donnie extracted the 'jello' from the mashed potatoes, placed it back in the original container, and defiantly ate it while the group laughed. The next day he was back again and this time Don took his milk and poured half of it on top of his tossed salad. Having had enough, Marin moved to another table, and he never sat with us again for the remainder of the year.

In class, students like Marin were often ostracized in other, more subtle ways: by having their pencils or papers ripped off, their gym bags stolen, or being the focus of jokes and comments in class. One boy, Dave, was alternately called a 'greaser' by many of the girls because of his long and admittedly dirty-looking hair and a 'stoner' by many of the guys because he was always talking about his drug trips – 'taking reds,' having a good supplier for hash, 'getting lids' cheaper than anyone else and so on. Everyone admitted they did not like him, yet Don was not above scrounging cigarettes from him for his after-lunch smoke. As the year wore on, students generally grew tired of him ('he thinks he knows everything,' was the common complaint) and by the eighth grade he was obviously on everyone's 'dump' list. I felt sorry for Dave but dared not tell the group to lay off for fear of appearing too much like a teacher.

There were two crucial elements to being accepted by mainstream groups at Harold Spencer. The first was some minimal conformity to the implicit standards of the group. Conformity was required in a number of areas: actions, interests, talk, dress, attitude toward school, toward peers, etc. There were a number of reasons why Donnie had never been accepted by most of the groups. His dress and personal habits did not endear him greatly to many of the students: sometimes his socks did not match, he tended to wear 'high waters' (pants whose cuffs were a few inches above the ankles), and colors that did not match. Additionally, he was ostracized for what was perceived as his all too close relations with teachers, that is, his constant desire to be helpful. One of the accepted norms of students centered around preserving a distance between the students and other adults and such helpfulness as practiced by Donnie was considered unacceptable by the group.

Conformity was required in other areas as well. When Dave got into difficulty with Marty, Tony and some of the others, one reason was because he called a girl who had been dating a friend of most of the guys in this group. That was simply not done by friends and Dave's indiscretion in calling Cheryl was the symbolic act that proved to the group that he was not part of their circle. If he had really wanted to be, he would have never done what he did. Other important norms included a trust not to 'narc' on anyone no matter how serious it might be, not to be too aggressive to do work, and not to display knowledge disproportionately so as to appear better than anyone else. The idea was to fit, for anything making the person stand out in an unacceptable manner could lead to exclusion.

A second and related condition of acceptance is illustrated in the incident involving Dave. Earlier, Tony had made the statement that Dave was in trouble with them because he thought he was so big. An individual who was indiscreetly immodest invariably was not well accepted by relevant groups within the school. As a rule, the students who were most popular and uniformly accepted were those who had obvious talents in the area of academics, athletics, music, art, drama but who did not play up their talents, but rather 'leveled' themselves to be as much like the 'average student' as possible. In contrast, the students least well accepted attempted to insure that everyone knew of their accomplishments, whether they be in academics, getting drugs, or athletic feats.

Summary and conclusions

In this chapter I have described the classroom world of the student at Harold Spencer. First, I pointed out major and persistent regularities of life in classrooms, highlighting how students spend their time within the classroom, the demands that instructional processes place on students, and the modal instructional system to which students are exposed. Next, I handed the story over to the students, permitting them to describe two important aspects of their institutional life – work and teachers, and the activities of teachers. Finally I raised the issue (to be followed in detail in much of what follows in this book) that activities normally associated with 'schooling' (that is, classroom instruction) are not the only activities of critical importance in understanding the student culture in junior high school.

I wish now to synthesize these major points, with a view toward understanding how organizational regularities and indeed the institution itself is maintained through the very manner by which the 'work' of students creates a specific and class-based cultural process.

If the information in Chapter 3 indicates anything, it is that the modal form of instruction at Harold Spencer does not demand much of the student's time in school. Over all, only slightly more than half of the time a student spends in school is occupied by instructional activities, a figure that is cause for reflection considering the six-and-a-half hours a day a student spends in school. Nor did instructional tasks, on the average, seem to demand much in the way of intellectual effort from students. It was relatively easy, for example, for John and Steve to discuss intramural football games while, almost subconsciously, working on a social studies assignment, a practice indicative of the intensity of intellectual work demanded of the students in the school. Student reaction to such work demands seemed more to be one of fitting it in to their ongoing personal agendas than having to adopt a radically different cognitive framework in order to complete the work successfully.

The culminating effect of the above findings is somewhat surprising. Some critics have come to see schools and the instructional procedures that go on within them almost analogous to a casting machine, stamping out children as products in a mold, with these products then being available for standardized use as parts for an automobile. In fact, Bowles and Gintis discuss the functions of the educational system as a method of disciplining children in the interest of producing a subordinate adult population. They say:

> Prompt and obedient response to bureaucratically sanctioned authority is, of course, a must. But sheer coercion is out of keeping with the modern educator's view of the child and the larger social needs for a self-controlled – not just controlled – citizenry and work force. Discipline is still the theme, but the variations more often center on the 'internalization of behavior norms,' on equipping the child with a built-in supervisor than on mere obedience to external authority and material sanctions.[6]

This rigid, almost deterministic force hardly seems borne out in the case of Harold Spencer. In fact, in so far as instructional practice is concerned, the amount of unrestrained time, coupled with a minimization of rigorous cognitive processing, seems to illustrate almost the opposite of a system of disciplining, and instead appears to be a system bordering on benign neglect. To the extent that this is the case, how do such activities affect the structure of student relations to the cultural patterns emerging from and created by those patterns?

The minimization of a rigid, all-consuming system of instruction where learning is under the close and conscious domination of instructional agents should not be taken to mean that a deep system of cognitive and cultural development is not ongoing here, nor that there does not exist a steady signal consistently but interminably sent out and received, albeit in almost a subconscious fashion. That is, there does exist a system of knowledge reinforced within the instructional modalities of a school like Spencer. Equally important there is a systematic definition and reinforcement of what is known and, equally important, how it is known. The system of instruction, by defining the social relationships among people in the school and through the constitutive process by which what is known is defined, then sets forth epistemological regularities that are defined, established, and maintained. To the extent that knowledge is so defined, then so is the labor process of those who produce and consume.

Harold Spencer defined and reinforced a particular epistemological system – a specific set of rules for ascertaining what is known and how it is known. That type of knowledge, what we will call 'reified knowledge,' is knowledge that while abstract, tenuous, and problematical, is treated as if it is concrete and 'real.' Such knowledge is treated unequivocally as a fact and as information to be used in the formation of real (empirical) relationships said to exist between those facts. It is, stated somewhat crudely, 'recipe' knowledge, or knowledge with components that are rather mechanistically added toward the creation of some predefined product. In emphasizing and reinforcing such a system of knowledge, it is the ends, the utility of the knowledge, that are of utmost importance, not the means by which what is known is, in fact, known. The importance of 'the right answer' (phrase, cadence, musical sentence), the mechanistic process of 'individualized instruction' via mathematics and reading aptly points out the systemic basis of school knowledge perpetuated at Harold Spencer. The world of education is that which supplies objective facts, concrete and agreed upon, that are to be learned, manipulated, and applied in an empirical fashion towards predefined ends. This involves, then, a problem-applying orientation to the world, and the orientation toward reified knowledge translates into a strategy using information and applying it to a problem in the manner of and under the assumptions of how it has been defined as a problem. The assumptions used to define phrase and cadence as a problem to be learned, are then not raised, neither are the criteria by which those and other facts are identified as educational problems that are part of a system of knowing.

Pre-eminence and the pervasiveness of such a system of knowledge in the school is not explicitly and manifestly repressive, although it is preordinately instrumental. Knowledge and way of knowing are defined, the rules of knowing are assumed, and the means – ends continuum becomes accepted. The ease by which students could follow through on school work, all the while talking about football or discussing parties while in the library, simply meant that students, for the most part, had come to accept the epistemological system preordinate in the school and had learned the means – end relationship necessary to insure the modicum of success necessary or desired. In so adapting to that epistemological current, knowledge and its attributes was taken to be given, and its problematical nature was neither addressed nor was it intended to be addressed.

This instrumental basis of reified knowledge was recognized by 'students', for the belief system of students on 'work' and on 'teachers' illustrates clearly the pervasiveness of reified knowledge and how that pervasiveness becomes incorporated into the belief systems of cultural groups. Students understood 'work' as a process defined and controlled by teachers, and that it was something over which students themselves played but a small part in determining its essential direction. The control and determination of labor, then, was an essential determinant that students used to classify 'work.' This is especially true when we note that the same objective tasks could be designated as 'work' or 'non-work' by students, dependent not on the nature of the tasks, but upon how or by whom the nature and outcome of the task was determined. As Anna indicated, for example, writing a story in Richards's class was 'work' because Richards required the task, but performing the same task in English class was deemed not to be work because she initiated the project.

This same segmented, concretistic notion of work is evident as well in student understandings of those who assigned work – the teachers. We find little evidence of student understandings of teachers as historical figures, as human beings in their contextual fabric facing their own dilemmas, making their own history. Instead they are, by and large, authority figures – individuals with the power to make the students do things they do not want to do and, ultimately, to apply sanctions if those things are not completed. Teachers' role behavior, according to the students, consisted largely of assigning work ('piling it on,' 'giving work,') and evaluating or assigning symbols called grades '(grade us,' 'correct papers'). The affective dimension of the teacher role as understood by students rarely was representative of the range of emotions normally present in any adult population, but rather was skewed toward dimensions of the teacher's official role as an individual providing factual information and enforcing the proper conditions to facilitate acquisition of that knowledge. So, according to what students knew, teachers spent much of their time 'being strict,' 'throwing people out,' and just plain 'watching.' Even so-called 'neat' teachers were so categorized not so much on the basis of how they taught but rather on how they interacted with students. Thus, they still gave 'work,' but were not as rigid in enforcing the conditions under which it got done.

There is a rather stable thread running through these outlooks on knowledge perpetuated in schools and what students must do to acquire it. That thread quite simply is that which is defined as 'work' is labor over which the student has little appropriation, or that which he/she must provide to another on the terms that the other has defined. Work thus done is present in an 'alienated' form in the sense that the student has little control over its definition and outcome and consequently is estranged from its fundamental properties. Work in schools, or at least that which students define as work, comes to be seen as labor not one's own, but that which inherently belongs to others.

The predominance of reified knowledge in the school and the manner by which students come to incorporate its premises and structure into their own cultural processes (thus using those premises to create their own existence) is analogous to the process wherein labour is turned into 'commodity production' which in turn becomes the basis of labor. In this process, as Marx explains, we first find that the control over labor – that very life activity that defines human existence and of which humans are conscious – is unequal, meaning that the worker does not control that activity that defines his/her existence in any situation. Due to this minimization of control, an antagonism is built up between the worker and the controller of work to the extent that what the worker does is contested. In this sense, then, the labor process to the worker is not engaged in because it produces something of value to the worker, because it is over this issue that the labor is contested (this inherent value of labor is what Marx called its 'use-value'). Instead, when labor is done and performed, it is performed for another value by the worker – that is called an 'exchange-value.' Herein, work becomes an intermediary process to produce a 'commodity' of value that can be exchanged for something else of value to the worker. To this extent, the worker becomes estranged from his or her work because the work is being performed for its exchange-value more than its use-value.

Marx continues and notes that, in capitalistic systems, because use-value and exchange-value are separated and labor tends to be estranged, recurrent crises occur as the system continually legitimizes the exchange-value of labor, thereby convincing laborers that the exchange-value is of sufficient importance to warrant them selling their labor power and thereby being estranged from their own labor. Accordingly, if the system is to survive, it must deal with the conflicts that are inherent in a situation where those who sell their labor power are subservient and thus provide for the profits of those in control of work. Managing such conflict becomes an important agenda of such a system, especially in the light of opposition to that system.

Reified knowledge and its predominance in schools such as Harold Spencer seems to be the basis of the early development of a labor process, the outcome of which is the creation of 'commodities' that have an exchange-value more than it is labor which has primary use-value. In this labor process, students viewed themselves as having little control over the productive process, and envisioned the role of and activity of teachers to be such that it was they who controlled the labor process and determined the outcomes of student labor. Work was then engaged in because the adults controlled its basic parameter, defined its content, and stipulated its outcomes. Students in turn produced commodities ('knowledge' or that so defined) in exchange for symbols of importance to them (grades, evaluations), or at least symbols they were told were important to them. To the extent that these symbols were not critically important, at least being together in class was important and, under the circumstances, worth the price of having to do 'work.'

When we think of it, 'working' in school and learning to accept the premises of reified knowledge is a natural way for young people to come to realize that work, for most of us, usually is that which we are told to do given the standards within which work is defined. In so coming to accept the premises of alienated labor, we can begin to understand the concurrent realization that the selling of one's labor power is the 'natural' process within labor, and that the owners of capital have the 'right' to control the labor of those they employ. Reified knowledge, then, with its emphasis upon concreteness and factualism, the origins of which are relatively unimportant but the application of which forms the *raison d'être* of the production of exchange-value, extends a fundamental cultural regularity of capitalism deep into the cultural processes within schools – indeed even into the informal social structures that students themselves generate.

As reified knowledge is incorporated into the belief system, and subsequent actions of junior high school adolescents, we can see the very process by which a culture creates and re-creates itself and, in the process, builds those very social structural arrangements we have come to see as given and impermeable. History is both living and lived, and through living we create a history for ourselves and those who follow us. In this sense the organizational culture of the school – the teachers, students, the knowledge system that emanates through instructional processes – all are constitutive elements that build what we sometimes see as 'objective' conditions. It is in this sense that the junior high students' culture becomes a living and breathing process, integrating what appear to be unrelated processes into a way of life we come to take for granted as something 'out there.' Thus, in the case of the junior high school, it is in the welding of this system of reified knowledge with processes by which students interpret and make themselves in the institution that the fundamental elements of a labor process and the very precepts on which it is based are re-created, built upon, and reconstituted. It is this interpretive process that is the subject of our next two chapters.

4
The world of Don's group

In the life of a young man the most essential thing for happiness is the gift of friendship (Sir William Osler).

I first became acquainted with Don and his friends as sixth-graders while doing pilot work for the present study. I had been at the school they attended for six weeks – hanging around with different students, trying to understand more fully what issues were of concern to them and what they did in school. The evaluation project on which I was working desired to obtain data on the relationship between sociometric choice and academic achievement, so I helped administer a sociometric instrument for this purpose. Analyzing these data revealed two pertinent facts. First, Don was nominated as one of the more popular boys in the sixth grade in the school. Second, a number of students were absent the day during which the instrument was administered, among them Don, Steve, and two girls – Karen and Delilah. This absence turned out to have a remarkable significance.

A few days after first administering the instrument, I came across Karen in the playground and asked her to complete the short form. Naturally, I was surprised when she turned her back and refused to talk to me. Spotting Carrie, a friend of hers, I asked her why Karen was perturbed. After coaxing and promising I would not tell anyone if she told me, Carrie finally revealed that Karen was mad at me for 'narcing' on her for skipping school the day the instruments were originally scheduled. Of course, I knew nothing about why Karen believed this, so I waited a few days for her to cool off before approaching her again. Karen said, hesitantly at first but then with increasing confidence. 'Well, some of us skipped on Friday; afterwards somebody called my mother and told her that we skipped and also told her where we were, and whoever the person was that called told my mother that his name was Bob, so we figured it was you.'

I finally convinced Karen I had nothing to do with all this, that the resemblance between 'Bob' and myself was in name only. Yet the event gave me occasion to talk to Don, Roger, and Steve about some of their activities and to learn if they, too, were suspicious of my motives. They were not, but our discussion convinced me that they would be a good group for me to join next year when they attended Harold Spencer. They were open, friendly, and seemed not to be threatened by my presence. One of the more popular groups of boys, they were regarded (both by themselves and the teachers) as average students who, while they did not sparkle in class, did what was expected of them (two teachers thought Don was very smart and could do much better 'if only he had applied himself'). Finally they provided a different view of the school than was provided by Chris and his friends who, even at the sixth-grade level, were more fully integrated into the academic and extracurricular structure of the school.

The people

Don's group consisted of a nucleus of three boys (Don, Steve, and Roger) together with three more peripheral members (Gary, Dave and Gordon).[1] The six spent most of their free time together in school and three of them interacted frequently outside the school. Perhaps this division was evident because the three key members had attended the same grade school together, while the other three boys had come to Harold Spencer from three different schools and only became attached to the group at the beginning of the seventh grade. Thus, the time that Don, Steve, and Roger had spent together over the years made it only natural that, at the beginning of my year at Harold Spencer, the three of them would be close.

Don was the leader of this group. His opinions and perspectives, while not blindly followed, still set the pace for the group's activities both within and outside of school. I saw him as the most mature member of the group, but maturity is a relative term because of the wide range of behavior exhibited among boys of this age. Don, a fairly good-looking boy, was somewhat tall for his age and had a strong build even though he never participated in interscholastic athletics. His hair was somewhat long and he dressed the part of a typical junior high boy of the day – faded blue jeans and 'Adidas.' During the winter months, a well-worn and cracked brown leather jacket was the trademark that set him off from the crowds of other students at Harold Spencer.

Roger, another member of this group, was somewhat shorter than Don and more 'homely' in appearance. Roger often participated in many activities just to be a part of the group, and was more a follower than a leader. He appeared somewhat insecure as he frequently made himself the center of attention and in the process brought undue attention to other members of the group. It was this characteristic, coupled with what Dave and Don came to see as his immaturity, which slowly eroded the degree of acceptance that the group held for him.

Steve, the third main member of the group, was the group's 'ladies' man.' Don did not become seriously interested in girls until the eighth grade, and Roger often ingratiated himself with the girls by being too forward. Steve, on the other hand, was the object of many girls' early infatuations and, while rarely aggressive, he relished being the recipient of the fleeting adorations of the typical junior high girl.

Steve too was more a follower, allowing Don to make major suggestions as to what to do. Steve participated in after-school and leisure-time stunts like stealing cigarettes from the local supermarket or riding around on motor cycles or in cars after school at the insistence of Don and Roger, who often had to badger him into participating in such activities. Steve too was more cautious in some of the in-class activities in which the group participated. I cannot ever recall Steve being called to the office for any disciplinary problems during the two years I was at Harold Spencer, whereas Don occasionally was summoned (usually for skipping classes) and Roger was a frequent visitor to Mr Pall.

Gary, Dave, and Gordon, while they hung around with the other three during the seventh grade, were more peripheral to the group. Their interests were also somewhat disparate and these activities tended to separate them from active involvement in the group by the eighth grade. Gary, for example, did not seem very interested in anything other than goofing off in class and talking to girls. Dave was more subdued but relished participating with the other members in goofing off in class and the more general harassment of 'weirdos.' Dave and Gordon were both interested in athletics and eventually participated in interscholastic activities. While Dave was quite cynical about most things (almost every other word he emitted was 'stupid') and appeared rather disinterested in academics, he was committed to athletics and quite competitive in PE class and track.

Gordon, the smallest member of the group, was the school's star lightweight wrestler, an attribute he claimed to have gotten from his brother who had wrestled in the state championships for the past two years. Very competitive, Gordon was always in excellent physical shape and could run circles around anyone in the school. Gordon was the least academically inclined of all the boys in the group and seemed to take pride in the fact that he visited the school 'shrink' and was in a few remedial classes. Gordon attended Harold Spencer until late spring of the seventh grade when his family moved across the main highway into the other junior high school district.

I never discovered much about the families of the boys, primarily because they rarely talked about them. I knew Don lived with his mother part of the time and stayed at his older sister's home at other times. Don's parents were divorced and, even though his father lived within 50 miles of their home, Don never mentioned seeing him. His mother, who worked as a secretary for a local business concern, apparently was concerned about some of his activities (at least the ones that she knew about) such as smoking marijuana and frequently hanging around with older boys who had what seemed to be ready access to alcohol. Occasionally he mentioned that she had confined him to the house for associating with the wrong crowd, but such was the extent of any conversation about his family.

Other background information that I gathered on the members of Don's group was the result of checking records in the school district's office. Roger's father worked in machine maintenance for a local construction company. Gordon's parents, who were his guardians rather than natural parents, both worked, he as a custodian and she in a local tavern. Dave's father was an accountant for one of the larger retail discount houses and his mother worked as a secretary for the city. Steve's father was retired from the military (I don't know if he was doing anything else but assumed he was) and his mother was a secretary for a large building products company.

This information reinforces the general occupational and social class character of the school district as described in Chapter 2 – higher proportions of people working in blue-collar or service industries. The family characteristics of Don's group also illuminate another statistic relevant to contemporary American society – the growing trend toward more than one breadwinner within the family. Of the six members of Don's group, the women worked in at least four of those families.

While somewhat disparate, the group was bound together by a collectively shared understanding of school life. 'It's the people I hang out with' came to be *the* defining factor of life for Don and his friends throughout the two years that I knew them. Indeed, the most significant aspects of those two years revolved around what they did together, how they thought together, and what they shared together. Most importantly, their collective interaction generated a separate knowledge system – one in opposition to the formal knowledge characteristically stressed by the school. We turn now to a description of the cultural process that generated such a knowledge system.

Activities and perspectives

Seventh grade

Beginning seventh grade was an experience to which students looked forward. In many ways it represented a rite of passage symbolizing the transition from childhood to adolescence. It meant going from a setting in which students were the oldest and dominant student group in the school, to one where they were the youngest and subservient group within the school. Transition to junior high meant too no more of the things associated with being in elementary school, like staying with the same teacher the entire day, recess, PE without showers, and a scarcity of extra-curricular activities.

Junior high school also meant something else about which students were aware but the consequences of which were never explicit. That 'something else' was the simple yet profound fact that student relationships with other students would become immensely more important than they had been in elementary school. That these relationships would become their stated prime reason for coming to school was central for them; that these relationships would serve as the basis for the generation of a meaning system about social institutions is important for us to understand.

'Hey, Roger, what'd Pall say to you?' Gary asked as Roger placed his lunch tray on the table and sat with those of us who had just come from Richards's social studies class. Roger had been called out of the class to go to Mr Pall's office for some misbehavior in English class the previous day.

'Yeah, Rog, what happened, what were you doing down there?' asked Dave, unenthusiastically eating a peanut butter and jelly sandwich.

'Ahh, that Burton (Roger's English teacher) sent me to Mr Pall for not doing any work. She said, "no pencil, no paper, you never do anything; just get down there to Mr Pall and you can tell him about it."'

'So what happened?'

'So, Pall talked to me for a few minutes and told me he was going to give me one more chance to behave and to show that I could be trusted. I said, "yeah, no sweat, I can be trusted."' Everyone at the table laughed and Steve said, 'Sure Roger, you can be trusted.'

The next day at lunch Roger told us that he had been transferred from Burton's English class into another class. When I asked him why, he said, 'We had some sentences to do in class and were supposed to use the words "excitement" and "enjoy." So I wrote, "I don't enjoy Mrs Burton's class and it's not very exciting."' When they had read the sentences in class, Burton had said, 'That's it, Roger, that's the last straw.' Roger added, 'I guess she knew all along that I didn't like her very well.'

As a result of periodic absences from school, Don too incurred the displeasure of the administration. These absences precipitated confrontations with the administration and plagued Don on and off for the two years that I knew him. Early in the fall of seventh grade, Don began the practice of skipping school, usually for the entire day. While he didn't skip frequently, his absences were regular, usually Fridays or Mondays. Sometimes he skipped with Steve, occasionally with Roger, but more often with Bob, an eighth-grader who, as the year went on, participated in many of the activities in which Don's friends participated. Don's problem was that when he returned to school, he rarely had an excuse from home, since his mother worked and he did not want her to know he was skipping. One day in late October Don was suspended from school until he could provide evidence that his absences were authorized. When he finally returned I asked him what had been happening.

Don replied, 'Well, I'll tell you old man, I got kicked out for skipping.'

'You did? What happened?'

'I don't know, I came Monday and I guess they knew I had been skipping so they told me I couldn't come back into school until I got a note from my mom. She came in and said she didn't know I had been skipping.'

I asked him what he and Steve did while they were playing truant.

'Had a ball. Went over to Bob's house and then all of us went over to this guy's house and got his sister's car. She didn't know we had it 'cause she was asleep so we just took it out for a little drive, gassed it up, then came back to the house and drank a little wine and listened to a little music. It was really cool, a lot better than coming to school.'

I asked him why he decided to skip on Friday (Don always skipped on a Friday or Monday).

'Oh I don't know, I thought that since it was the end of the quarter and the report cards would be out pretty soon that it really wouldn't make that much difference because there wouldn't be that much happening. I just thought it would be a good day to skip, there wouldn't be that much to miss.'

Incidents reflecting minor and sometimes major altercations with the 'authorities,' be they within or outside the school, were often the topic of conversation of the group. For example, although only Don, Roger and possibly Steve seemed to be into smoking, the subject of how, where, and who did was often addressed. Once, Dave (the 'weirdo'), who had been sitting at the same lunch table with us in the early months of the seventh grade, had been caught smoking, the penalty for which was attendance at a 'smoking clinic' which the district had recently adopted to reduce the problems of smoking within the schools.[2] The day after Dave's first class (held in the evenings in the library at Harold Spencer), Don asked him at lunchtime what they did in the class.

'Nothing,' replied Dave, 'the doctor who was supposed to teach it never showed up.'

'He never showed?' Steve laughed, 'man, what a farce. Are you sure you were at the right place?'

'Of course ya dingbat. If I was at the wrong place then so was everyone else 'cause we all waited an hour.'

Ron continued, 'So, if you waited an hour, what'd ya do for an hour, jerk your chain?'

The group all laughed and Dave said, 'Yeah, yeah, forty guys out there all . . . no, some of us went to the parking lot and just lit up while we were waiting.' That brought even more laughs from the group, as they envisioned a smoking clinic with guys waiting around for the event to start, and all passing the time smoking cigarettes.

It did not take long with this group for me to realize that one of the fundamental threads to their relationship was their often explicit opposition to authority and being told to do anything. Especially for Don, who spent significant amounts of his free time with boys in the high school, 'raising hell' was something they really enjoyed. Of course, members of the group did this to various extents, with Don and Roger the most conspicuous. Yet these activities were bounded, as all group members confined their most explicit opposition to authority to those activities outside of school, saving school time to share them and plan new ones. Indeed, even their inter-group conflicts did not usually spill over into serious violations of school authority.

While friendships were very important to the meaning of life at Harold Spencer Junior High, for most in Don's group such friendships were not always harmonious or free of conflict. In fact, altercations ranging from joking, name calling and teasing were somewhat frequent. Occasional serious incidents – those that threatened to erode the normative structure of the group – did happen; one occurred a few months after I had been with the group.

Serious incidents that strained group relationships were often precipitated by seemingly innocuous incidents, and such was the case at lunch one day. As was typical, comments about the food were being made, related to what looked bad, what tasted even worse, and the usual bargaining and bartering over different items of food available in the lunch proceeded as usual. On this particular day, Roger did not like his 'key lime jello' (as it was described in the menu) and Gary did not like his 'creamy coleslaw,' so they agreed to swap. Gary, sitting on the other side of the table and three spaces from Roger, took his plastic bowl of coleslaw and slid it down the table, whereupon a corner of the bowl caught on the edge of a tray and the slaw spilled on to Roger's shirt. Roger became angry, not appreciating the ridicule from his peers. 'You bastard,' he said to Gary, 'why don't you watch what the hell you're doing.'

Gary too laughed uncontrollably as he looked at the white sauce dripping from Roger's dark blue shirt. 'Hey, man, it was an accident,' he replied between fits of laughter.

'Yeah,' said Roger, taking a handful of coleslaw and flicking it at Gary, 'well, this is not an accident.'

'Wow, all over his hair! Good shot, Rog,' someone shouted.

The laughter continued as Gary took a handful of 'jello' and began in hot pursuit of Roger, who sprinted out the door of the cafeteria on to the lawn beside the school. They both returned a few moments later, huffing and puffing, but visibly laughing at each other. Don and Gordy, however, were not content to let such an interesting event stop there. With Roger sitting at the far end of the table now, Don and Gordon baited Gary to continue.

'Rog sure get's excited easily, doesn't he?' Gordon began.

'Yeah,' said Don, 'I don't know why he got so bent out of shape, I mean, you didn't try to get his shirt all messed up, did you Gary?'

'Hell no,' Gary replied, 'the dummy just got bent out of shape over nothing, that's all.'

'I'd get back at him,' Don continued as he and Gordon attempted to keep the drama alive. 'I have fifty cents, we ought to hire someone to do it.'

'You're on,' Gordon said excitedly as he held out his hand for the money from Don. Don thought for a moment then decided that he'd rather not give the money away as he wanted to buy some ice cream after lunch. By this time, Gary was convinced that retribution was called for.

'Shit, man, I'll do it without the money,' he said as he got up, grabbed a bowl of coleslaw, walked around the table behind where Roger was sitting and nonchalantly turned the bowl upside down on Roger's full and curly hair. Immediately the cry of 'fight' went up as Gary and Roger wrestled each other to the floor. This all brought the attention of Hawkeye, standing nearby, who came over and ordered everyone to clean up the mess on the floor and then banned Gary and Roger to a separate table.

Their punishment, as it turned out, was to spend the next two weeks after lunch cleaning the cafeteria, a punishment that was not too severe in that it only involved five or so minutes every day. I noted that, within five minutes after they had been separated, Gary and Roger returned to their usual joking and laughing as if nothing had happened. By the next day the entire incident had been forgotten and at lunch Gary and Roger were plotting how to eat their lunch slowly so that they would not have as much time to work for Hawkeye.

This serious an altercation was not normal within the group, but degrees of it were not uncommon. Conflict ran throughout the group and was a subject that occupied a great deal of students' time during the seventh grade. While Don's group had more than their share of fights, I came to discover that fights themselves were a common point of discussion for the student body in general.

Much of the conflict that characterized the life of Don's group was group-centered conflict. It involved not just one individual pitted against another, but the group as a collective in conflict with individuals or groups of individuals external to the group. I found this to be true early in the Fall as Don's group appeared to be in a continuous state of conflict with three boys in one other group, a group for which they obviously had little use. The two groups seemed to be getting at each other continually, and an implicit mutual defense pact existed where any attack on one member of the group was considered a violation on all.

In situations such as this, the slightest incident could spark an ongoing series of debates and exchanges that eventually would rally all members to the scene. While in math class one day, for example, Roger had just completed taking a test and was waiting for the aide to finish grading it. Rog had nothing to do, so he sat at his table bothering one of the girls who was assigned to the table with him. Just then, the loudspeaker came on: 'Mr Glenn, would you send Keith James and Mike Proudy [a member of the group in conflict with Don's group] down to the office please?'

'Right away,' called Mr Glenn, who was working with some students on the other side of the room at the time. Keith and Mike, who were at the table adjacent to Roger's, got up to go down to the office.

Roger leaned over and said, 'What'd you two do, get caught faggin' together?'

In an immediate and aggressive tone, Mike replied, 'I can beat the hell out of you, Anderson [Roger].'

Roger retorted, 'Yeah, well if you can, how come you didn't meet me after school the other day, you chicken?'

'If I didn't meet you it's my business. If I want to fight you, I'll fight you when I feel like it.'

By this time, Mr Glenn heard the commotion and told Keith and Mike to hurry down to the office. Don, Steve, and Gary had heard much of the talk and they immediately began talking about how much they hated 'those fags.'

Steve said, 'That James, he's such a fag.'

Throughout the remainder of the morning, the group discussed how they were going to 'get' Keith, Mike, and Tom and they figured they'd challenge them to a fight after school. Sure enough at lunch, Roger and Don walked over to the table where the three of them were sitting and attempted to schedule a fight after school. They talked for about five minutes and when they returned to our table, Gary asked them what had happened.

'They're all chicken,' said Don triumphantly.

'Yeah,' added Roger, 'they want to fight up near Andrews school. That way they'll be close to James's house so they can get that guy with the gun to come out again if they're losing.'

'So what happened?' I asked.

'Nothing, but we'll get them next time.' The next week Roger told me that he and Gordon had gone to see *Planet of the Apes* at the theatre and that they had run into Mike and Tom there. They tried to get them into a fight while in the movie but Mike and Tom refused. About the only thing that Roger and Gordon accomplished was getting kicked out of the theatre for making too much noise.

Such conflicts among groups of students often erupted into mass spectacles for part of the student population. For example, a well-known incident late in the winter involved, directly or indirectly, significant numbers of students who I knew at Harold Spencer. We were walking from math class in the morning when we heard this tremendous commotion in the hall. Instantaneously, a large group gathered to watch two boys slug it out in a very ferocious manner. Bodies clashed and twisted on the floor, bouncing against the metal lockers on the side of the hall.

'Come on, Jerry, let him have it,' shouted Don as we moved up to the edge of the crowd. I could hear students on the fringes of the crowd rooting for the other participant, and it was obvious that each belligerent had his own group of supporters and rooters in attendance. It was then that I saw that this was more than a minor scuffle; these guys were serious in destroying each other, and I was immediately struck with the fact that I might have to break it up, or else someone could seriously become injured.[3] Luckily (for me) I did not have to make that choice, as Mr Franks pushed his way through the crowd in an attempt to break up the fight. The whole incident was over almost as quickly as it had begun.

Or almost so. The fight was the subject of conversation for quite a few days thereafter. Jerry, a friend of Don's, apparently had taken the worst licks in the fight (he had to have an operation to save his sight in one eye; later on in the year, we heard that Jerry's parents were going to sue the family of the other protagonist), but the victor was in even greater trouble.

'He's had it,' said Don, 'everyone's goin' to be out to get him now. He'll be afraid to even come back to school, 'cause all Jerry's friends are going to really lay into him. No way can he come back to Spencer without a bodyguard – that is if he can find anyone.' The group seemed to agree, but I was not at all sure about why the whole event had occurred in the first place.

'You mean those two dudes just went out there swinging?' I asked the group.

'Naw,' said Roger, 'they've been at each other for a few weeks.'

Don took a bite of his sandwich and said rather philosophically, 'Yeah, I think Denny stole a bottle of scotch from Jerry's house a few weeks ago and ever since then they've been itching for a fight. Jerry said that if he did not bring it back he was really going to coldcock him and then some friends of Denny's began pushing some of Jerry's friends around and, well – you know how those things go. Shit, I thought they'd have been at it long before this.'

Such conflicts were always discussed rather routinely, as if they were a natural part of the life of students within the school. And indeed to a great extent they were, so we might expect that students would handle them in a rather routine fashion. I once asked Don if conflicts such as that between Gary and Rog, or the fight between Jerry and the other student were typical. His reply was that they were but they were 'no big deal' because 'kids at school are always hassling each other, trying to create a little space, trying to see who your friends are.' His rationale made sense, for it seemed that in a school like Spencer, based as it is on the linearity of knowledge and the prerogatives of teachers to 'teach' that knowledge, students would search for strategies in which they could create their own rules. Conflict, its resolution, and its continuance was simply one of those strategies because it was one of the few areas where the students could make and enforce their own rules rather than following those of the institution. Through conflicts the students resisted the production system of the school that defined them as entities whose fundamental function was to produce teacher-defined and controlled 'work.'

It is clear by now that individual students at Harold Spencer coalesced into somewhat fluid social units which they called 'groups.' Each group had, in turn, a somewhat unique social fabric, consisting of the mores, beliefs and actions of the group and out of and through which they both interpreted and created their specific role in the school. With Don's group, such processes were culturally based activities that facilitated the group glorifying its independence from other people or situations, activities that illustrated their proclivity to make what seemed to be facile decisions about acceptable and non-acceptable situations and behavior, and those activities congruent with their understanding of themselves as 'in control' of their destiny despite a school structure that moved against the legitimacy of their possessing such control. For Don and his friends, such control was reasserted via the constitutive process through which they wove their own social fabric – through such processes as trading insults, practical joking, and making fun of girls. Such processes served the contradictory functions of providing an interpretive basis for collectively defining school as well as sowing the seeds for the gradual dissolvement of the group. 'Jiving,' teasing, joking – all were typical actions of Don and his group. Particularly unattractive girls ('dogs') were often the focus of barbs and jokes. Sitting at the lunch table, Gordon and Dave often barked like a dog when Denise and Patty passed by, just to let them know how they felt about them. And Gordon had his repertoire of 'dream jokes' – stories he made up in simile form and to which group members occasionally added.

'That Denise,' Gordon would say, 'is like a carpenter's dream, flat as a board.'

Dave then would add, 'Yeah, but Karen is like a skin diver's dream, a real treasure chest.' And on it would go, with the quality of the lines varying inversely to the number spun out at any one time.

Any expression of interest in a girl during the seventh grade was likely to be met with a mild form of ridicule and laughter from the group. Sometimes this ridicule was serious, more often it was offered in a joking manner which, if accepted in the same vein, went unnoticed or at least was not seriously regarded. This was especially true for those within a friendship group (such as Don's or Chris's), or those outside the group but still on good terms with the group. Norm, the real ladies' man of the seventh grade (with the exception of Steve), was constantly teased about his involvement with the girls, yet it seemed to be taken in good stride. Around Christmas, for example, we were eating lunch when Dave noticed Norm coming into the cafeteria holding a girl's hand.

'Wow, look at Norm, really making time,' said Dave.

Don looked up and watched them approach. 'Hey yeah, gettin' it on with Pamela Jenkins, how long's he been going with her?'

'Beats me,' said Dave, and just as Norm passed by with Pamela, Dave, Don, and Steve began sighing in long, breathy sighs, lying down on the tables.

'Oh, here comes Norman . . .'

'I think I love him, he's everything I always wanted in a boy.' Norman tried to ignore all of this and Pamela's face rapidly turned red.

'And that girl he's with, who could she be? Why I think it's . . .'

'Pamela Jenkins.'

Gordon got up on the bench, kneeled with his hands slightly bent to emulate a dog sitting, and then began a series of long mournful howls. 'Wooooo, Wooooo,' he clamored. Pamela took her purse and gave Gordon a good-natured hit on the head with it.

'Gordon, shut up, will you?'

'Of course, my dear,' replied Gordon.

The romantic involvement of any other members of the group was rare, and happened only with Steve and Don. Ironically, it was over the same girl, Karen. This competition over Karen brought a slowly developing tension between Don and Steve to the surface and this tension ultimately affected their relationship for the rest of the year.

I first noticed the underlying frictions about Christmas-time while at lunch. While sipping milk shakes, Don brought up the subject of Steve and Karen's alleged interest in each other.

'You know that Steve, how he likes Karen and all that . . .?'

Dave butted in and added, 'Yeah, and she likes him too.'

Don then launched into a critical analysis of Steve. 'Yeah, I know he does, but he sure doesn't act like he likes her at all. You know a couple of days ago we were walking down the sidewalk outside the 'B' building and he was walking right behind her, not even walking next to her. I'll bet he hasn't gone further than just holding her hand. We were kidding about this a while ago, making fun of him for being such a pussy, and you know what he did? He goes home and tells his sister about it and has his sister stick up for him. He won't even walk home with us anymore, he's just acting like a big baby.'

'That's what happens when you fall in love,' said Dave in a facetious manner.

'Naw, he didn't used to be like that, you just don't know him.'

Dave agreed, 'Yeah, I can't believe he would be like that. That doesn't sound like him.'

Don continued, 'Well, you don't really know him. I mean like we're over at this chick's house a while ago, and this chick is pretty mature you know, and he could have had a good time with her. Instead what's he do? Say he has to go home to fix his motor cycle.'

The group members laughed, and as they walked away Don was telling them that he (Don) knew how girls wanted to be treated far better than did Steve.

Yet such criticism of Steve was of a relatively mild form; more characteristic of student group behavior was what appeared to be the crass manner in which they often treated each other. Cursing and obscenities, name calling and insults, tricks played on each other, and physical activity bordering on fights – all were common among friends within Don's group. Yet, rather than this being merely crass and insulting behavior, I found it to be distinctive of the internal dynamics of the group and important for group maintenance. Indeed, cursing, obscenities, name calling and jokes were often symbolic of group solidarity.

Almost everything was regularly cursed. The 'goddamn' lunch line or the 'shitty' food were regularly assailed as were such rules and regulations as not being able to leave the cafeteria area after lunch and the random enforcement of dress codes. Obscenities were usually saved for comments among those within the group. 'Fuck' was commonly used in its many variations, and during moments of heated expression, 'fuck' was often followed by a string of other obscenities, such as the time when Roger and Gary were involved in their food fight and during which time Roger called Gary a 'dirty fucking son of a bitching bastard.' Often, discussions engendered considerable controversy and, accordingly, mutual vituperation. For example, on one occasion the group was discussing what classes they were going to take for the Interim which was to begin immediately after Christmas. Don and Dave had signed up to take skiing, and Gary said he was thinking about it. Pete, an acquaintance of Don and Roger, and an eighth-grader, raised the question of how much it cost to go skiing.

'Costs about $80,' said Don.

'Does not, more like $60,' replied Dave.

Pete, who had taken skiing the previous year, voiced his opinion that the whole thing cost about $85 last year.

'See, told ya,' Don said as he turned to Dave.

'Look, you asshole, all I know is what Hawkeye told me last week and he said "60",' Dave said emphatically.

Then Steve added, 'You guys don't know what you're talking about, it's about $70.'

The whole group turned on Dave. 'Your ass,' said Gary, 'how the fuck do you know?'

'My brother told me.'

'Your brother? If he's as dumb as you are, he doesn't even know how to tie his shoes in the morning.'

'Fuck you, man, I know a lot more than you do.'

Dave, tired of the whole conversation, picked up his tray to return to the kitchen area.

'God,' he said walking away, 'what a bunch of assholes!'

Such conversations were common, and I came to regard them as an acceptable way of communication within the confines of the group. The use of obscenities could occur between members of a group or between members of two or more groups, although they were used with greater rapidity and intensity within the group than they were between groups. In either case, a distinguishing mark seemed to be the ability to carry on such dialogues without conflict. The fact that these interactions could continue and be immediately forgotten signaled the somewhat ritualistic flavor and the manner in which epithets were regarded.

A similar form of interaction involved name calling and the trading insults between group members. The greetings exchanged by students between classes were one example of name calling. The terms that were used changed rapidly to account for differing situations, but the following were used throughout the year: 'stoner' for anyone who came to school after smoking dope or having done some drinking with friends, 'weirdo' for anyone who happened to wear different clothes for a few days, 'spaz' referring to a poor showing in PE class or during an intramural game, 'dildo' as a generally insulting term.

The most common form of 'disrespectful' interaction within the group was in the form of tricks and jokes which they often played on each other. Early in the year, Roger and Don were out one week-end smoking a joint with Dan, one of Don's friends. Don and Dan decided it would be a great idea to get Rog drunk, so somewhere they procured a bottle of *crème de menthe* and told Rog it was great stuff and that he should drink some of it. They gave him so much of it that, between the high proof of the liqueur and the joints, he got, as they said, 'fucked up.' The next Monday at lunch the story of this incident was discussed with great interest as Don recounted Roger's condition.

Soon, however, Roger appeared embarrassed by all this, but was able to laugh along with the group as he became the focus of their laughter. Throughout the next few weeks Roger was teased about drinking *crème de menthe* for lunch, a teasing that soon evolved into more insults and name calling.

'I'll bring some green food dye with me tomorrow so we can watch you get stoned,' Gordon stated one day.

Rog, getting tired of the whole thing, replied, 'Fuck you, Gordy.'

'What's the matter, Rog, don't you like green lemonade?' Gary asked sarcastically.

'None of your business.'

'Hey, guys, ol' Rog doesn't like limeade after all,' interjected Dave.

Even though it was at someone else's expense, the *crème de menthe* incident was a source of unity for the group, as the teasing and joking symbolized the crystallization of a primary relationship for some time to come. 'The hill,' responsible for students being late to class, for their coming to class covered with dirt, and for the ongoing attention of teachers and the administration, was another.

The hill was nothing more that its name implies, a hill. It paralleled a sidewalk on the north side of the school near the athletic fields. It was not a particularly steep hill; but it had the advantage of being immediately adjacent to the sidewalk, which meant that one could bump into people ('accidentally,' of course) and roll them down the hill, dry and grassy in the Fall but muddy and sloppy in the winter and spring.

Dave and Steve were the best at rolling people down the hill. They rarely picked on Don because he was too big, but Gordon was just right. They often met him between first and second period and the strategy was quite simple: Steve walked in front of Dave and, when he saw Gordon approach, stopped to talk to Dave for a moment. As Gordon approached, Steve and Dave both dropped their books, grabbed Gordon, and tossed him down the hill. Dave and Steve then ran down the hallway, laughing with glee as Gordon climbed up the hill after them. While Dave, Steve and Gordon pushed other students down the hill, these incidents were qualitatively different. For the important symbolism of 'the hill' rested, as did name calling and trading practical jokes, in the extent to which being pushed down the hill could be accepted within the bounds of friendship without engendering conflict or hostility. For example Larry (the 'weirdo') was pushed down the hill too, but it was not a fun event; rather he was shoved with very little laughter or accompanying glee, more as a way of harassment than a symbol of friendship. The hill and the actions associated with it were symbolic of the interpretive structure of meaning built by students as they came to gain greater control over everyday life at Spencer.

The absence of reciprocity between individuals often was indicative of the absence of a shared perspective and thus group membership. A good example of this was a group-sponsored conspiracy to raise money for lunchtime milk shakes. One day Roger produced some tickets that simply said 'Admit One' on them and which he had received at a festival held at the elementary school the year before. He was thumbing through them when Steve got the idea for a good trick.

'Let's sell them to somebody, somebody really dumb like Marin.'

Just then Roger saw a student called Mark, whom they did not like, approaching the table. 'Hey, let's sell them to Waller for a nickel, then tell him he can get a milk shake with them. Waller,' he shouted, 'come over here and sit.'

Roger and Steve played it very cool. They did not pressure or badger him, they simply went about their business and allowed him to eat his lunch. Then Roger looked at Waller and, in a very courteous voice, said, 'Mark, want to get in on a good deal?'

'What deal?'

'I got these tickets good for a milk shake. Got them for selling magazines during the magazine drive. I'll sell them to you for a nickel each.' While Mark began digging into his pockets, Steve and Dave could hardly contain the laughter.

'Something fishy about this,' Mark said, looking for money. 'How come you guys don't want them?'

'Listen man,' said Dave, 'we've had so many shakes in the past week we could hardly look at another. Rather have the coin.'

Waller handed Roger a quarter and Roger counted out five tickets. Then Waller walked up to the ice cream window with everyone at the table straining to see what would happen. He ordered a milk shake and handed the lady a ticket, but we could see her shaking her head. The group burst out laughing and Mark returned to the table, obviously upset.

'OK, you guys give me back my quarter.'

'Sorry, man, it's not our fault they won't take the tickets. They must have expired.'

'Come on, you don't expect me to believe that, do you?'

'We don't care what you believe, that's the way it goes so why don't you just buzz off?'

By this time Mark was almost in tears, 'I'll go tell Hawkeye, he'll get the money back.'

'Look,' Dave threatened, 'you tell Hawkeye and you'll get the shit beat out of you.' Mark left the table and, to the best of anyone's knowledge, never did tell Hawkeye.

Here the rules were the same but were interpreted differently, as selling the tickets to Mark (as well as other acts such as stealing food from kids or teasing them about personal appearance or mannerisms) raised hostility and some degree of animosity between participants, whereas the same activity conducted among friends did not. Thus, while jokes and tricks were a form of permitted disrespect among friends, they served as acts of hostility if friendship was not involved. With the case of Mark, no relationship existed wherein custom permitted disrespect or over which no offense would be taken. While behavior was the same between friends and outsiders, the interpretations of it were different and thus the cursing at each other, the use of obscenities, the name calling and the insults, the tricks and the jokes were not taken to mean the same thing. The behavior among those who understood the meaning symbolized an expression of group understanding and trust. It helped set a group apart from others, to provide a sense of identity in a school of 1000 other students and in classes where students were primarily one of many.

Some may have concluded by now that Don and his group were totally disinterested in academic pursuits and consequently must have performed poorly on assigned tasks. Despite the fact that little mention has been made of the group's instructional activities, most members performed adequately. Don got into more than his share of petty trouble, and even though he played truant with considerable regularity, it did not appear to affect his grades adversely. I was surprised, in fact, that he took care to insure his grades did not suffer unduly from repeated absences. For example, after he had skipped off and on for about a month, I told Don that Mr Pall would become wise to his pattern of skipping on Mondays or Fridays.

'Yeah,' he said, 'I know, but I don't plan on skipping too much anymore.'

'Oh, turning over a new leaf, eh?' I asked.

'Not necessarily, I just don't want to get too far behind in my work. I think what I'll do is try to get a little ahead, that way I can take off again for awhile.'

Roger was the only member of the group who avoided doing much school work. In fact, he was transferred from a number of classes during the seventh grade because the teachers could not get him to do the minimal amount of work. I never knew from one week to the next where Roger would be, and if he did not attend a particular class for a while I assumed the teacher had grown weary of his antics and had requested that he be transferred. More often than not, I was correct.

Yet Roger had always said that school was a waste of time for him because all he wanted to do was to drive a truck. Despite this, Rog indicated that his mother and father got into arguments about his work in school.

'The boy will never amount to anything if he doesn't start doing better than this,' he reported his mother saying one day after I had mentioned that I saw her in the principal's office.

'What difference does it make,' he said that his father replied, 'that school is worthless anyhow, what do you expect the boy to do?'

According to Roger, his father then launched into a speech about how he paid taxes, that most teachers 'sat on their asses most of the time anyway,' and that the mere fact that they rarely sent any homework home with Roger proved the fact that most of them did very little.

In general, then, most of the group did what was expected of them with a minimal amount of complaining or resistance. Assignments were completed more or less on time, tests taken and passed and everyone in the group (with the exception of Roger) had a C/B average in all subject areas. Such a grade average was not difficult to maintain, as indicated by the fact that the members of this group could spend as much time as they did talking in class about things they did and were interested in, yet still be considered relatively successful within the context of the demands of the school.

Two notable patterns emerged in the spring and characterized the end of the year as well as the life history of the group within the seventh grade. First, strains appeared in the group coalition as individual members began to branch into other interests. Gordon told us in the middle of January that he would be attending the other junior high school in the district because his parents were moving. Gordon left Harold Spencer in February and I saw him once more that year, during a track meet, when he came back to his alma mater to beat some of his friends in the 440.

Dave began to spend more time doing athletics and with other students interested in sports. Seventh-graders were allowed to participate in interscholastic track and basketball, and Dave tried out for the track team and became one of the school's sprinters for the seventh-grade team. While he continued to eat lunch with the group and goof off in class (especially in Marcy's class where most of the group was fifth period) his interests were slowly shifting toward sports-oriented activities.

Don, Roger, and Steve continued to do much together after school and during their free time at week-ends. Many of their activities centered around 'hell-raising' and early experimentation with drugs (mostly marijuana) and alcohol, activities that would consume much of their attention during the eighth grade.

Even by the spring of seventh grade, drugs and alcohol were a topic of increasing interest to group members and thus was a second issue to affect the group. Quite often Don came to school on

Mondays looking rather red-eyed and tired, and proceeded to tell of his week-end exploits. He and Steve had been to a friend's house one week-end, and during lunch at school relived many of the things they had done.

'Far out stuff,' said Don.

'Great,' added Steve.

'What did you guys do?' Gary inquired.

'Southern Comfort, bitchin good stuff,' Don asserted, shaking his head in the affirmative. 'Pulled an "American Graffiti" too.'

Gary was getting curious. 'What the hell's that?'

'Had this bet,' Steve replied, 'went to the drive-in and we bet Dan five dollars that he wouldn't streak in front of the screen and then go over and moon some car. So the idiot takes off his clothes, sprints in front of the screen, comes back to the car next to us and sticks his butt right next to the rear window. Funnier than shit.'

The whole group was laughing at the thought of such an incident, but Dave just sat there shaking his head. 'You guys are crazy,' he said, 'really crazy. You all are going to end up in the nut house some day.'

Don laughed, 'What a way to go nuts, drinkin' good stuff, tokin' up on a joint. FAR OUT.'

Once the weather became warm, students returned to wearing Adidas every day and brought out the beer T-shirts that had laid dormant since last fall – the ones that said 'Primo,' 'Bud,' 'Blue Ribbon,' or 'Oly' on them. Dave spent most of his afternoons at track practice, Gary began spending time helping his father in his construction work, and Don, Steve, and Roger spent varying amounts of time getting their motor cycles ready again and partying at week-ends. There was more of the typical horseplay, stealing gym bags, rolling friends down the hill, chasing Mike around before Marcy's class, that kind of thing. Seventh grade ended, and I did not see the group again until Fall.

Eighth grade

Eighth grade was important because it meant that, at long last, the eighth-graders no longer were the youngest group in the school. Most eighth-graders reminded themselves of that during the first few weeks of school by noting publicly that the new seventh-graders were little and immature, neophytes to the ways of life at Harold Spencer.

Some of the changes in the composition of Don's group that began at the end of the seventh grade continued into eighth grade. The class schedule, too, affected some important shifts that had already begun. For example, Gary and Steve remained rather close because they shared some of the same classes. But Gary was in few classes with other members of the group and his lunch schedule precluded him from eating lunch with other members of Don's group. It was almost one month before I saw Gary for the first time and I rarely saw him throughout the remainder of the year.

Dave's interests led him to more involvement with the athletic group. His math and social studies classes were the same as Gary's and the two of them frequently goofed off together during class. Occasionally, he ate lunch with Steve who ate during the same period as he did, but those were the only regular interactions with members of the old group. Gary did become a member of the football squad during the Fall of eighth grade, and involvement with fellow squad members was by far his most consuming social activity, both in terms of time and intensity.

Gordon, of course, had moved, so that left Roger, Steve, and Don in the original coalition that had begun in the seventh grade. Their activities increasingly were the 'wilder' events and hell raising, drinking, and a growing involvement in drugs came to typify their actions for the year. The summer apparently had permitted their contact with some other students who were ninth-graders and high school students who had access to cars. Thus, almost every day during class, before school, and especially during lunch, the three of them would relive the frolics of the previous night or the week-end.

More than ever, Don, Roger, and Steve became seen as 'bad apples' by some teachers. This perception became especially pronounced in PE because it was the first class in the morning, and Steve and Don were often late arriving. Their activities and the teacher's views of them were typified one day during the third week of school. I was standing on the sidelines watching a soccer game being played by the first period PE class when, fifteen minutes after the class had begun, Don and Steve both sauntered leisurely up to me. 'Where have you guys been?' I asked.

'Late night, last night,' answered Don, looking at me with droopy eyes. 'Should have stayed home today but my mom kicked me out of the house.'

'Late night, eh? Doing what?'

'Where do you want to start?' said Steve groggily.

'Went to the fair last night with Dan and Dennis [there was a large state fair every year in a nearby town],' Don began. 'Cops chasing us around the fair grounds, the whole bit. You should have been there, Bob, had some really good stuff this time. Ever drink "Black Velvet"?' I told him that I hadn't. They then continued to relate how they got into trouble at the fair, ended up pouring Coca-Cola in a vendor's change box, and how that led to the police searching for them.

'Wow,' said Steve, looking out at the class playing soccer, 'I could no more go out there and play soccer than I could take another drink right now.'

About then Mr Walters, the PE coach, walked over.

'Where you two characters been?' he asked, obviously irritated by their tardiness.

'Got here late, didn't have time to suit up,' Don answered.

'Second time in the past two weeks, isn't it? Maybe you think it's a joke, but you two birds can flunk this class by doing this; maybe you ought to think about that instead of sitting around here chewing the fat. Go on over there and sit,' he added, motioning to the other end of the field.

As they walked away, Walters looked at me and said, 'What do you know about those two?'

'Well,' I replied, 'they seem to do a lot more than I did when I was in eighth grade.'

'You'd better believe it. Really a pity too, those guys are just gettin' in with the wrong crowd, a bunch of rotten apples. I see it every year too, these guys who pull this not suitin' up crap, you get more and more of them in the eighth grade and even more in the ninth grade. Most of them turn out to be bad characters too and most of them I'd rather not waste my time with. But Don, that guy could be different. Ever see him during touch football? The kid has talent,' Walters continued, 'the kid could be a real good end, he catches well, runs well, and is really aggressive. I know Jerry [the football coach] tried to get him to come out for football, but he isn't interested. How do you get a kid to turn some of that energy and talent into something useful instead of just running around with bums?'

I agreed that it was a problem.

'Can't spend all the time social working every kid in the school,' Walters said as he headed back to the soccer field. 'Bob, there's just too many of them and not enough time for us to do with what we have. Sure hate to see a kid like that go down the tubes though.'

There was little doubt by now that Don, Steve, and Roger were finding the requirements of school to be unfulfilling and alienating. They resisted teacher attempts to involve them in the classroom because to become so involved would be tantamount to admitting that the reified knowledge of the school was legitimate – that they could accept selling their labor power and produce products that had primarily an exchange-value. Don and his friends were interested in the present, not the future, and no amount of cajoling or ridiculing by teachers could convince them that this alienative work was for the better. Their goals were simply to consume as much of the products that liberal capitalism had produced as possible, thus to be exercising their own control of their own fate, rather than having to wait for some unknown time when they could cash in their talents for some unknown career. What's more, their daily life in the school reinforced even more these tendencies, for if reappropriation of control, independence, and certainty were what they were after, what better way to gain these experiences than to drink, run around in cars, smoke dope, and so on. And what less frequent of an opportunity to do it than being in the school where their labor was appropriated from them, they were placed in largely dependent statuses, and were always unsure of the criteria for certainty. Eighth grade, then, found the group still actively involved in those cultural processes within the school that led to the weaving of their own self-determined social and cultural fabric.

We find then the joking relationship between Don, Steve, and others in the group continuing into the eighth grade much the same as it had existed during the seventh grade.

One particularly memorable incident along these lines occurred early on in the eighth grade. Don, Chris, and I were walking out of the gym toward the main part of the school when Steve came up behind us.

'Wait for me you guys.'

'Hey it's Stev-o, how's Cindy?' Don said as Steve caught up with us.

'Get lost with that Cindy jazz, will you?' Steve replied with what seemed to be a twinge of embarrassment. Chris, not knowing anything about what was prompting all of the discussion about Cindy, began pumping Don for the details.

'You don't know about that? Funniest thing in weeks,' Don continued. 'Me and Dan set old Steve here up with Cindy Jones . . .'

'That slut!' Chris interrupted.

'Yeah, now wait a minute. We had him set up for a good evening. She said she was going to take good care of you, Steve, call you around 9.30 when she's ready. Got a good deal too, $12 for the week-end rate.'

'Don't waste your time,' Steve replied, ' 'cause if she calls I'm not gonna be home.'

'Oh yeah you will,' Chris said, laughing at the prospect of the little game being played, 'I hear she's really good.' Steve said nothing as he went to science class while we continued down the hall.

The incident did not end there but continued on into the next week. At lunch one day, Karen and a few of her friends came over to our table to talk to Steve, sitting at the other end of the table. As Karen placed her tray down on the table and sat down across from me, she turned to Steve and said, 'Hey, Steve, what'd you do this week-end?'

Steve looked quizzically at her, and shook his head, 'Nothing,' he replied.

Karen smiled and began laughing in a taunting manner, 'That's not what I heard. Did you hear that, Winters?' she said, turning to one of her friends.

'No way, I heard it was a real special week-end.'

Steve began laughing, but in a manner that indicated that the conversation was not totally amusing to him. 'What do you mean that's not what you heard, what do you mean?'

'You know what I mean,' Karen replied.

Steve slammed his fork down on his tray, 'Who told you . . . Don?'

'No, Louise [a ninth-grade friend of Don's] said that there was some chick you were lined up with for Saturday night.'

'No way,' Steve said vehemently, 'no way would I touch that bitch.'

Winters turned to Steve and said, 'Did she ever call you?'

'I don't know, I wasn't home all day Saturday.'

By this time Dave and the others sitting at the table were discussing the series of events and making fun of Steve for staying away from home intentionally so that he would not have to answer the phone, but Steve took this in his stride and the event seemed to be forgotten.

Or was it? A subtle but significant change was occurring between Don and Steve. Close friends for the one and a half years I had known them (and according to them, for some years before that) they seemed to be in the process of selecting new friends and forming new groups with whom to associate on a more or less continual basis. Not that they rejected each other, rather that the attractions were not as strong. While in PE one day, the class was playing basketball and Don, a boy named Walt, and I were standing on the sidelines waiting for another group to finish using the court. Don was discussing some of his after-school antics in which Steve happened to be involved.

'Is Steve very tough?' Walt asked.

'No,' Don replied, shaking his head, 'in fact he's gettin' to be kind of a pussy. See how fat he's getting,' he said, pointing to Steve out on the court. 'He's puttin' on weight, he never does anything.'

'Yeah,' Wally replied, 'he's always trying to get away without doing any exercises when he's in my group in PE.'

Don continued, 'He's really a chicken, he's always afraid of going to Schwartz Hall [the juvenile home] all the time. Every time we are doing something, he just runs. Like sometimes we are walkin' along the street and a car pulls up with some guys in it, he just runs into the bushes. You know like last month when we got busted at Seven-Eleven, Dan's brother is outside screeching his tires and the owner calls the cops, all Steve is worried about is whether we're goin' to Schwartz. Here it is 2.00 a.m. and the pigs are takin' us back to our houses and Steve's askin' them if they're taking us to Schwartz Hall. Every time we are going to do something cool, like throw smoke bombs inside the theatre, he doesn't want to. That's why he's getting fat, he never wants to do anything.'

That, according to Don, was the real reason for the slow erosion of their friendship. Don was interested in more adventuresome activities while Steve was apprehensive about becoming involved. Soon, Steve was practicing with the football team (although he did not play much) and associating with a different circle of people, and I saw relatively little of him for the remainder of the year.

Don's behavior in class coupled with his playing truant and the company he kept led to his being 'marked' by Hawkeye and Pall as someone to watch. About half-way through eighth grade some of the teachers' cars in the parking lot had incurred minor damage (scratches on the side, radio antennas ripped off, a few hubcaps missing) and Don was brought to the office to answer for that. Don denied any involvement, but Hawkeye told him that they had witnesses who said he was seen in the parking lot standing near the cars. Later in the day Hawkeye told me, 'We're just waiting to get the goods on Don. It's a matter of time before we catch him. With the company he's keeping, we'll have them all out of this school before the year's over.'

To Don, much of this was a game between the administration and himself; he learned the strategies that they used to 'make you confess' and was not about to get caught in the web.

'I know how they work,' he explained to me, 'but it won't work on me. First they try to browbeat you into confessing to somethin', they try to scare you; that shit doesn't work with me. When that doesn't work, they try this psychology crap, like Pall said, "OK, Don, I know you're not a bad kid; you get good grades, you're pretty smart, now I can't believe you'd do what you were sent down here for." They try to soften you up with that "good guy" approach.'

Don had begun regular associations with a new network of friends, a group that, while not excluding past friendships (Steve and Roger were occasionally included), still was not dependent upon them. His closest immediate contact in this group turned out to be Bob, a ninth-grader who had contacts with older students in the high school. These students had access to cars, quality liquor, and what seemed to be a steady supply of marijuana and pills. The group also included Jack, who was involved in many of the same activities but often with a different group of friends. Much of their talk centered upon smoking dope and drinking alcohol and the context within which it was done. They always spoke knowledgeably regarding the subject, and I never had any real reason to doubt the veracity of their statements. Yet, since I never participated with them in these activities I wondered how much stories were stretched just a little to make them more exciting.

By January, I learned, however, that most of it was true. January was when the regular school year came to a halt for three weeks while students took 'enrichment courses' such as swimming, automobile maintenance, fishing, and skiing. I took skiing, not only because I wanted to learn to ski (I never did, at least never very well) but mainly because many in Don's group went too. In actual fact, they did not go just to ski; I learned that when I embarked on the bus at 6.30 a.m. for the trip to the ski area.

'Hey, Hippie, come on back here with us,' I heard one morning as I got on. It was Don, sitting in the back with Dan and a few girls. He was waving a brown paper sack at me, so I made my way to the back of the bus and sat down.

'What's in the bag?' I asked.

'My lunch,' he laughed, as everyone around joined in the laughter. 'Want to see?' he said, opening the bag and showing me two bottles of Olympia. 'Want a swig?'

'You must be nuts,' I replied, 'I couldn't drink a beer at this hour if my life depended on it.' I settled down for the long trip, while Don, Dan, and a few of the others took turns occasionally passing around the beer, in between talking and snoozes.

A few beers on the bus was not the only extra-curricular activity afforded by the escape from the confines of the school. For example, it was easy to have a smoke on the slopes by simply slipping into a grove of trees on the way down the hill and lighting up. (Jack told me he figured that when the snow melted they'd find thousands of butts in one grove where they always stopped.) Better yet, was to light up a joint on the chairlift going up the hill.

Such led to problems. Boarding the bus for the return from the ski area, I found no seats in the rear and had to sit in the front near one of the teachers. As it turned out, this was one of the times I was glad not to have been with Don and his friends. Half an hour after we left the ski area the chaperon, Ms Hummel, turned to me and said, 'Do you smell anything?'

The odor of marijuana was unmistakable and I knew instinctively its source. I tried to act dumb, and when Ms Hummel turned toward the front I immediately turned in my seat to get the attention of Don, Dan, and Jack. Placing my hands in the air to get their attention, I raised my fingers to my lips as if smoking a cigarette and pointed to Hummel in front of me.

'Darnit, I smell smoke back there,' Hummel said as she got up and headed for the rear of the bus. As she made her way to the rear,

I could hear her say, 'Somebody smoking back here?' A few minutes later she returned, 'They're smoking dope back there, can you believe that?'

'Who is it?' I asked.

'I'm not sure, but Dan was in the lavatory when I went back there and the whole rear of the bus smelled like grass. Do you think I should turn them in?'

'Wouldn't do much good if you didn't actually catch anyone,' I replied as if I knew what I was talking about. 'It'd just be your word against theirs.' Hummel sat down in her seat. 'Boy,' she mumbled, 'Larry [the person in charge of the ski program] would shit if he knew about this.'

After we reached the school and got off the bus, I asked Don and Jack if they didn't realize how strong the smell of the marijuana was.

'That stupid shit, Dan,' Don replied. 'We had the greatest set-up goin' and he ruins it. You should have seen it, Bob, it was perfect. You can go in that rest-room in the rear of the bus and when you shut the door it creates a draft out the vent in there so you can light up and there's no smell. Perfect! Then that stupid Dan leaves a joint in there burning for me to go in and take a toke, 'cept he leaves the door open a crack so the smoke blows out of the john into the bus instead of out of the bus. I could kill him for that.'

About a week later, I heard that Don's friend Dan had been suspended from school for stealing. 'Stupid shit, it served him right to get busted,' Don said with little emotion. I was somewhat surprised at his apparent lack of sympathy, expecting instead his usual barrage of how Pall and the principal had Dan earmarked and were just ready and waiting to bust him for anything they could.

'How come you say that?' I asked, 'You think he deserved it?'

'Listen Bob, anyone that goes into the locker room and rips off a pair of Adidas [tennis shoes] deserves to be caught. What a stupid thing to do. Why go around ripping off stuff like that, it's just asking for trouble? You know,' he said philosophically, 'this school isn't that bad if you don't go around doing stupid things; you can still get away with a lot, you know, skipping, smoke a little, goof off, things like that.'

'You mean guys really get in trouble if they push it too much?'

'Sure, look at Roger and his friend, "Rat." They're both stupid 'cause they come to class stoned half the time. Everyone knows they're stoned, even the teachers, so naturally they're always going to be suspicious of them. Guys like that are always going to be in trouble because they're always watched for everything they do. I can do a lot of what those guys do and not get in trouble because I'm more careful and they aren't watching me.'

There is a very important message in Don's rejection of the school, the expulsion of his friend Dan, and Don's recognition of how to control deviant experiences in the school without being expelled or to be in such serious trouble that all was lost. That message was simply that one should conform to the requirements of the school in sufficient detail so as to 'get by,' all the while creating a separate culture that permitted the maximum elements of self-determination. This, I believe, is an extremely important aspect of junior high schools and helps to explain the extent to which the organization serves as a bridge between the elementary school and high school. This bridge is created to the extent that the student groups, dependent upon their own interpretation of the organizational environment, come to reconcile the contradictions in their own labor – the essence of their own being – and that practice of selling labor power for exchange-value. Students thus made 'adjustments' and went through stages where they seemed to accept the premises of the control over their labor in school. In this sense, then, these contradictions were 'worked out' for some period of time. But then new forces and new interpretations generated further contradictions which also became the basis of subsequent actions. Students tired of handing in work to gain only a 'grade' at the end of the quarter. Threats of detention wore off as detention itself became a symbol of group unity. For Don and his friends, it was a continual process of finding a place where they could be left alone and in return, where they would agree to violate school standards minimally.

Junior high students are working through these contradictions in part because of the nature of the organization they inhabit. Here they are, for the first time in their lives, in an institution that is devoted to and organized around standardizing human behavior in such a fashion so as to create relatively predictable outcomes. By that I mean that the junior high school, unlike most elementary schools, operates on a fairly rigid schedule of timed classes that permits little variation, moves students from one experience to another in large groups or 'batches,' and is so organized as to assume that students realize the authority of the teacher as the fundamental source of knowledge and be willing to abide by that. Thus, classes are organized where teachers dispense information, where little dialog is encouraged, and where the control of knowledge rests with the adults within the organization. It is no wonder then that young adolescents in schools like Spencer fit all the characteristics of most junior high students – unpredictable, erratic, verging on hyperactivity. They are attempting to work out a system of control over their own labor (in the school, this is called 'work') for the first time in their lives, within an environment that denies this right to them. As those adolescents come to learn that the school does in fact deny them control over knowledge and its use, they begin to seek out other arenas for control, and they discover that they can at least attempt to control the social processes within their own group networks. Since the students in the school all interact within the same materialistic world (the organization of the school), they then come to constitute a social class because their relation to the productive forces of the school is approximately the same. Thus the junior high school consists of an organization in which the majority class (students) is denied basic control over the fundamental labor processes they perform in that organization. Their efforts to create new knowledge in this environment helps explain their unpredictability, their apparent hyperactivity.

So, the Don we saw at the beginning of eighth grade could be much different by the end of the eighth grade, yet still be the same. All of it depended upon the manner in which he had interpreted how to 'get by' near the end of eighth grade.

I noticed Don, Jack, Steve, Karen and Morrie, one of the football players, standing around the hall talking and laughing. I hardly recognized Don as he had had a haircut and now looked very 'respectable.' I went over to see what was happening.

'Hey, Bob,' said Morrie, 'I ran into Jim over at Firtree [the junior high school] yesterday.'

'Hey, really,' I replied, remembering that Morrie had been one of the people selected by the student council to make an exchange visit to the school. 'How is it over there?'

'They're all a bunch of fairies over there,' he replied.

'Yeah, and he said Jim's eyes were all bloodshot, like he's been stoned for a week,' Steve added.

'Knowing him, he probably has,' Karen said, looking at Don. We all began walking down the hall toward the science rooms. 'So, what kind of stuff you into now, Don?' I asked.

'Signed up for Kung-Fu lessons,' he replied, 'and might take scuba lessons this summer.'

'Sounds serious,' I replied.

'Just trying to get my head screwed on a little bit,' he said casually.

Just then Jack turned around. 'Hey, you guys, my brother says he and some guys from the high school are going to put on a kegger next week over in Forest Grove. I'll bet we could get a ride over.'

'OK,' Steve said emphatically.

'Can you get a bag?' Jack said, looking at Don.

'I'll manage.' Don smiled on his way into the science room. As we sat down, the four of them – Jack, Don, Steve, and Morris – began a chorus of their favorite song.

> And I said no-no-no-no, I don't smoke it no more,
> I'm tired of waking up on the floor;
> No thank you, please, it only makes me sneeze,
> And then it makes it hard to find the door.

The bell rang. Mr Franks barked out, 'Class, turn to page 328 in your science books. And stop the singing back there. Now, yesterday you remember . . ., I told you about igneous rocks . . .'

Summary and conclusions

Before we discuss the fundamental significances brought out in our understanding of Don and his friends, I think it useful to note that there is little material in this chapter focusing explicitly on the manifest purposes of schooling – the formalized instruction of students discussed in Chapter 3. There are two reasons for the absence of material on what we may imagine should be the focus of a discussion about a group of boys in the junior high school. First, the group's learning experiences fit quite well with the discussion of the roots of knowledge in Chapter 3, and there seems little reason to detail those experiences again here. The second and more basic reason why learning and the topic of learning is absent from the material in this chapter is that it was rarely interjected by anyone within the group. For learning, as I have pointed out, both for good students as well as poor, simply was not an issue over which groups concerned themselves. This is true because academic learning is not the central precipitator for the formation of groups and coalitions of students. The basis for group formation is more social than academic, and involves the interests and perspectives of people as they interpret *their* place in the organizational matrix of the school. Thus, for most in Don's group, banding together had little to do with instructional activities but rather was oriented around their common and shared interest in motor cycles, smoking 'dope' and general hell-raising outside the school. The daily scene, then, revealed a constant, albeit subtle, tension between the group fulfilling its own agenda and, at the same time, paying the necessary attention to the requirements of completion of a grade or course.

If academics were not particularly salient to group activities, then how successful were individual students at meeting the minimal academic requirements of Harold Spencer? Most in Don's group did fairly well. At the end of the last semester of the eighth grade, Don had one A, three B's, a P (pass) and a F (fail). (For the two years I was at Spencer, he compiled a 2.75, or B−, average.) He received the F in shop during the eighth grade because he said he was not interested in doing required projects and would much rather have done projects that he originated himself. Others in the group managed to do about as well with B's, C's and a smattering of D's here and there. (With the exception of Roger, all in the group had a two-year average of between 2.1 and 2.9; Roger's was 1.6.) The point, then, is that most group members met the requirements of the school despite a consuming interest in their own activities and the seemingly ambivalent manner in which they treated anything having to do with academics. The school demanded relatively little from them, and they gave what was required but certainly no more.

Our examination of the predominant impact of group collegial relations in the everyday life of Don and his group suggests a second type of knowledge system associated with the process of schooling in an organizational context. This knowledge is legitimated and reinforced through, and based upon the collective ties between, individuals whose relationship to productive forces is roughly equivalent and who share common world-views that grow out of and eventually may re-create those very productive forces – a social class. Such a knowledge system, based on mutuality of communication within a 'community' (such as that of students), may be termed 'regenerative' because it is created, maintained, and re-created through the continuous interaction of people in a community setting and because what is known is, in part, dependent upon the historical forces emerging from within the community setting. Because such knowledge grows out of and is based on social interaction and the specific context of social interaction, regenerative knowledge is interpretively rather than empirically based. In this frame of reference, then, reality is not 'known' or preordained (as in reified knowledge), but rather is socially constructed and reconstructed as definitions, meanings and values are arrived at through collective communication.

The important characteristic of regenerative knowledge is that it is contextually based, meaning that understanding comes out of the specific historical context in which the actors are immersed. What, then, is known, or what is said to be, grows out of and in fact is part of the cultural process wherein people actively make and define their world again 'under very definite assumptions and conditions.' Regenerative knowledge is that which is imbedded in the constitutive processes that make history and, in opposition to reified knowledge, is generated by social groups as a natural process.

The contextual, collective dimensions of regenerative knowledge clearly are borne out throughout the description of the daily routine of Don's group, most especially the role of conflict. Fights and the activities built around them, for example, often seemed to integrate the student groups as they also disintegrated the student community (as one might suspect) and provided the elements of regenerative knowledge that built up among students. Also, the fights were usually only manifestations of a system of meaning of greater complexity. For fights did not just 'happen,' but rather usually built up over extended periods of time, and the fight itself was the culmination of events between two antagonists, for disagreements, insults, name calling and the like had preceded the actual fight itself for a considerable length of time. Only when this preliminary activity had run its course – when the insults and pushing in the hall no longer served a useful purpose – did the fight itself actually occur. There then was a social process to the act of fighting whereby one step escalated into another, and finally when the physical fight emerged as the only manner by which the objectives could be resolved. The school provided no institutionalized forum for resolving social differences among students, and thus the fight represented the students' own invented forum. It is only natural that if the student's daily life in the school is concerned largely with activities outside of the normal and formalized agenda of the school, that the resolution of conflicts in that life would also occur outside that formalized agenda.

Other forms of what appeared to be conflict were often little more than the creation and extension of the regenerative knowledge and thus the group consensuality. 'It seems they can never get along, all this insulting each other,' was a comment I heard from a teacher one day in the faculty lounge. Yet the fact of the matter was that all this name calling was *not* necessarily any indication that they did not get along; rather, it often was indicative of how well they *did* get along. The typical 'joking relationship' in the form of insults, practical jokes, rolls down the hill and the like, symbolized a bond of understanding and intimacy that could only be understood by those participating in the act, a fact that in itself demonstrated the true understanding that the group had of its own patterns. Further, there was a fine line between the interminable cursing, pushing down the hill, insults, and practical jokes as a form of joking behavior and an act that could escalate into a fight. Why could Dave push Gordon down the hill and have it be taken as a form of friendship, yet if he pushed Dave (the 'greaser') down the hill, it surely would mean a fight? Quite simply, while the acts were the same, the meaning was different. Joking behavior was done between friends, thus was symbolic of friendship; on the other hand, the same act between two persons who were not intimate did not symbolize friendship, but rather hostility. By knowing the degree of group intimacy, then, one could predict the interpretive structure within which actions were placed.

The use of profanity, tendencies toward deviant behavior, the varying use of drugs and alcohol, all may lead the reader to believe that Spencer was a veritable 'blackboard jungle' full of budding criminals and candidates for the juvenile courts. However, there are no places in this story describing instances of disrespect to a teacher or someone in the administration. Nor is there any indication of malicious and wanton destruction of property (the unscrewing of door nameplates and a few desks aside) or evidence of vandalism.

The absence of information on disrespect, threats to teachers, or vandalism is so because there was so little of it. Harold Spencer was an efficiently run school, with students apparently 'knowing their place' quite well. If a student was told to do something in class, he or she usually did it with little or no argument – Don, Steve, and Roger included. If the group became involved in a food-throwing incident at lunch (such as that between Roger and Gary) and Hawkeye broke it up, those involved stopped and listened dutifully as Hawkeye reprimanded them and meted out the punishment. The building generally was clean, with little evidence of carving on desks, spray paint on walls, clutter on the grounds, or signs of vandalism. Don and his friends (as well as the student body in general) seemed to respect the authority structure of the school and the facilities that they attended every day. Most principals would be envious of such a student body.

As such, then, activities that brought trouble to any in Don's group were not things like theft, insubordination, or drugs, but rather activities that upset the organizational routine – such as skipping, smoking, and goofing off in class. Yet, even group members recognized the necessity of boundaries. I was quite surprised, for example, at Don's and Jack's lack of respect of Dan for ripping off the tennis shoes. This displeasure seemed to symbolize a more general perspective that violations of school codes were acceptable as long as they did not drastically jeopardize one's over-all chances for survival in the school world as established by adults. One was literally 'stupid' if he blatantly challenged the school procedures by engaging in acts that, if caught, could lead to 'real' trouble.

In the final analysis, then, group-centered activity was an important part of the daily life of Don's group, and was the foundation out of which a regenerative system of knowledge emerged. Regenerative knowledge is of particular import because it is characterized by some fundamental factors that differentiate it from reified knowledge. In fact, regenerative knowledge stands in opposition to reified knowledge – it contradicts reified knowledge because of the very constitutive processes by which such knowledge grows out of collective human interaction. Accordingly, regenerative knowledge contradicts reified knowledge because it is interpretively based rather than empirically based, subjective more than objective, contextual rather than absolutist, symbolically oriented rather than factually oriented. Regenerative knowledge is of a *Gemeinschaft* and the organic solidarity of community; it grows out of cultural process and is the knowledge of groups as they create their own reality – as they make themselves through the production of their own means of life.

This contradiction between reified and regenerative knowledge may exist in more than just form as it seems to be present in content as well. We will discuss this at greater length in Chapter 5, but suffice it to say that the cultural processes manifested in Don's group – fights, conflicts, profanity, drugs, drinking, the incipient stages of sexism – all were outcroppings of growing anti-social forms that probably would develop greater pre-eminence as Don, Roger, Steve, and their friends moved through the school, and as the symbolic value of grades held less meaning as the structure of reified knowledge diminished in importance.[4] At Spencer, such anti-school activities, or those denying or serving to deny the prerequisites of reified knowledge, were carried out all the while that group members maintained adequate grades, but this does not mean that group members necessarily internalized or finally had appropriated proper forms of reified knowledge. It means simply that most put up with them as a price to pay for their own activities to be generated.

The key question to be answered, however, is what that price was, and whether some students pay higher prices owing, in part, to their location in the larger system of economic stratification. Later I will want to argue that they do, and that the content as well as the form of the regenerative knowledge-system plays a part in the price extracted. Suffice it to say here that such regenerative knowledge may represent what Willis has termed a 'partial penetration' by students of the basic labor process engaged in within schools, later to be transported to the labor process within the modern workplace. By the term 'partial penetration,' Willis means that students collectively understand that conformism to school rules and procedures holds few rewards and that to conform 'is to give up all possibilities of independence.'[5] That the school does not legitimate the presence of student cultures is clear by the fact that it establishes no formal mechanisms for collective expression and/or control by students. Recognizing this, students initiate expression and control through self-generated, interpretive dimensions that provide what appears to be some modicum of control over some dimensions of their role as members of the school proletariat. In the case of Don's group, then, regenerative knowledge and the meaning of life in the school did serve as an opposition form to the reified knowledge emphasized by the school. It opposed the predefined, ostensibly certain, passively acquisitional characteristics of reified knowledge through an emergent, interpretive, active process built up through group interaction. Regenerative knowledge and its creation and re-creation among students reveals that the deterministic forces of the school, as exemplified by reified knowledge, do not always take root and in fact may scarcely be paid attention to at all. The student culture and the regenerative knowledge that grows from it may serve to resist that alienative aspect of learning by creating oppositional forms that contradict the mechanistic processes of school learning. And the dynamic forces of opposition are ongoing as well for those students who may not be so 'anti-school,' as we see in the next chapter on Chris and his group.

5
The world of Chris's group

Laugh then at any but at fools or foes;
These but you anger, and you mend not those.
Laugh at your friends, and if your friends are sore,
So much the better, you may laugh the more.
(Alexander Pope, *Imitations of Horace*)

I was not surprised to see Chris's name on the list of students nominated by sixth-grade teachers to be above average in academic ability. I had heard that he was an outstanding student as well as sixth-grade class president, and the little I knew of him indicated he was popular among other students, a fact confirmed by the sociometric measures.

Chris attended the same elementary school as Don and Steve, and Chris counted them as his good friends, but he also told me that he associated with Phil, Barry, and especially John, who all lived nearby. All were part of a nucleus who had been together for most of their days in elementary school and who had shared many good times together. All were good students at Garfield, all interested in sports, all rather clean-cut kids, well respected among their peers, both boys and girls. The next year at Spencer, Marty, who had come from a different elementary school, joined the coalition, which remained inviolate through the seventh grade and part of the eighth.

The people

Chris was a good student while at Garfield Elementary School and continued to be a good student while at Spencer.[1] He was well known by all students at Harold Spencer, the brains as well as the 'weirdos' and the troublemakers, and got along well with everyone. Not only was he articulate, but he had a good sense of humor. Most teachers, with the exception of Von Hoffman, enjoyed having him in their class.

Chris was rather small in height when I first met him, but grew rapidly over the two years of the study. In other respects, Chris was pleasing in appearance with somewhat long but well-kept hair (it was shorter in the eighth grade after his father insisted that he have a haircut) and a well-kept manner with regards to clothing. Chris's closest companion during the seventh grade was John, who was nicknamed 'Choo-choo' or 'Railroad tracks' by his friends because of the braces he wore on his teeth. John was less outgoing than Chris, and did not participate in class work as actively as Chris. He was content to 'get by,' but he got by quite well in that he was a 'B' student for the two years I knew him.

Barry, another member of the group, was short and chunky, and appeared in the seventh grade as if he should have been in fifth grade. Barry's last name was Simmons so he was, at some time before I knew him, dubbed 'couch' – the name he was called by Chris, John, and others who knew him well. More academically oriented than the others in the group, Barry did what was expected of him in class, yet seemed to do it more promptly and regularly than either John or Chris, and was not as prone to goofing off in class. Barry too liked sports, and in fact he went out for the eighth-grade football team although he rarely played. He and Chris enjoyed talking about one of their favorite sports, hockey, and often made friendly wagers on the 'Peter Puck' games shown on national TV at the week-ends.

It is useful here to mention two other individuals who, while not members of the group for the duration of my time at Spencer and while not as closely linked to the coalition, were still important 'significant others.' The first of these was Phil who, while fairly intimate with the group in the early part of the seventh grade, was obviously, purposefully, and slowly ostracized from the group by the end of the year. Phil too was quite interested in sports and, like the rest of the group, spent considerable time in school discussing athletic activities. Phil talked as if he was a very good athlete, and he always criticized others whom he thought could not match up to his athletic ability. Phil too was a good student, and while he had a greater propensity to goof off than Barry, he did not 'act up' as consistently as either Chris or John.

Marty was the only member of the group to come from an elementary school other than Garfield. Unknown to the group in the early part of the seventh grade, he did not share in their collective experiences until later in the year and into the eighth grade. Nevertheless, he became important, especially to Chris who said that Marty was one of his closest friends during that year. Marty maintained the lowest GPA (Grade Point Average) over the two-year period, a C average. Marty too was a 'sportaholic,' and was in the school wrestling team for two years (one of the years, the first, with Gordon). Marty, in some respects, was a cross between a typical member of Chris's group and Don's group for, especially in the eighth grade, he talked more and more about his involvement with marijuana and his ability to get supplies of beer and occasionally liquor.

Chris discussed his family life more than any other member of the group but, here again, these discussions were rare and came about only as a result of talking about something else wherein the characteristics of home life would be brought out. I knew Chris's father worked for the state in the area of fiscal analysis while his mother worked as a clerk in one of the state agencies.

Barry, who lived near Harold Spencer in a modest one-storey ranch house, once mentioned to me that his father worked for a small 'food place' in one of the nearby shopping centers. By checking the records, I found that his occupation was listed as being a 'sales clerk' at a nearby delicatessen which had a reputation for selling quality meats and seafoods. While he did not mention it himself, I also found out that his mother was not employed outside the home. Phil, who lived within a few blocks of Barry in a similar home, was like Chris in that both of his parents worked. His father was a civilian electronics technician for a nearby military installation and his mother worked as a clerk for the military base. John lived close to Chris in a newer tract of homes. John's father was a teacher in one of the adjoining school districts, a fact that John never mentioned until late in the study. Marty lived with his aunt, who worked as a machine operator for a local wood products firm. I did not know why he lived with his aunt and never asked; nobody else did either. Once Chris told me that Marty could not have much money as he was eligible for a free lunch program for students from low-income families. Because of this, Marty was popular at lunch, especially during wrestling season when he had to restrict his food intake. Often Marty would simply get a lunch and then give it free or at reduced cost to anyone who wanted it.

The family characteristics of Chris's group were not significantly different from those of Don's group. The women worked in three of the families, and the father's occupation, with the exception of John's father, tended toward skilled technical work or semi-skilled operative work. All families, with the exception of Barry's who had moved to the district when he was in the third grade, had resided in the area since the boys were born and all had relatives living in the area. In that these characteristics represented features of most families in the area who sent their children to Spencer, the group and its origin was fairly typical.

Activities and perspectives

Seventh grade

'What's the score?'

'You have zero.'

'I thought I had one point.'

'Come on, Bob, that one didn't count, I moved my thumbs on that one.'

'That's your problem, not mine,' I replied.

'Poor sport,' John interjected.

'Come on, line up, I'm ready,' Barry said impatiently.

Chris placed his two index fingers parellel to each other on the desk and touched his thumbs to the desk so that the parallel fingers served as an upright. Barry spun the quarter, waited for it to stabilize, then attempted to flick it over Chris's outstretched hands. The quarter zinged over the bar and struck Chris on the chin.

'A George Blanda special,' Barry said emphatically, 'I'm even with you now, Chris, the score's three to three.' Just then the bell rang, signaling the beginning of the first period.

The year had begun at Harold Spencer. More specifically, the year with Chris and his group had begun and, in their case, every day began with math class first period. The few moments before math class often began with the omnipresent 'coin games' among

Chris, John, Phil, Barry, and myself, wherein we kept a running score, often used to determine who would buy milk shakes in the cafeteria after lunch. The year also began as it had for every year that any teacher in the school could remember – with a magazine drive.

At about 8.50 the loudspeaker came on: 'All students in building B should now proceed to the cafeteria for the assembly.' Books were slammed shut and we all waited for the signal to proceed to the cafeteria. 'Sit in your assigned seats,' yelled Mr Charles as we moved out through the door.

'Wonder what this thing is all about,' Barry said innocently as we moved down the halls filled with noisy students. 'I KNOW what it's about,' John said confidently, 'my brother told me some old dude tries to get you to hustle magazines and you get some dinky prizes if you sell the most. Big deal.'

I sat between Chris and John about half-way from the front of the auditorium, and we waited for the assembly to begin while students from other classes continued to pour into the auditorium. Following the 'pledge of allegiance,' Mr Pall introduced an elderly man who had been running these magazine drives for a long time. He began his presentation with some jokes (few people laughed) and some salutary comments about how he always liked to come to Harold Spencer every year because the student body was so energetic and responsive (almost everybody, especially the eighth- and ninth-graders, laughed). The salesman then proceeded into his speech, designed to convince the students on the art of selling. After providing directions on the procedures of how to fill out the subscription forms, and rattling off the list of prizes (the top room, on any given day, received free ice cream cones at the school cafeteria; the top individual seller, for any one day, was eligible for a drawing on one of the three ten-speed bikes; anyone selling at least three subscriptions could choose from a variety of large posters), the class was excused and we all returned to math class.

'Told you, Barry,' John said as we entered the room. 'Did you see those neat prizes, a poster of Captain Kangaroo for your very own. Just sell three magazines.'

'Big deal,' Don added from across the room, 'I'm not selling any of their baby magazines.'

'Bet you do,' Chris shot back jokingly.

'Bet,' Don answered, extending his hand as if to bet. 'Naw, you probably won't,' Chris replied, taking his seat. Mr Glenn then came in with a big stack of subscription forms and gave them to Chris.

'Well,' he said, as he handed Chris the forms, 'you're the representative to the student government from this room, so I guess it's your job to hand these out and collect the money every day.' He turned to the class and gave the instructions that people were to get the forms from Chris and that the first five to ten minutes of every class from now until the end of the magazine drive (one week) were to be used to hand the money in to Chris. Chris thus began his first obligations commensurate with his newly elected post as class representative to the student government.

The student government at Harold Spencer was a body elected by the students. Any student running for school-wide office had to have a 2.5 average. There were no grade requirements for room representatives, although if students elected what any one teacher thought was a 'goof off,' (meaning a person who would not handle the responsibilities of the office) teachers did their best to dissuade the class and, if necessary, used their authority to veto the decision. The school-wide council – president, vice-president, secretary, and treasurer – was elected in the spring and thus consisted of eighth- and ninth-graders. Room representatives were elected early in the Fall and seventh-, eighth-, and ninth-graders were equally represented.

The first meeting of the year was held early in October. As was to be the case for the two years I attended these meetings, few, if any, students knew before the meeting what was to transpire. Chris and I entered the room where the meeting was to be held and sat in the rear near the window where some of the other seventh-graders were sitting (since seventh-graders often did not know many of the older students, they tended to cluster together for security until the middle of the year when they felt more comfortable). Mrs Patterson, the adviser to the student council, began the meeting by introducing a gentleman 'who has a product you may be interested in buying with your student body funds.' The man had a large case which he placed on the table before him. Before proceeding, he asked a girl sitting in front for the name of the school mascot. Upon being told it was a stallion, the salesman taped a large piece of paper to the chalkboard behind him, took out a stencil of a horse from his sales kit, placed it on the paper, then, with a can of spray paint he took from his kit, sprayed an outline of a red horse on the paper.

The students watched attentively as the salesman continued with his demonstration.

'OK, who do you guys have your next football game with?'

'Stonebrook,' the football players and cheerleaders said in unison.

'OK, then here we go,' he said, taking some large letters from his kit and beginning to spray the letters G-O S-T-A-L-L-I-O-N-S B-E-A-T S-T-O-N-E-B-R-O-O-K.

'Hey, far out,' said one of the cheerleaders.

'Yeah, better than those crummy signs we have now,' one of the football players added.

'Shut up, Jackson,' the cheerleader said in jest. 'We work hard on those signs, just so you guys might win a game once in a while.'

'My kid sister makes better signs,' a football player added.

'My kid brother plays football better,' the cheerleader retorted. The salesman laughed at all this while continuing his pitch on the versatility of the sign kit, its use for athletic events, dances, holiday signs, special events and the like. 'It's guaranteed too, if any of these rubber stencils break we'll replace it free,' he added.

Chris raised his hand. 'How much does it cost?'

'We'll get to that in a minute,' he said as he dragged out umpteen bottles of spray paint to show all the different colors. He began spraying a new sign, demonstrating how different colors could be combined. Taking Chris's cue, another student asked how much the paint cost.

'Twenty-four dollars for a case of 12 . . .'

'What!' a student interrupted, 'I can get it for one dollar and thirty-nine cents at Red Front [a local discount store].' The salesman appeared a little unnerved by this comment, so he extolled how this was a special paint and that it would last longer. Another student raised his hand to ask him how much the whole kit cost. 'Let me show you one thing and then we'll get to that,' the salesman replied.

Chris leaned over and said to me, 'Sure sounds like he's stalling on that price.'

'That, my boy, is the art of salesmanship,' I replied. By now it was 9.15 and the period was almost finished. The salesman finally got to the discussion of price. 'These kits range in size, with the small portable kit like this one [holds kit up] costing one ninety-five, to the large kit which has everything you could possibly want. Plus, with this large kit we'll throw in sixty dollars worth of extra silhouettes or paint free.'

'How much?' Chris said impatiently from the rear of the room.

'For the large kit, three forty-five.'

'You mean a dollar ninety-five for that little one and three forty-five for the big one? Heck, that's not bad.'

'Yeah, we ought to get it,' the talkative cheerleader added.

The salesman smiled, 'No, it's one hundred ninety-five dollars for the portable one and three hundred forty-five dollars for the large kit.' The gasp in the room was loud and clear. 'Three hundred forty-five dollars for THAT?' someone said. Chris said loudly, 'What a rip-off.'

Mrs Patterson looked embarrassed, but just then the bell rang to end the period. 'Can you come back tomorrow so we can make a decision on this?' she asked the salesman. He said he could not as he had to be out of town. 'OK,' Mrs Patterson said as the group filed out of the room, 'we'll have another meeting first period tomorrow to make a decision on this.'

The next day a meeting was held to decide whether to buy the sign kit. Terry, the president of the student council, had not been at the meeting the previous day, so Mrs Patterson took a few moments to fill him in. While we were waiting, Chris told Jim, another seventh-grade representative, that the whole thing was a waste of money. Jim shrugged his shoulders but was preoccupied with copying John's English paper for an assignment due that afternoon. After a few more moments Terry asked if there was any discussion on the purchase.

'Wait a minute,' said Chris, 'how do we know we have enough money to buy this thing?' People in the front turned around, somewhat surprised that someone should ask such a question, especially a seventh-grader. The treasurer of the class, busily talking to one of her friends, looked up and said in a very matter-of-fact manner, 'Oh, shoot, that's not a problem, we have a couple of thousand bucks.'

'Well, let's vote on it then,' prompted Terry. 'How many want to buy this thing?' Led by the cheerleaders and the football players, who were urging everyone to get their hands up, the vast majority of the student council voted to purchase the super stencil kit for $345. Chris was one of the few who did not raise his hand.

I did not get an opportunity to see Chris again until the next period when I saw him in music class.

'Well, what'd you think of your first student council meeting?' I asked while we were waiting for Hackett who was, as usual, late to class.

'It was a waste.'

'Did you vote to buy the sign kit?'

'Are you kidding,' he replied emphatically. 'They could have made that thing in the shop for half that price. I'm pissed!'

I did not doubt Chris's frustration at what had transpired in the meeting. However, as I attended similar meetings over the two years I remained in touch with the school, I became convinced that the school-based domination of meeting agendas was not the most significant issue in the operation of the student council. Instead, what seemed most clear was the over-all lack of concern most students had for the business conducted within the council or indeed the very presence of the council itself. Thus while students who were elected usually attended the meetings and often dealt with the agendas presented to them, the business of the council seemed little different from the business conducted in most of the classes. The reasons for this are complex, but are not unrelated to the very culture students built and through which they came to interpret their place in the school. A description of some of the recurrent activities of Chris and his group will illuminate this point.

The games before class, as noted earlier, typified the routine of Chris and his group. So too did a general accommodation to classroom requirements. There was, however, one notable exception. Chris and his friends had great difficulties with one teacher, Mr Von Hoffman, and it was here that the group developed the reputation of being troublemakers.

Von Hoffman was perceived by students and teachers alike to be a poor teacher. He had been teaching for over fifteen years, and although the administration would have liked to have him fired, this was difficult. Chris, John, and Barry tried their best, however, to drive him out of teaching but Von Hoffman seemed able to outlast them.

One day it seemed Von Hoffman could not take it any more. John, Chris, and Barry had been goofing for the entire period, despite frequent admonitions from Von Hoffman. But they kept getting up, walking around, talking to each other.

Suddenly, Von Hoffman stomped to the rear of the room. 'You, you, you, you and you,' he said pointing to Chris, John, Mark, and two other boys, 'you five come with me; we're going down to the office right now.'

'ME?' Chris responded incredulously, smiling as he said it.

'I didn't do anything,' John added.

'How about Barry?' Mark said, pointing to Barry who was in his seat doubled over in laughter. 'He ain't been in his seat at all.'

'Don't say "ain't" in this class,' Von Hoffman said almost automatically. Chris looked over at Barry in his seat. 'Hey, don't flip Mr Von Hoffman the bird,' he exclaimed. By this time Von Hoffman was visibly upset and he marched the five to the office for a conference with Mr Pall. Sitting down outside Mr Pall's office, I could catch glimpses of the conversation inside.

'I'm sick and tired of these hoodlums disrupting things. . . . I want them all transferred.'

'But Mr Von Hoffman, you know I'm doing better, better than I was doing before.' It was Chris, using his PR skills as usual.

'I guess so, but I want the rest of them transferred . . .' The conversation went on for about five more minutes. Finally they came out and returned to the room. I poked my head in Pall's office.

'What happened?' I asked.

'I transferred three of them,' he sighed. 'They should have gotten rid of that idiot years ago, but nobody has the guts.'

John was not transferred, and the group was fairly well behaved for the next few days. Soon, however, they reverted back to their original form. Chris and John began discussing (as they had in the past) how they thought that Von Hoffman was 'crazy' and that he had been in a mental institution at one time. They concocted games of looking at his habits and idiosyncrasies and 'typing' them as being the characteristics of someone who is a little bit unbalanced.

Little incidents continued to build up, with Chris, John, and Barry in the middle. The next day Chris and John, sitting next to the window, happened to look out at the nearby road and saw some students strolling by.

'Hey, those are Spencer kids,' said John in a loud voice. Von Hoffman looked up from his desk. 'Knock it off and get to work,' he said, pointing a pencil at John.

Chris ignored Von Hoffman's warning and continued, 'Yeah, that's Jon Smith and he's in my science class. Wonder what he's doing out there?' The whole class was peering toward the road by this time, and Von Hoffman too had been lured over to the window.

'Must be playing hookey or skipping,' John said nonchalantly. By this time Von Hoffman had swallowed the bait.

'Are those kids really from Spencer?' he asked.

'Sure,' Chris replied, 'one of them is in my science class.' Von Hoffman turned around abruptly and headed for the door, which he opened half-way before pausing. Apparently thinking twice about leaving the room unsupervised, he re-entered it and flipped on the loudspeaker switch to the office.

'Office.'

'Yes, this is Mr Von Hoffman, would you [in the meantime, controlled and almost uncontrolled laughter from Chris and John, covering their mouths, looking out the window, doing everything they could to keep from giving the whole thing away] tell Mr Pall that there are some boys out front trying to skip school.'

'OK.'

It was a well-executed trick and Chris and John had pulled it off perfectly.

Within the week, events in the class reached their lowest point of the year. John, Chris, and Barry had been especially persistent in their bugging of Von Hoffman to the point where some of the girls were even picking up on the activities (a fairly rare occurrence). On Thursday, Von Hoffman tired of the two girls near the back talking, so he sent one of them out of the room. The other girl pleaded to be sent out too, saying she promised that she would not get in any trouble, but he refused. Chris and Barry, sitting near the window and the heater, were plopping small objects down the vents, causing a 'bing-bing' sound when the objects hit the fan blades.

'Knock that off over there,' Von Hoffman yelled. 'You boys get away from that heater.' The two of them slowly moved their desks, being careful in the process to scrape them as loud as possible on the tile floors. Von Hoffman turned his back to the window to talk to the girl again.

Meanwhile, the girl in the hall was looking in the window of the door, pointing to people, laughing, and trying to make them read her lips through the window. Chris, watching the girl in the window, suddenly called out, 'Hey, quit flipping Mr Von Hoffman the bird.'

That did it. Von Hoffman was back at Chris's desk in a flash, standing above him. 'You little smart guy,' he said in an emotional tone, 'it's about time you start learning some respect,' whereupon he grabbed Chris by the shoulder and began shaking him.

'Oh, my shoulder, I'm dying,' Chris moaned.

'Sue him, Chris,' John said, continuing to flip paper into the heater.

'I'll sue,' he said.

'Get up in your seat,' Von Hoffman ordered, 'and start your assignment.' Chris got up and sat in his chair while Von Hoffman continued to glare at him. Finally, Chris picked up his pencil and poised it on the paper, as if ready to write. He looked at Von Hoffman and asked quietly, 'What's the date?'

The juxtaposition of the irate Von Hoffman and Chris's refusal to take the incident seriously was too much. 'Out-out,' Von Hoffman shouted and Chris walked out the door, banned to the hall for the remainder of the period.

The next day Chris told me that his penalty was to go to the library to write 'I will not talk in class' 500 times, and that he could not return to class until the sentences were finished. All of which was just fine for Chris because he spent the next two weeks in the library writing fifty sentences a day and reading books most of the time. He told me that he was thinking of getting a transfer, but that since it was already the second semester it was probably too late. 'Besides,' he said, 'Barry and John miss me. They say the class is boring and that there's nobody else to goof off with.'

Von Hoffman's class was both hated and loved by the members of Chris's group, and through this contradiction we can see the manner in which they came to interpret their presence in it. In the first place, the class was nothing but 'work' to the students in it – in fact, the class was the epitome of reified knowledge described in Chapter 3. Students did what they were told to do, were provided little if any flexibility in controlling the formal basis of their work, and were given tasks the purpose of which quite often seemed more related to filling up the time than to the achievement of any specified instrumental end. Yet the personality of Von Hoffman as an authority figure was something students found incongruous as well. Here was an individual who was supposed to be 'a boss' because of his age and experience, yet he seemed unable to carry out the imperatives of his position. In this sense, then, students found not only the work they did to be alienative, but found themselves estranged from the individual in authority who parceled out the work to carry out.

Given this context, they created their own knowledge system, permitting control over the dynamics within the classroom as well as the person who had authority in the classroom. This system of knowledge was based upon the mutuality of shared experience as perceived by students removed from meaningful work and from appropriate understanding of the nature of work they did. Thus, going to Von Hoffman's class became a game – one that proved to be somewhat entertaining – that Chris and his group played whenever they felt it appropriate. To the extent they controlled the game, its rules, its outcome, and understood the basis on which it was played, the class was somewhat enjoyable, and the perspective students created within it proved to be another constitutive element of their culture within the junior high school.

As with Don and his friends, Chris's group spent significant amounts of time actively comparing themselves to other students in the school. The process of and results from this comparative process constituted another dynamic in the creation of the group's distinctive belief system.

Picking on other students (usually 'weirdos') occupied much of the group's time, not only outside but also within class. Sam was one boy who was the constant target of both Chris's group and Don's. Sam was apt to be ridiculed in the lunch line, as he walked down the hall, in class, in virtually any place he went. Typically, Sam was teased for the clothes he wore, the food he ate, the motor cycle he could not fix – actually everything. Sam's typical response was to try to ignore these taunts and hope the perpetrators would tire and leave.

The group made it a practice of joking with girls with equal fervor. Usually, this was accepted with equanimity, but occasionally it was not and the good-natured joking then backfired. One day the group was in science class with nothing in particular to do (it was a day to 'catch up' on assignments, meaning, for most, a time to sit around and talk). Sitting behind us was a girl named Kathy who wore braces on her teeth, as well as a cumbersome neck brace. I overheard one of her friends saying to her, 'Did you ever fly on an airplane with that thing on [motioning to the brace]?'

'No, why?'

'Well, I could imagine that if you tried to go through the security gate, the metal brace would make the buzzer go off and you'd probably have to take your shirt off so they could see it was really a brace and not a bomb you were carrying.'

Chris and John, who had been talking to Don, overheard the same conversation and turned around to Kathy and the girls with whom she had been talking.

'You couldn't get on anyway,' Chris remarked, 'they don't allow dogs to ride on airplanes.'

'Or if they do they have to ride in the luggage compartment,' John added.

'That's all right, there are plenty of dogs back there to keep you company.'

'Yeah, especially if girls from this school are riding the plane,' Don said from the front. 'Kathy looks like an X-15 space pilot!'

'Why don't you boys turn around and mind your own business,' one of the girls said.

'Yeah, buzz off, you creeps,' another added.

John and Chris finally turned around but five minutes later Andy, one of the boys in the class, came over to John. 'What'd you guys do to Kathy?'

'What do you mean what did we do?'

'Look,' he said, pointing to the back of the room where Kathy had her head down on the desk, sobbing loudly. All her friends were around her trying to console her, telling her not to take it all so seriously.

'What's she bawling about?' John asked, unimpressed by all the dramatics.

'She says that she's tired of being picked on because of the way she looks,' Andy said.

'She ought to,' Chris said, looking into his microscope. 'Hey, look at this worm here!'

All of this banter and ridiculing accentuated the minimal discussion among group members about classwork, grades, or intellectual pursuits. I knew that group members did well in class, and especially compared to Don's group, and I expected to hear the group mention classroom-related experiences more than they did. Yet they didn't, and this puzzled me.

I explored this situation one day at lunch with Chris, Phil, John, and Barry.

'Barry, you told me a few weeks ago that you didn't like one of your classes because you didn't have any friends in there and that there was nothing to do. How important is it to have people to hang around with here in school?'

'Well, if you don't have anybody to be friends with, you get done and there is nothing to do because there is nobody to talk to. If you have somebody to talk to in class, even if it means getting in trouble, at least you have friends to pass the time with and to sit by in the lunch-room. If you don't have many friends, what are you going to do here except sit around and do nothing all day. Just being by yourself, sitting at lunch all by yourself every day, not being able to talk to anybody, it just wouldn't be any fun.'

'So, you're saying that if you guys didn't hang out together that . . .'

'School would be a bore,' John interjected.

Chris added, 'That's really what this place is all about, you know the social bit. I mean, that's what I look forward to every day, the little dumb things we do, telling jokes, goofing off in Von Hoffman's class, catching up on the latest gossip, bumming money from you, Bob. By the way, got a dime for an ice cream?'

'Get lost, will you,' I laughed. 'How about grades, isn't that important? What if you had the choice between getting a D or F on a test and being with your friends in class or at lunch, which would be more important?'

'I wouldn't care,' Chris answered immediately. He continued, 'If you have friends you don't need that good of a report card and all that. You could have a 4.0 average and still not be able to talk to anybody, but you could have a zero average and have friends, good friends and that is more important, that's what I think.'

To a large extent, it was. Most in the group had the internal motivation to do passing work in school. But such work was not important for group membership and thus was not a topic of conversation within the group. Classroom instruction pertained to individuals and was not a factor in social relations. The group reaffirmed this point time and time again.

The low level of student involvement in academic matters was reaffirmed even in school-based agendas that would seem to be of interest to students. This fact has been noted in the episode with the sign kit described earlier. After this, the student council lay dormant until late November (meetings were usually called by some member of the administration in order to settle one issue or another). The purpose for the November meeting was to pass out instructions to room representatives for taking orders for class and individual pictures. After Pall spent about ten minutes describing the procedures for taking orders on pictures, the meeting was open to discuss any issue of concern to the students. A few questions were raised about the use of the sign kit, but little interest seemed evident about it.

Little else related to student council affairs (or the lack of them) occurred until late in the winter when there was some talk about holding a school dance (only the second one of the year). There were preliminary plans to hire a band from outside the school at a cost of about $150, but those plans were in the process of being vetoed by Mr Edwards because he felt the students should not spend that much money. The next actual student council meeting was in March and was called by Mr Edwards in order to make some announcements to the council. We all waited a few moments but somebody called over the loudspeaker to announce that Edwards would be a few moments late. Tony decided to open up the floor for both old and new business. It turned out to be one of the few times when the council expressed any collective displeasure with what they had and had not been doing.

'Let's appoint a new dance committee,' someone said immediately.

'Yeah, maybe we can get some decent dances at last.'

'I think that the dances have been turned over to Mr Pall now,' Tony announced, looking cautiously at Mrs Patterson in the back, 'so maybe we can get some decent dances for once.'

'How about a new committee?' the original spokesman reiterated.

'OK, let's have a vote,' Tony said. 'How many want a new committee? [two hands] How many don't? [four hands] How many don't care? [the most hands] OK, we'll keep the same committee.'

Another girl then raised her hand. 'If we're going to keep the same dance committee, how about scheduling some noonies [informal dances held at lunchtime]?'

'The last time we asked Edwards, he said no.' Tony replied.

'We asked Mr Pall and he said it was OK,' the girl responded.

'Yeah, except that everything has to go through Mr Edwards.'

'Typical,' a girl replied.

'Figures,' Chris added.

'How come we can't have one?' one of the cheerleaders asked.

Tony was put on the spot but he did not have the answers. 'I don't know, he just won't go along with it. I've talked to him a couple of times and we just can't get anything going.'

'What if we get up a petition,' Chris offered.

'They won't accept it.'

'Let's talk to Pall.'

'He's out of town until Monday,' Mrs Patterson offered.

'So what, we don't have to have the dance until Monday.' That sparked a small amount of laughter.

One of the cheerleaders had an idea. 'Hey, what if we got a petition and had all of our parents sign it, then they'd really have trouble turning us down.'

'You'll never get all the parents to sign it and they wouldn't listen to that either.'

'Why not?'

'Because it has to be certified.'

'Certified? What's that?'

'A lawyer has to sign it and say it was a real petition. If you can get a lawyer to certify it, then it's a real petition.'

'Where'd you learn that, in history class?' someone from across the room asked.

A person in his history class replied, 'No, he sleeps in there.'

It was clear that students were displeased over what they saw to be the high-handed manner in which Edwards controlled the funds and decisions pertinent to the council. Yet it was also evident that their displeasure was readily displaced into the usual general apathy that characterized much of student life in school. Out of this apathy arose the bantering and joking that smoothed out the rough edges of the apathy and provided the students with some sense of control and direction. But this too wore off and frustration, intermittently connected with humor and resignation, all worked together to reveal the core of the student's internalization of Edwards controlling even the very funds that they raised for themselves in the annual magazine drive.

The meeting then continued.

'Tony, let's get this thing going before Mr Edwards gets here,' said Mrs Patterson from the back of the room. Tony said that the dance committee would try again and asked if there was any other old business.

'No.'

'Good, let's get out of here.'

'No,' said Tony, 'that's all the old business, we still have the new business.'

'Crap.'

'Hurry up.'

Tony went on. 'OK, new business. You know those signs some of the schools have in front of their buildings, like Stonebrook Wildcats or Woodtown Red Devils? Well, some people think that we ought to have something like that in front of our school so people will know what school it is. Is there any discussion on that?'

'Yeah, I can just see it, Spencer Stallions. Big deal.'

'Who wants a stallion?'

'Hey, I have an idea,' said a girl in the back of the room. 'How about putting a stuffed horse in front of the school. That would really be different.'

'Yeah, Stonebrook has a wildcat in front of their school, how come we can't get a stuffed horse?'

'Come on you guys, get serious,' remarked Tony impatiently, but to no avail.

'Sure, I can see a stuffed horse in this place; where would we put it?'

'In the cafeteria, it would fit the food.'

Bill, one of Chris's friends, said bitterly, 'This meeting sucks.'

'Is that what it is?' Chris replied.

'Hey, I got another idea,' suggested the girl who offered the idea of a stuffed horse in the first place, 'How about a work horse, one of those really big ones you know.'

'He'd have to be big all over,' one of the football players replied.

'What do you mean?' asked the girl.

'Just big ALL over, ha, ha.'

'Tough to take.'

'Hey, that's what I'd expect coming from you, Bruce,' the girl replied as her face turned slightly red.

'Come on, you guys, you're out of order; you're all out of order.' Tony was getting impatient.

'Order? Yeah, I'll take a Big Mac.'

'Two fries and a vanilla shake – to go.'

Tony kept on trying. 'Any more discussion?'

'Yeah, how much is all this going to cost?'

'I don't know,' Tony replied. 'I'll have to find out.'

'How can we vote if we don't know how much it's going to cost?'

'Yeah, where's all the money going to come from?'

'Where do you think?' Chris said out loud.

'Never mind, I know,' the girl replied, slouching down in her seat.

Tony continued his attempts to keep the conversation moving. 'We have over one thousand dollars in the student treasury and Mrs Patterson said we're supposed to leave something for the school.'

'La-de-dah.'

'I hate these meetings,' shouted a ninth-grade boy. 'Three years of sitting in these stupid things and it's always the same old . . .'

'Shit.'

'Hey, quiet you guys,' called out a boy near the door. 'Here comes Edwards.'

Mr Edwards walked in and said that he had a few announcements. First, he had been talking with a representative from a copy machine company who wanted to place a copy machine in the library. The student body would derive $30 a month in rental fees, so Edwards said that he had accepted the machine on behalf of the student council and asked if there were any objections. There were none. Next he announced that he had arranged with a scrap paper company to place a large container in the rear of the school, and that there would be an all-school paper drive the last week of the month, proceeds going to the girls' athletic program. He asked if there were any objections to that and there were not. With that he left. Mrs Patterson remained.

As soon as he walked out of the door one of the cheerleaders raised her hand. 'New question,' she said. 'Why can't we use some of this money to buy trash containers and picnic benches so we can eat out on the patio when the weather's nice?'

'They'll get ripped off at night,' a student responded.

'Chain them down, they do that in all the parks.'

'Listen guys,' Tony said with a sigh. 'I've already gone through that, too. Mr Edwards doesn't think that would be a good idea. He doesn't think the kids would use the trash cans and there would be paper lying all over the patio.'

'How does he know; he hasn't tried it yet.'

'He doesn't trust us, that's all.'

'Why can't we have a chance?'

'Yeah, they bring in that xerox machine on a trial basis like it's a big deal, but they never ask us until after they've decided. Why can't we have picnic tables on a trial basis?'

'I've already told you, man,' Tony replied, 'I talked to him on this and it's not going anywhere. Some of the teachers have asked him too and he won't go along with it.'

'I hate this place and I hate these meetings,' the same boy reiterated. 'I can't wait to get out of here this year.'

'Lucky.'

'Let's go in there again and talk to him about it.'

'Look,' Tony reiterated, 'you could send 30–40 kids to work him over and it wouldn't convince him.'

'Wanna bet.'

By this time the period was over. Tony announced that they would have two meetings the following week, one on dances and one on 'nooners' (they were never held). As we walked out of the room Chris complained how nothing ever got done in the meetings. Bill suggested that they put a statue of a horse on the front of the school, only they make it a dead horse.

The council never resolved the issue of the horse, the picnic tables never got past Edwards, and the council only met one more time that year. And although there was more grumbling about the absence of noonies and picnic tables, most students soon forgot about it and went back to hanging out, making jokes and bugging Von Hoffman. Expecting the students to be indignant, I found that they were, but got over it and soon were more blasé about the situation than anything else. At first I was bothered by such a lack of concern, but I came to understand it as I realized that control over issues such as a horse on the front lawn or picnic tables did not matter to most of the students anyway because few of them shared much of an institutional loyalty. After all, the schooling process rarely placed much credence on the intrinsic nature of student labor, so student presence in the school was based more on the exchange-value of their labor than the value of the work. Certainly picnic tables and the like had little intrinsic significance to students because they knew that Edwards would ultimately control their use. As far as the effort placed into raising the money, that money was raised almost totally by the seventh-graders, who sold magazines for Led Zeppelin posters and free ice cream cones as prizes. The eighth- and ninth-graders had long since seen through the shallowness of such prizes, and expended little effort over selling subscriptions.

That maybe already they knew that they would have little proprietary rights over the fruit of their own labor which existed outside the school was, it seems, a very telling lesson they had learned.

Eighth grade

Chris's and Marty's favorite class this year was history. The class seemed relatively enjoyable for them, as usually there was considerable discussion on issues such as the death penalty, world famine, and race relations. With few exceptions, however, Chris and his circle of colleagues continued to place more emphasis on the creation and sustaining of their own system of meaning in the class than they did on the discussion of salient issues. For example, for one week in the course, the class had been working on a unit on worldwide hunger. One day the discussion centered on the obligation of the developed nations to help out those who were less fortunate. As always, Chris and Marty were in the thick of it with their witticisms. After taking roll and dispensing with the preliminary formalities, the teacher, Mrs Paul, began the discussion. 'All right, class, let me have your opinions on the obligation that we as citizens of a wealthy country have to help those less fortunate than we.'

'Let them starve,' Tom laughed.

'Right on,' commented Linda, 'we've worked hard for what we have so why can't everyone else?'

'Linda,' Chris exclaimed in surprise, 'where's your charity, your sense of concern for your fellow man?'

'Shut up, will you, Chris,' Linda retorted.

Sally raised her hand and volunteered that 'the people in India all had a chance to come here at one time; they knew about this place; why didn't they come?'

Chris added a very uncharacteristic comment, 'The only reason that all the blacks came here was that they were strong and stupid.'

Melvin, the only black in the class, did not like it either. 'I'll get the Panthers after you,' he said half jokingly, but obviously upset as well. 'Besides,' he went on, 'blacks weren't dumb; it was a black that invented the cotton gin and a white guy stole it away from him.'

A girl commented that all the people in India deserved to starve when they had all those cows around but still did not eat them.

'Yeah, but cows are sacred in India,' argued a girl.

'If you were starving and a cow walked in front of you, you'd eat it, wouldn't you.'

'Would you eat an eagle?' Chris asked.

'An eagle! What's that got to do with it?'

'Well, the eagle is sacred to us, isn't it? Religions teach you certain things and that's why the people of India act the way they do. Our family is Catholic and there used to be this thing about eating meat on Fridays so that if you did eat meat you felt real bad inside.'

'I didn't know you were Catholic,' Marty said across the room to Chris. 'What do you do, eat Romans?' That comment brought loud ripples of laughter from across the room. Mrs Paul attempted to keep the conversation going, but by this time the humor and plays on words had become contagious and things were deteriorating. In my subsequent discussions with Mrs Paul, she said that she knew better than to expect more, but still was frustrated when students such as Chris, 'good students' (as she said), did not take the class seriously but instead 'make light of everything.' I could see how that could be frustrating, but on the other hand those such as Chris and John had learned to depend upon their group-generated behaviors to make sense of their mostly subservient role within the school. The fact that Mrs Paul's class was one of the few classes in which student dialog on academic issues was actually encouraged was not an easy point for most students to recognize. Daily attendance in classes such as Richards's and Von Hoffman's had a cumulative and dulling effect, almost overpowering those few instances where reified knowledge was somewhat de-emphasized. Chris's group agenda setting and Mrs Paul's frustration were clear indications that the segmentation of knowledge as it existed at Spencer was so pervasive that individual efforts by a few teachers were simply swallowed by the cultural process created by students as they interacted in the material world of the school.

The new president of the student council had been elected at the end of seventh grade; new room representatives had been elected as well and Chris had been elected to represent first period PE. After the first meeting of the year he told me, 'You know, those meetings are the same old shit over and over again. Just like where we left off last year. Nothing happens, just a complete waste of time.'

The next student council meeting was in October. This meeting, like all others, was called by the administration specifically to (a) elect two representatives to go to a leadership conference sponsored by the Red Cross, (b) to ask the student council to authorize spending $50 for the school-wide openhouse to be spent that week. The tone of the meeting was not all that different either, except that now I realized that the dynamics of student council meetings were little different than those in most classrooms. That is, there existed an obvious underlife continuing on and running both parallel and in opposition to the formal agenda of the meeting. Again, the underlife was illustrative of the separate culture that students created within the organizational context of the meeting.

Patterson opened the meeting, explained the leadership conference, and then turned the meeting over to Steve, the president.

'OK, who do you guys want to have go to this leadership conference?'

'Who wants to go?'

'Big deal.'

'Are you going to Thespians tonight?' (Chris, overheard talking to a ninth-grade girl.)

'Yes, are you?'

'Let's send Yates [the school brain who had almost been elected secretary of the student council last year as a joke].'

'Send Yates!'

'Did you hear that Marie and Jimmie broke up?' (Overheard behind where I was sitting.)

'Yes, I couldn't believe it. Is she here today?'

'I don't know, I haven't seen her yet.'

'We want Yates to go.'

'How embarrassing.'

'Why not, he'd like to go, then one of us won't have to go.'

Patterson stepped in front of the group with the letter from the Red Cross in her hand. 'The letter encourages you to send people who are in leadership positions in student government. Now, that is the intent of the letter and, of course, if you want to violate the intent, that's up to you.'

'I hear they might not do the play they had been thinking of for the Interim.' (Overheard between Chris and the girl he had been talking to.)

'Why not?'

'Not enough people and the wrong kind of people for the parts.'

'What are they going to do?'

'I'm not sure, I heard Calamity Jane.'

'Who broke it off?' (The girl behind me continued to talk about Jimmie and Marie.)

'Marie; Jimmie was acting like an ass and she just grew tired of it.'

'I'm glad, I never liked him that much myself; thinks he's a super stud.'

They then voted on who would go to the leadership conference. Yates came in third. Steve, the student body president, and one of the cheerleaders were chosen to go.

'New business?' Steve asked.

'I've got a super idea,' queried a ninth-grade girl. 'Why don't we have a slave auction like the high school does? We could auction off people to do a certain thing and then give the money for some cause or something.'

'Hey that sounds like a super idea,' was a response, and the excitement built.

'Yeah, why not, we could auction off Yates.'

'Better yet,' said one of the football players, 'we could auction off Janson [a well-endowed ninth-grade girl of 'questionable' reputation].'

'For sure, I'll go for that.' This was followed by general laughter and conversation among a group of boys sitting together.

'Come on, you guys, get serious,' said the girl who brought up the idea of an auction.

'We are,' one of the boys replied laughing, making a panting noise.

Steve tried to get the group on target again, 'Well, I'll talk to Mr Edwards about it,' he said, pausing to think for a moment. 'But I don't think he'll let us do it.'

'Why not?' asked the girl.

''Cause he just won't.'

The girl behind me leaned over toward her friend. 'Fuck him,' she said, and then continued her conversation. 'If we don't see Marie today, let's call her after school . . .'

I had talked to Chris during the two years about his feelings regarding the student government. In the spring of the seventh grade, I asked for his thoughts after a year as a room representative in the student council. He told me: 'I don't think it has really done as much as it should do but even if we do get together there's not that much we can do without having some kind of trouble from the administration. Like with that dance thing, it really worked out crummy because Edwards would only give us thirty-five dollars to hire a band so what are you going to do? They say you can have a live band and everyone gets all excited, like we have a real opportunity to do all this but then he says, "Oh, wait a second, I forgot to tell you, you can hire a live band but you only have thirty-five dollars to do it with . . ." We have money we could do things with but we just can't do it.'

The next year, near the end of the eighth grade, he was equally as displeased. Chris had mentioned throughout the year that he was going to run for student council president in order to rectify some of those issues. I asked him what he would do if he were elected. His reply was that his main goal should be to keep the administration from controlling the student council. After this conversation I thought Chris was all fired up to run for office. Yet I had overlooked his comments that he did not know what he would do if he had to confront Edwards on some major issue, and that there was probably little he could do. I also had forgotten that most students really did not care that much about the student council and that there would be little support from Chris's peers for such a confrontation. When petitions were being circulated for the student council president, I felt sure I would see one bearing his name. The deadline passed: no petition.

The next day I saw Chris in PE class. I walked up to him, obviously a little irritated (but more importantly, disappointed) that he had not run. 'Damn it, Chris,' I said, 'from all that talk a few weeks ago, I thought for sure you were going to run for student council president. What happened?'

'Yeah, Chris,' John said jokingly, 'we need some LEADERSHIP.'

Don stopped bouncing the basketball for a moment. 'Mr President,' he said, turning to Chris, 'I vote for a vending machine for joints.'

'I chickened out,' Chris replied to my original question while trying not to be too serious amid all the joking. 'I guess I figured that if I had been elected and said what I said I would, I'd be kicked out of school.' He grabbed the ball from Don, went for a lay up (missed) and the three of them took a few shots as if the student council was the furthest topic from their minds.

It's useful here to pick up on the activities of some people who have 'disappeared' from our story this year, that is, individuals who were close friends for most of the seventh grade but who became involved in different activities and interests during the eighth grade. I'm talking of John, Barry, and Dave (from Don's group) in particular. To discover what happened to them in the eighth grade, we enter, if only for a brief time, the 'athletic group.'

When I first began eating lunch with this group, early in the eighth grade, most of them were involved in eighth-grade football. About a month into the season one common understanding, a dislike of the coach, Mr Jerald, served as a common point of discussion. The team members constantly complained about him and blamed him for the team's first two losses.

'Did you hear what he said at practice yesterday?' Dave said to Harry. 'What a dumb thing to say.'

'What did he say?' I asked.

'Called us "shitheads,"' Dave replied. 'He said we were all shitty players and he didn't care how we played because he was getting paid to coach so it didn't make any difference to him whether we won or lost.'

The next week they were actually able to say something funny about the coach and at the same time knock Phil, who was Chris's and John's old friend. As Rick told the story, one of the players had dropped a pass and Jerald sent Phil in at end to replace him. Rick said he was standing along the sidelines and said to a teammate, 'He's sending Palmer [Phil] in, the coach really is a dumb bastard.' The coach, overhearing this, turned around and wanted to know who had said that; of course, nobody owned up. But, on the way to losing 18–0, Rick and John said they had a good time on the sidelines laughing about calling Jerald dumb.

Athletics, then, were not much different from classes and the student council. Students continually opposed the required activities when and where they could, given their understanding of what they opposed. In class, the athletic group was not much different from other groups of students with regard to their posture toward classes. Most did what they were told and got by, some better than others. I once asked Wally how he did in his classes, since I had never heard him (or anyone else at the table for that matter) discuss grades.

'I do all right,' was his reply.

'What's that mean?'

'It means I get by, you know, screw up once in a while but I'm not going to get uptight about it.' I asked him what he thought he was getting out of Spencer in terms of things that interested him, and his only reply was that he liked to be there with Rick and Dale and Chuck and John, that they had a good time together 'in a lot of ways' and 'what else is there? I got a B on my English essay yesterday, that's not slackin' now, is it?' Wally showed me the essay, titled 'The Funniest Thing I Ever Saw.'

> Last night we went to play basketball at the barn. When we got there somebody lit up a joint. There was [red penciled with a 'were'] two cows in the barn at the time, one mother and one baby. They kept watching us toke away on it, so we were feelin' good and we gave the cows nose hits. They got stoned, so did we.
>
> We started playing basketball and we played for a while. Then both cows started mooing and we went to see what the matter was. The cow had stuck his head in the door. It yelled and yelled, and we got him out and he was chasing us around the barn. We ran down to the store to get some munchies, then we went to Chuck's house to play poker.

'That's really great, Wally,' I said.

Toward the end of basketball season, I heard increasing discussion about the drinking parties and the smoking of pot over the week-ends. Not everyone was equally involved (I rarely heard Dave or John mention much about their participation) but it seemed, nevertheless, that at least Wally, Dale, and Clint discussed cases of beer and 'nickle bags' with increasing regularity. Clint said it did not affect his game performance because he usually tipped a few only on week-ends. Their involvement and interest in drinking and marijuana appeared small compared to that of Don and some of his group.

Barry disappeared from my observations during the eighth grade, despite my attempts to keep track of him by keeping track of Chris, John, Bill, and the others with whom he associated in the seventh grade. His lunch schedule was altered a few times, so I don't think I ate lunch with him more than once during the entire eighth grade. He tried to hang around with the athletes but, because he did not have the skills to play, he never fitted in. The last I heard of him was during basketball season, when I saw him at a basketball game as the scoreboard operator.

Summary and conclusions

Chris's group, consisting of Chris, John, and Barry and, to some degree, Phil (in the seventh grade) and Marty (in the eighth grade), was somewhat 'straighter' than Don's group. Yet like those in Don's group, the members saw themselves in a relatively nondescript fashion – as a group trying to fit into the social fabric of the school. Being with friends, constructing humorous incidents in class, bugging the teachers, some minimal involvement in student government – all constituted the daily routine of Chris and his group throughout the seventh and eighth grade.

The everyday behavior of Chris's group is important because it illustrates, although in a qualitatively different fashion, the process whereby social groups give rise to regenerative knowledge through cultural processes present among junior high school adolescents. The cultural processes evident with Chris and his friends reveal that, even among the more 'mainstream' students, resistance to the regularities of organized school life are common and that oppositional forms to formal organizational procedures arise. Such opposition can and often does develop as a contradiction to school knowledge. The complexities of this process become more clear as we re-examine the nature of student involvement in school government, the purpose of humor and joking relations for students, the import of these conditions for student cultures, and the manner by which these cultural processes contribute to the reproduction of the larger social structure in which they occur.

Toward the end of my second year at Spencer, a colleague working in the same project attended a meeting of a Jefferson citizens' advisory board which served as a liaison between the school board and the larger community. The next day he told me that the vice-president of the student council at Harold Spencer had attended the meeting and complained quite vociferously about how Edwards controlled the students' money in the school and how he constantly vetoed their every request. The board discussed this with her for about twenty minutes and a district official in attendance promised he would look into the situation. To the best of my knowledge, the subject was not raised again.

I was somewhat puzzled by this student's willingness to express herself so openly before such high-ranking officials, especially since this rarely was done within the school itself. I questioned her at lunch one day as to what had prompted her to raise the issue and what (if anything) she knew about any outcome. She and the friends sitting with her laughed at my question. The whole incident, they told me, came about as the result of 'a bet' which her friends had made as to whether or not she had the 'guts' to go before the advisory board and express her views. Because the father of one of the boys sitting at the lunch table happened to be the president of the advisory board, the whole incident was viewed with irony in that the girl indicated how the father pulled out various regulation books to support the stand on why students could not have certain activities. In the final analysis, the confrontation, while connected with complaints that the students had articulated over the past few years, was not motivated by any seething resentment on the part of the student council vice-president. Rather, it was seen as a joke and in that sense represented another form students created based upon their interpretation of their interaction in the material world of Harold Spencer.

I suppose that I placed much more faith in the involvement of students in student governance than could reasonably be expected. First, one could see that school officials rarely were facilitative in their attempts to get students involved in a viable policy forum. Given the circumstances, then, I had to agree with Chris in his decision not to run for student body president. What was there he could do? Teachers had confronted Edwards on his dominance of student council activities and funds and to no avail, and it was certainly not reasonable to expect that Chris or any other student, for that matter, would meet with any greater degree of success.

Yet how involved could the majority of students ever be in a forum such as the student council? The creation and operation of such a body assumes that the topics to be dealt with are of high saliency to the students in the school; it was obvious that most were not. Few students cared about putting a stallion on the front lawn and only the cheerleaders (supported by the athletes) pushed for buying the sign machine. Even though school dances were discussed and summarily vetoed by Edwards, it was only a small group (again the cheerleaders and some of their friends) who ever pushed for dances, 'nooners,' or picnic tables on the outside patio. Most did not care one way or the other. When Chris told Karen and Linda in art class that Edwards would not permit much money to be spent on dances or parties the girls appeared ambivalent and reacted more strongly to the fact that Tony (the student council president) 'kissed like a fish' than the fact that the money was being expropriated from them.

Yet the minimal involvement of students in school governance can be examined as still another organizational regularity based upon reified knowledge. The governance of school activities, indeed the definition of who has power over what, is preselected within defined parameters through tradition, and attempts at maintenance are made by those in control. Issues that do emerge or are allowed to emerge in student government are not salient to the vast majority of students because such issues have more to do with the ongoing history of the school organization (such as the stallion) or the image of the school to outside agents (the sign machine, sending a representative to the leadership seminar), and these are not of particular concern to most students because, since they pass through the school in three years, they have little stake in institutional permanency or image. Still, the fact that issues and processes of school governance are predefined, absolute, and treated as 'real' indicates that reified knowledge can and does occur through more forms than those pertaining to the academic instruction of students. Rather, such knowledge is an integral part of a school organization that reproduces a specific system of social relations in a hierarchically oriented society, predicated on unequal access to control of the means of production. This is more than Marxian rhetoric, for limited access to the means of production signifies, in the case of the production of political power, that student government is little more than a reconfirmation and re-creation of an ideology that political decision-making is done within the limits that others have defined as the scope of legitimate political action. This ideology is important, pervasive, and dominant as the young become adults.

This is why such minimal control by students is so critical even though the students themselves appear largely unconcerned about it. It points to the manner in which activities that play such a small role in the lives of most students in schools come to take on such a great importance. We need ask ourselves what it is that is being learned here, and how students are being taught about political decision-making in an ostensibly democratic society. For it seems they are learning at minimum that there is no useful role for them, that their involvement has been established and regulated, and thus that their apathy is a reasonable accommodation. Consequently, the fact that students seem so unconcerned (and that 'no harm' has come to them) is, in fact, the wrong observation. In a democratic society, depending as it must on the active participation of its citizens, we should be concerned that the students are so resigned to this condition.

In the absence of critical involvement in school-based knowledge, the play on words during student council meetings, the jokes about the Spencer stallion, and other forms through which cultural processes work make more 'sense,' given the organizational and institutional context within which they are created. The telling of stories and jokes was a trademark of Chris's group and provided them with an identity unavailable to other coalitions of students. There was no doubt that Chris, Marty and, later, Pete were very good at telling jokes. Communicating these jokes served three purposes in so far as a group identity was concerned. First, it meant that members had to have access to new and funny jokes, a point about which there was some pride. Second, joke telling required a certain dramatic skill and there was no doubt that Chris and Pete had the skills to tell good jokes. Finally, and perhaps most importantly, the telling of certain types of jokes symbolized an understanding of group membership – who would understand certain types of jokes and who would counter with equally complex and sometimes obscure lines. I remember once, in math class, that Chris told a joke to Ralph, a rather immature student, who did not even understand the joke. Later, in history class, Chris told the same joke to Pete and Marty who doubled up in laughter and Marty immediately countered with an Italian joke. Such jokes required a certain level of sophistication and not everyone could counter with jokes equally as sophisticated and novel. Thus most joke telling usually was carried on within the group or between groups of equal understanding.

Wisecracking in class, while it served many purposes (some of these will be discussed more fully in Chapter 7) was a demonstration of superior perceptiveness or creativity, and a creative wisecracker was one who had a higher social standing among his peers. Ordering a 'Big Mac' in the student council meeting, Marty asking Chris if he 'ate Romans,' Chris asking Mr Von Hoffman what the date was while Von Hoffman was standing above him in a state of rage – all these served to demonstrate the wit and craftiness of the perpetrator. I clearly remember the awe in which Wally, one of the athletes, was held in the eighth grade as a result of his wisecracking in English class. The class had been studying poetry and their assignment was to bring a short poem to class, read it, and tell what type of poem it was. That day, poems by Wordsworth, Keats, Browning – all the 'classic' poets – were read before the class. Then it was Wally's turn.

'What type of poem are you going to read, Wally?' asked Mr Vincent.

'Uh, this will be blank, uh, blank, whatever it is.'

'Blank verse, Wally,' Vincent filled in.

'Yeah, that's what it will be.'

'OK, we're ready, you may go ahead.'

Wally stood before the class, smiled slightly, and then rattled off in perfect style: 'Two all beef patties, special sauce, lettuce, cheese, pickles, onions, on a sesame seed bun.' He then sat down amid roars of laughter.

'What was THAT?' asked Vincent.

'My poem,' replied Wally, 'in blank verse.'

'You've got to be kidding,' replied Vincent, 'how can that be a poem?'

'I don't know,' Wally said in a straight voice. 'All I know is that McDonald's had this contest and if you went in and could say the ingredients of a "Big Mac" without making a mistake, you got a free shake. I did it and the guy said it was poetic.' The whole eighth grade talked about Wally for the next two days.

All in all, then, humor and its uses served to establish and reinforce social identities, demonstrate social acceptance, and to provide a means of boundary maintenance between and within the social group. Rather than just being 'something that junior high kids do,' it became something they did for a specific purpose although it was not always an immediately recognizable purpose. Perhaps Chris summarized it best when I asked him what held him, Mike, Marty, and Pete together during the eighth grade. Speaking of Mike, he said: 'We hang around together because we can goof off together and if I say something funny, he thinks it's funny; if he says something funny, I think it's funny. It's mostly just the relationship between a bunch of guys goofing off and having a good time.'

In humor, jokes, and joking relationships we see the very forms that are the basis of regenerative knowledge. These cultural forms are extended by students against the school's control of time, space, and organizational outcome. In the process, students appropriate for themselves a commodity over which they have full control – the ability to joke, interject, and to interpret as humorous the most mundane of activities. The importance of humor and its dimensions lies in the fact that it is the group out of which humor is generated and defined that decides what is funny and what is not, what can be taken to be irreverent and what is sacred. In this respect, Don, Roger, and Gary decided when throwing 'jello' was funny and when it was not; and Chris and his friends gained a sense of pride, almost as if they possessed a secret code, because teachers thought that rough-housing was violent when in fact it often symbolized intimacy. That only participants, out of context and through communication and interpretation, could define such incidents and build upon them is critical, and anchors firmly what often appears to be the 'squirliness' of junior high social life.

So, with Chris and his group we see, as with Don and his friends, existence of opposition and resistance to the pervasive nature of reified knowledge and the forms in which it is transmitted in the school. This resistance occurs in part because of the exclusion of students from crucial decisions about the nature of their labor, from their failure to see their labor as much beyond labor power that has exchange-value, and from their lack of understanding about the very 'value' of the commodity that they had produced through their labor. Clearly, even for those students who did moderately well in school, the demands of the institution were relatively minimal and sporadic. Time was something that students 'filled in' because the school could not fill much of it in and, even when it did, the value of the requirement was questionable to the students. That Wally could get a 'B' for his story about the cows then symbolized both the ritualistic manner in which students viewed work and the limits to which the institution would go to accept anything for the sake of legitimitizing the demands it made of students and having students accept those demands.

In schools, then, that are the backbone of formal education in modern capitalistic societies, the knowledge of youth – that interpretive, contextually generated knowledge of community or subcommunities – is built up through social forms that are largely unrecognized, indeed even separate, from those official channels through which reified knowledge is transmitted. There is then a disjuncture – a chasm – between the assumptions of reified and regenerative knowledge systems, and it is the extent of the interface between the two that is particularly crucial. This is so because it is the content of regenerative knowledge (as well as its structure), as it increasingly contradicts the content of reified knowledge, that serves as a discriminator between and among students and school knowledge, thereby 'allocating' students ultimately to particular organizational patterns. Note that I am talking about the cultural process of knowledge generation, and not the determining factors of school structure in and of itself. The degree of disjuncture is well illustrated in the case of John and Chris. In Chris's instance, his father spent considerable time discussing politics and 'philosophy' with him; with John, his father was a teacher and one could assume certain predispositions there. These factors contributed to a closer integration between the knowledge system demanded by the school and the content of the regenerative knowledge that grew out of their interpretive setting. Thus the activities of John and Chris, unlike many of those of Don and his friends, skirted around and teased the predominance of reified knowledge but did not reject or transcend it. Chris and his friends resisted to a considerable extent but, in the end, adapted to the imperatives of reified knowledge. Even Chris, in his opposition to Von Hoffman's inane procedures, realized the ultimate importance of 'knowing' the way the school required knowing and the proper social relations to 'know' in that way.

In the case of Don and his friends, that opposition took on a more 'anti-school' form, despite the adequate grades that group members received. Certainly Don and Steve 'got by,' but it was obvious to me that both were finding it more difficult to make that accommodation in eighth grade than they had in seventh. To them, the reconciliation between the reified knowledge of the school and the regenerative knowledge they created as they interpreted their existence in school was more difficult because they had little or no additional sources (parents or families) to make them believe that the reified knowledge and its attendant behavioral dispositions had any value to them. Thus their own participation in the school became increasingly self-determined, which in turn alienated them even more from whatever value there might be in accepting the premises of school knowledge.

We begin now to get the glimmerings of how schools contribute to the reproduction of social differentiation in a class-based society. This happens not so much in a deterministic, 'knee-jerk' fashion but rather through the constitutive processes by which knowledge is produced, used, and modified, and the nexus of knowledge systems. It is, again, a materialist process – a process that occurs as actors create their history in a material world, in ongoing systems of labor and exchange. It is also in a materialist world that students come to form their understandings and interpretations of these forces of production and their place in those forces. To understand better the incremental process by which students come to interpret their place in the reified world, we need to pry more deeply into the daily routine at Harold Spencer – by 'goofing off.'

6
'What did you *do* in English today?' 'Nothing, just goofed off'

> The general spirit of the bureaucracy is the secret, the mystery, preserved within itself by the hierarchy and against the outside world by being a closed corporation. Avowed political spirit, as also political mindedness, therefore appear to the bureaucracy as treason against its mystery. Hence, authority is the basis of its knowledge, and the deification of authority its conviction (Karl Marx, Contribution to the *Critique of Hegel's 'Philosophy of the Right'*, J. O'Malley (ed.), Cambridge University Press, 1970).

The students' map of the school

I was leaving Marcy's English class, after the period ended, and finally caught up with Don and Mike as they were proceeding down the hall on the way to science. Walking through the halls we met John, who called out as Don went by.

'Hey, Randall, what'd you guys do in English class today?' Don stopped for a moment, then continued down the hall, looked over his shoulder and said in a very nonchalant way, 'Oh nothing, just goofed off.'

In this chapter we will examine the activity called 'goofing off' as it is part of the social process by which the ties of *Gemeinschaft* are built and from which meaning is defined. This meaning, and the interpretive process by which meaning is created and sustained, is an especially important dimension in the creation of regenerative knowledge. Goofing off also raises explicitly the existence of contradictions to the schooling process that are generated by that very process itself.

Table 6.1 What students do in school

What students do in school	Go to the cans.	Smoke.	
		Smoke a joint.	
		Shit.	
	Work.	Do tests.	
		Write essays.	
		Do math.	
		Do assignments.	
		Take notes.	
	Pick on kids.	Give them flat tires.	
		Harass them.	
		Pick on Mike.	
		Pick on Kathy.	
		Throw their books on the floor.	
		Threaten them.	
		Steal their food.	
	Get busted.		
	Fight.		
	Mess around.		
	Goof around.		
	Skip.	To the park.	
		To the mall.	
		At home.	
		A period.	
	Go to class.	Daydream.	
		Make time go by . . .	Goof off.
			Push the clock.
			Daydream.
			Bug the teacher.
		Be teacher's pet . . .	Grade papers.
			Pass out books.
			Take out attendance slips.
			Record stuff in grade book.
			Go to office for them.
			Get out of class.
			Get out of spelling tests.
		Get in trouble.	
		Sit on our asses.	
		Don't do much.	
		Do as little as I can.	
		Sit and rot.	
		Sleep.	
		Get detention.	
		Get points.	
	Go to lunch.	Goof around . . .	Chase kids to courtyard.
			Go to lockers.
			Wait outside classes.
		Eat lunch.	
		Scrounge.	
		Talk.	
	Goof off.	Shoot things . . .	Rubber bands.
			Paper clips.
			Paper wads.

What students do in school

- Slam books down.
- Break pencil points.
- Have pencil fights.
- Throw paper in wastepaper basket.
- Borrow paper from someone.
- Hock a loogey.
- Do anything you're not supposed to.
- Talk.
- Throw things . . .
  - Chalk.
  - Erasers.
  - Gym bags.
  - Books.
  - Mike.
- Bug teachers . . .
  - Talk.
  - Bug substitutes.
  - Do your push-ups screwy.
  - Chew gum.
  - Defy them.
  - Be late on purpose.
  - Pretend you are chewing gum.
  - Pass notes with nothing on them.
  - Talk about them.
  - Talk about them and let them hear you.
  - Tap pencils.
  - Tap feet.
  - Laugh.
  - Kid them about the way.
  - Flip intercom switch.
  - Flip lights on and off.
  - Flip teacher off.
  - Ask teacher to repeat questions.
  - Not do work.
  - Wear hat in class.
  - Wear coats in class.
  - Be late and don't bring slip.
  - Laugh when they yell at you.
  - Move slow when they tell you to do something.
  - Not be in seat when bell rings.
  - Lay your head on the desk.
- Write notes.
- Crawl behind chairs.
- Take someone's books and have them chase you.
- Punch other kids around.

Reading, writing and resistance

In Table 6.1, I have outlined the activities that students said they engaged in while in school. Even though, at one time or another, I witnessed most of the activities noted, I did not compose the list from my own observations of life at Harold Spencer. Rather the list represents a picture, a 'map,' if you will, of the school as seen from the inside by a cross-section of the students themselves. In the rest of this section, I will point to some major 'intersections' on the map, places where students' self-described activities came together. This should be useful to understand better the total milieu into which goofing off fits.

Drawing the lines

In any setting in which physical and emotional activity abounds, conflict is probable. Yet aside from the activity factor, the structure of the school reinforces the existence and continuation of conflict. Students are formally separated from teachers and are continuously differentiating among themselves in the few ways they can take the initiative – along social lines. Since social groups continually jockey for position *vis-à-vis* one another – drawing the lines between themselves and the adults 'in control' – conflict is inevitable. More importantly for our purposes here, however, a perusal of Table 6.1 supports the notion that varying degrees of conflict are indeed descriptive of the life of junior high students. Conflict seems to abound as kids 'pick' on each other, 'fight,' and through 'bugging the teacher.'

Poor Larry, I often thought as we stood outside Marcy's English class every day after lunch. I wonder what he really thinks as Don, Dave, and Steven continually harass him and purposefully single him out as the brunt of their sometimes almost inhumane jokes and ridicules. I never could see Larry as doing that much to deserve such persistent treatment. Yet Larry was considered a 'weirdo,' and the way he and others like him were treated served to illustrate how some students were singled out and 'picked on.' Don and some of his friends derived great pleasure in ridiculing the way in which Larry walked – up on his tiptoes in a bouncy manner. Sometimes Don and another boy, Bill, followed Larry around before class, walking on their toes with their shoulders hunched up as a form of mimicking him. Others were continually dumping his books on the floor in social studies and, at lunch, his tray frequently was picked clean by students stealing his food.

While 'picking on kids' was one form of conflict with other students, 'fighting' was probably the most physical and in some respects most serious expression of conflict. Fights were not that significant in terms of numbers of people who fought; of all the people with whom I was associated, only Dave, the 'greaser,' seemed to be regularly involved in fights, and he lost most of those. But fights were significant because *everyone* heard about them, talked about them, and discussed the issues. Friends of the fighters lined up with one party or another, making the competition of fights between groups of people rather than simply between the antagonists themselves.

Yet, the underlying and ongoing conflict between the student and the teacher, in many respects the two prime antagonists in the conflict arena, was even more pervasive than the conflicts between students. According to Table 6.1, there were two main interactions that students had with teachers. A somewhat passive activity occurred when students described what they did in class, using such terms as 'daydreaming,' 'not doing our work,' or 'sitting on our asses.' The other main interaction with teachers was more conflict oriented, as epitomized by 'bugging the teachers.'

The term 'conflict' immediately conjures up visions of the 'blackboard jungle,' vicious fights, continual challenge of teachers' authority and other images of outright warfare. Nothing could be further from the truth with the students at Harold Spencer Junior High. I never once saw a knife fight of any kind, and although there were occasional bloody noses from fights in the hall, these were no different from the same fights I witnessed in my own days as a student, nor any worse than those I broke up as a junior high teacher. Yet that does not change the fact that teachers had dominance over students in a forced environment and this situation guaranteed some degree of resistance by students against the all encompassing authority of the teacher. Accordingly, conflict, in terms of 'bugging the teacher' and its part in the ideational system of the students' world, seemed a preordained consequence of the formal organization of the school.

Work and going to class

There are two reasons why it is useful to review the subject of 'work' and 'classes' as something that students say they do in school (Table 6.1). One reason is because work was not often discussed and thus students did not view it as an important element in the student collective existence.

A second reason for reviewing the subject of work is also found in Table 6.1, wherein there are indications that classes were something students endured or, in some circumstances, that they attempted to alter in some way. Terms such as 'daydream,' or 'do as little as I can,' and 'skip' are signals of how students saw classes as something to put up with – to endure. While not all classes were seen in the same way, even those minimally approved of were regarded cautiously.

Some students attempted to circumvent the need to endure classes by 'being teacher's pet,' one reason why students, especially girls, talked about 'being a pet.' To be a pet meant getting out of class work and thereby doing something more than enduring the time put in. Being a pet also meant activities that set the pet apart from the other students who had to be involved in classroom activities required by the teacher. Being a pet thus meant the possession of some control over the scope of involvement in the activities of the school, and for some students such control was worth the ridicule from other students. For pets were ridiculed if they actively solicited favors from the teacher. Yet, to show again the importance of the student-generated interpretive structure, students who performed the same acts could be held in regard by fellow students if the frequency of such favors was low and if the student did not seek them out.

The social context of goofing off

I will focus now upon only one of the activities mentioned in Table 6.1, that of 'goofing off.' Even though we will examine student life through 'goofing off,' many elements of Table 6.1 are involved. In fact, I have chosen to examine goofing off primarily because it is so uniformly perceived as the *raison d'être* of the school. Therein was generated the very essence of student activity and regenerative knowledge, and it symbolized the separate culture created in opposition to the reified knowledge of the school.

We can begin our understanding of goofing off by returning to a class we have visited before – the social studies class taught jointly by Mr Richards and Mr Bruce. While most students tolerated Bruce, few students liked Richards, in part because he appeared excessively authoritarian, unbending, and insistent on exactness for every paper or project. It had to be done his way ('right') or not at all, and most of the students resisted such an uncompromising position and reacted against it.

One day's experience was typical of this class. We entered the room and sat down in the assigned seats. The bell rang and the aid, Mrs Rose, stood at the front taking attendance by seat number. After attendance, Richards said, 'On your desks you will see textbooks. The first thing you will do is turn to page 204. That is where the section on Bulgaria begins. I want you to read carefully pages 204–210, and when I say carefully, I mean carefully! For those who have poor memories and forget the assignment, it is also written on the board to your right. I will pass out worksheets on which are listed ten questions from the reading, and what I want you to do is to answer the questions, being sure to write in *complete* sentences, capitalizing the first word of each sentence. Are there any questions? Well, if there are not, there shouldn't be any excuse for not doing a good job.'

Chris, who was sitting in front of me, leaned over to Marty as he opened his book to the designated page. 'What a bunch of crap. Capitalize the first word,' he said, attempting to mimic Richards by being stern and direct. 'Hey, Marty, know what's for lunch today?'

Marty and Chris started reading, Chris finishing the six pages in about ten minutes. By that time, Richards had passed out the mimeographed sheets with the questions on them. Chris looked at them, then put them down and began thumbing through the book looking at the pictures.

'No good pictures, look like they're from the Dark Ages,' he mumbled.

Looking at the front of the book, Marty said, 'No wonder, look when the son of a bitch was printed, 1963.'

'Neat,' Chris acknowledged as he began to work on the questions, but not too energetically as he intermittently doodled on the desk, being careful to wipe it off after completing a design or a picture. Chris finished the questions in about fifteen minutes, and Richards, seeing that some students had finished, told them to 'find something to do' until everyone finished because they were going to review the answers in class. Chris pulled out a copy of Eric Von Daniken's *Chariot of the Gods* and began reading it.

After about ten minutes, Richards asked how many were not done. About ten people raised their hands and Richards said that he would give them five more minutes to finish up. 'I think some of you people better spend more time on the assignment and less time fooling around,' he said. 'It shouldn't be taking you forty minutes to do this assignment.'

Richards then told the class to get out their papers and he started reviewing the answers to the ten questions. He asked for volunteers for each question, but volunteers were slight, despite the presence of eighty people in the class. (The class was held in a large lecture hall, and the class size was one reason why it was taught by two teachers.) Slowly, Richards elicited answers to all the questions. Richards then asked everyone to pass in their papers. It was about five minutes before the end of the period.

'All right, keep it quiet till the bell rings or I'll find something for you to do. Martin, turn around.'

Richards started walking around the room. He was a stickler on people being quiet before the bell rang, and sometimes had the whole class sit straight for twenty seconds before he would let them go. As the bell rang, Chris and Martin vaulted out of their seats, walked rapidly to the door, and hurried to lunch.

After lunch, John, Chris, and I ambled over toward the "A" building for fifth-period English with Mr Von Hoffman. The assignment today was to give oral reports assigned almost one week ago. The reports were to be short (two to three minutes) and Von Hoffman stood near his desk recording grades as each student finished his report.

A girl began by giving a report on photography, but it was clear that few people were paying attention.

Von Hoffman interrupted the girl giving the report. 'People, have some courtesy for those giving reports and stop your talking. I'm sure you wouldn't want to be giving a report with half the class talking and not paying attention.'

'I don't care,' chipped in Mike on the other side of the room.

Chris stated, 'Hey, Mr Von Hoffman. If everybody talks we shouldn't have to give our reports, right?'

The girl continued. John had to give his report in about fifteen minutes, so he turned around to Chris sitting behind him.

'Chris, Chris.'

'Yeah.'

'Tell me something I can do for a report.'

'I don't know. How about Hickory, Dickory Dock?'

'No, I'm serious, what should I do?'

'Hey, I know. Why don't you tell some story about your rabbits? Like raising rabbits and how you do that. You could fake that for a few minutes.'

'That sounds, yeah, why not. Just about raising rabbits, something like that will keep him happy.' John then turned around and jotted a few notes on a scrap of paper.

After listening to reports on 'My Trip to Glacier' (National Park) and a slide show on Japan, it was then John's turn. He walked up to the front of the room, turned to face the class, caught Chris's eyes, and started laughing.

'Come on, John, give your report or sit down,' Von Hoffman directed. John started but began laughing again.

'Great report, Mr Von Hoffman,' said Mike, clapping, 'give him an A.'

'Outstanding,' Chris said, adding his support. 'Best report of the year.'

'OK, John, sit down please.'

'No, no. I'll give it. Tell Chris to stop laughing.'

Von Hoffman then walked to the back of the room, stood next to Chris's seat and said to John, 'Begin!'

'I have some pet rabbits at home and I'd like to tell you about raising them. First, you have to feed them and I feed them food that rabbits eat.'

Chris raised his hand. 'What kind of food do rabbits eat?'

John replied, 'They eat rabbit food which I buy at the rabbit food store [everyone in the class laughed]. They also eat food which comes from our table.' He went on, 'Rabbits do not like the cold ground so you have to build cages for them. The cage I have is off the ground so they don't get wet, and it is made of wire.'

Chris raised his hand again. 'John, where did you get the cage?'

John said that he had built it 'with scrap lumber and special materials that one gets from the rabbit store.' From then on, every time John spoke, Chris raised his hand and asked in a very serious and studious manner a question about something that John had said. Finally, Von Hoffman, irritated by Chris constantly raising his hand, asked him to not interrupt and let John finish his speech.

'But Mr Von Hoffman,' Chris said innocently, 'I'm just trying to find out more about rabbits and the only way I can learn is to ask questions of someone who knows.'

John continued, describing what rabbits like to do for entertainment and how even in winter if it gets cold you have to put a heater in their cage. Finally, John ended his report by saying that 'rabbits are also kind of stupid animals, in fact they are so stupid I butchered all of them last week and they do make very good stew.' With this, he sat down.

John, Chris, and Mike snickered to each other from across the room. I overheard some of the girls in the class saying 'Yuk,' or 'How could you kill those soft little bunnies.' One girl turned around to John and said 'None of that is very funny.' Chris continued to laugh and volunteered, 'Good speech old boy. Mr Von Hoffman, I think he deserves an A.'

Von Hoffman was obviously irritated. 'An "A" like mad. Just sit down and be quiet, both of you. I don't know why you can't take anything seriously enough to do a good job on it. I ask you to give one oral report a term and you have to make a big joke out of it.'

'Did you give John an "A," Mr Von Hoffman?'

'Chris, shut up. No more out of you for the rest of the period or you'll be down to visit Mr Pall.'

John turned around to Chris and said, 'What a sorehead.'

As the class was ready to leave, Von Hoffman told me that he was tired of 'that group always goofing off in here.' He said that they took nothing seriously and that even though John, Chris, and Mike were 'good students,' they seemed to think it was more fun to 'fool around' and be rude than it was to do their work. 'I can't understand why they have to act that way. There are some students in here who never give me any trouble. It's the same ones all the time.'

Von Hoffman's question, basic as it was, was a good one. Why was it that Von Hoffman always had trouble with 'that group' fooling around while Richards (in the class I described earlier) seemed to experience relatively little harassment from Chris, John, Mike, or Marty? Certainly, there was little doubt that Richards ran a much more regimented class, and consequently, it was difficult to get away with very much. Still, for Chris or John or others that was not necessarily a deterrent because, as individuals, they were often quite passive in classes that were equally as 'loosely' operated. For example, John basically put up with music during fifth period and Chris was untypically quiet in his second-period art class.

I gained some insights into the basis of collective action or inaction in class while we were sitting in science class the next day. John was recounting to Don the previous day's event in Von Hoffman's class and how he and Chris had been able to contrive this 'beautiful story' (about rabbits) on Von Hoffman. I then asked Chris, 'How come you goof off so much more in Von Hoffman's class than Richards's class? Do you like social studies that much better?'

'Are you kidding,' said John. 'Richards is a fag.'

'Yeah,' replied Mike. 'That class is a real bore and it's even worse when you have it the first period of the day. First period on Mondays with Richards? Man, I just count every second.'

I replied, 'Yeah, well I'm not in there first period, and I can't figure out why Chris doesn't goof off that much in Richards's class if you guys like it that little.'

Chris replied somewhat dejectedly, 'Well, I imagine if John and Mike and a couple of the other guys were in there I'd goof off in there too, but now I sit by a bunch of freaks. There is really nobody in there to goof off with.'

I asked if that was why he goofed off more in Von Hoffman's class.

'Yeah, that's a lot of it. It's really not too much fun in class if you don't have friends to goof off with. Like you know the other day when John was giving his report on rabbits? That wouldn't have been any fun if we were all in different classes.'

'How do you mean it wouldn't have been any fun?'

John said, 'Man, you always do stuff like that with a friend.'

'Really?' I asked.

Chris explained, 'We've got this deal, John, me, Mike, and a couple other guys, like when one says something the other guy backs him up, helps him so he doesn't get into a lot of trouble. That's why that rabbit story was so neat. I was able to help John out by asking questions so he could finish his report. He hadn't even started it until we talked about it in class.'

All of this began to make more sense to me. For John, Chris, Mike, and a few others (all were 'B' students), one of the most important determinants of whether or not they 'goofed off' was having friends in the class. Friends were important because they provided people with whom to interact either about subjects of importance or in activities that symbolized the significance of the group. Goofing off with friends was a way of acting in class in the same way that one did in informal situations when the person could choose his own associates. Later in the year, Bill, a person who knew Chris but was not really good friends with him, told me:

'If you don't have anybody to talk to, you just sit through the whole class, duh! And you don't get interested in the class. But if you have friends you can goof off with your friends.'

I asked him if this made the class more interesting, and he replied, 'Sure, you can goof off more.'

Since friends were so important in the goofing off process, then, by definition, there were people with whom Chris and his group either did not goof off with or who, to their way of thinking at least, did not goof off at all. Because goofing off occurred largely with friends, the students' perceptions of who goofed off and actualization of those perceptions into behavior provided what appeared to be a consistent and reliable way by which they drew boundaries around their own group of friends as set apart from other groups of students. Goofing off did not cause, but was associated with, the boundaries that had been drawn and were in the process of being drawn around the membership of relevant peer groups. In that sense, then, goofing off is quite indicative of the extent to which regenerative knowledge characterized the very nature of student groups and the patterns of student associations. Goofing off involved, as we have pointed out earlier, contextually based characteristics wherein students actively created and defined their world under the assumptions in which they have come to understand it. Goofing off resembles a shared speech community wherein collective interpretations of the relationship of the student to the productive process demanded by the school gives rise to collective actions. While certainly there existed different interpretive structures, different strategies for goofing off, all associated with different student groups, still goofing off itself was a uniformly perceived activity engaged in with friends through acts of self-determination. As I will go on to describe in the next section, the shared belief about the nature of 'goofing off' is indicative of the class position of junior high students within the world of Harold Spencer.

Ways to goof off

The interactional dimension

Thus far we have established that goofing off is an activity that students saw occurring among friends or, at least, among compatible people. While everyone 'goofed off,' different groups of people did it in their own way and qualitative differences existed between the types of goofing off. In this section we will learn that the items mentioned in Table 6.1 as ways to goof off were qualitatively different. Identification of these qualitative differences provides greater insight into the internal logic of goofing off as manifested by those who did it.

Table 6.2 provides an overview of ways to goof off which are avowedly interactional among students. That is, students perceived goofing off not to be a solo event, but involving explicit interaction among friends. This aspect of goofing off involved certain activities about which students were conscious.

Table 6.2 Ways to goof off pertaining to interaction among students

Write notes.	
Shoot things:	Paper wads. Rubber bands. Paper clips.
Break pencil points.	
Throw paper in wastebasket.	
Borrow paper from someone.	
Throw things:	Chalk. Erasers. Books. Gym bags.
Talk.	
Punch friends around.	

The interactional dimensions of goofing off are best illustrated if we can return to the classes of Richards and Von Hoffman. Remember first that Von Hoffman was quite frustrated over the course of the year as he witnessed John, Chris, Mike, and others playfully shoving each other over desks, into lockers, and on to lawns before, after, and during classes. Richards, the social studies teacher, thought that such behavior was 'disruptive' and 'juvenile' and said that he would never tolerate it in his class – and he usually didn't. His objections did not, however, change the nature of 'punching your friends' as a significant category describing ways students used to goof off as related to social interaction.

I asked Chris one day if there was any difference between picking on Larry or Dan before math class and the hitting and shoving he did with John before and after (sometimes even during) Von Hoffman's English class. Chris told me that there were two kinds of punching and hitting around, one was the 'kidding' kind and the other the 'serious' kind. The serious kind was related to 'picking on kids,' that is, students not liked or ones you considered to be 'weird.' The 'kidding' kind was reserved directly and specifically for friends, and for Chris that meant the kind he did with John, Mike, and others in his group. He said:

'Like with John in Von Hoffman's room, I'll pretend that I'm punching him or something then push him clear across the room. Or I'll call him steel teeth or choo-choo tracks [John wore braces] and he'll slug me and I'll fly across the room making all sorts of noises.'

Table 6.2 shows that a third cluster of categories of ways to goof off connected with social interaction consisted of throwing or shooting things: chalk, erasers, paper clips, rubber bands, paper wads, all were included. One incident of particular noteworthiness serves well to illustrate the interactional patterns of shooting things. Dave, Steve, and Don, and a few other students, were engaged in a paper wad fight with straws; I was sitting directly behind Dave on the right-hand side of the room near the windows. As before, when Marcy was not looking or was preoccupied, the group began their usual barrage of paper wads across the room. But this time I, too, was getting hit with paper wads, and it became apparent that I was the target for both Steve and Don who were sitting on the left-hand side of the room. At about that time, a boy named 'Wolfie' who was *persona non grata* with Don and his friends, began rolling his own paper wads, shooting them back to Steve and Don, neither of whom were at all interested in returning paper wads to Wolfie. Wolfie shot a few more wads toward Steve and Don, but they continued to ignore him as they shot wads toward Dave and me.

One of the basic tenets of spit wad fights seemed to rest in having an adequate supply of projectiles on hand because, in the heat of battle, it took too much time if one had to roll wads while others were shooting. There were two ways of obtaining a supply: making a supply in advance or having friends provide a supply by making them or picking up missiles from the floor. Wolfie had not made any wads in advance and he tried to pick some up from the floor to replenish his dwindling supply. Immediately, however, other students sitting near where the paper wads were landing began to pick them up and hand them to Dave in front of me.

'Come on, you guys, give me some of those,' Wolfie pleaded with Jim, who had been handing Dave paper wads. Jim ignored him and nonchalantly continued to lean over on the floor as Marcy turned her back.

'Bug off, will ya,' Jim said curtly as he tried to shake Wolfie away.

Dave continued to have a ready supply but Wolfie, having to roll his own and having his requests for more ammunition ignored, was limited to muzzle loading speed. Since nobody was shooting back at him, he was effectively limited from the non-verbal interaction of shooting spit wads and soon quit.

All such similar events now made more sense to me. I had seen eraser and chalk fights before class where Don and his group had been throwing erasers and where Yaeger had tried to join the festivities. But Yaeger too was denied participation in these activities by virtue of being ignored and eventually shoved out of the room. Don and his friends simply had no time for involvement with someone not part of their group. Yaeger was excluded because he had attempted to break into what was essentially an intricate and tightly closed communication system that existed between members of a social group. Because of the social characteristics of such activities as throwing and shooting things, they took on an important meaning to those who engaged in them. While 'disruptive' to teachers, they formed another strand in the activities of goofing off, representative of the complex culture of junior high students who actively created elements of their own culture.

Bugging the teacher. I have discussed goofing off as a form of social interaction among the students. In this context, we have examined the meaning system shared among members of the group as it pertains to the activities of the group. Reference to Table 6.1 demonstrates, however, that much goofing off was directly or indirectly related to someone other than students – that being teachers, and in the form of 'bugging the teacher.' Thus, 'bugging the teacher' and its variety of categories represented still another way by which groups of students were cemented together via the goofing off. It also represents the most obvious and pervasive strategy wherein students symbolized their opposition to selected elements of schooling. Bugging the teacher as a manifest action is therefore illustrative of how students represented their understanding of being estranged from much of their labor.

Bugging took many forms but one of the more common ones was to say something about a teacher so that they would overhear, but be unable to do much about it. Numerous 'Christie Love' incidents illustrated this. In an attempt to reduce some of the 'problems' with girls at the lunch hour, Edwards had released one of the women teachers to patrol rest rooms and halls during the lunch hour in order to catch smokers and break up minor disturbances ('Hawkeye' served in a similar capacity for boys). Many of the students dubbed the woman 'narc,' Mrs Hanslenski, as 'Christie Love,' (after the television show of a black policewoman). If Hanslenski approached a specific group at lunch, a member of the group almost invariably said 'here comes Christie' because they knew she disliked the label.

'Flipping the intercom switch' and 'flipping lights off and on' are two more illustrations of the interactional aspects of ways to bug the teacher. Flipping the intercom switch was perhaps the most 'exciting' of these two individual bugs in that it caused the teacher the most surprise and Don, Dave, and Steve were experts at this. Leaving the room at the end of class, Steve or Don pulled the 'call' button down on the intercom, located adjacent to the door. Marcy, at the front of the room organizing papers and putting away books, did not recognize what had happened (pulling the 'call' button signaled someone in the main office that the teacher wanted information for some reason). The office would then call back to the room, 'office.'

'I didn't call the office.'

'Well, *someone* called the office from your room, Mrs Marcy.'

Marcy muttered, 'It must have been those boys again. Oh *why* didn't they put that switch somewhere else?'

Bugging the teacher had two basic forms: one was socially initiated (that is, those initiated by two or more people), as indicated in Table 6.3. These activities included those just discussed.

Table 6.3 Ways to bug the teacher – socially initiated

Bug substitutes.
Talk about them.
Talk about them and let them hear you.
Tap feet.
Tap pencils.
Laugh.
Wear hat/coat in class.
Pass notes with nothing on them.
Flipping lights off and on.
Flipping intercom switch.

As opposed to ways to bug the teacher done in concert by two or more students, there were more 'individual' ways of bugging the teacher. These forms did not require the direct participation of other members to carry out the bug. This, then, is the second basic form of 'bugging the teacher,' and these categories are listed in Table 6.4. Even though these ways to bug the teacher were carried out by individual students, they were still socially significant and provided another interdependent link that helped to bind students together.

Table 6.4 Ways to bug the teacher – individually initiated

Chew gum.
Pretend to chew gum.
Be late on purpose.
Be class joker.
Flip teacher off.
Talk back.
Be late and don't bring slip.
Move slow when they tell you to do something.
Not be in your seat when the bell rings.
Lay your head on the desk during films.
Not do work.
Tap feet.
Tap pencils.

Chewing gum or pretending to chew gum in music class is illustrative of individual bugs and their practice to generate a 'we' feeling among the students. For example, I usually attended music with Chris and some of his friends. Mr Hackett, the music teacher, was usually late to class, and as he took the roll seemed in an angry mood. One day, while taking attendance he noted Lisa who apparently was moving her mouth in slow and calculating manner (I could not see for certain because I was sitting in the back of the class while she was to my right toward the front). Hackett burst out, 'Lisa, get rid of that gum – and you have thirty minutes tonight [meaning detention after school].'

'I don't have any gum.'

'Lisa, I saw you chewing it so don't tell me you don't have any.'

Lisa simply opened her mouth, lifted her tongue, and moved her head around to give Hackett a total picture. 'See, no gum.'

Hackett was caught, he could not do anything about it. He blurted out, 'OK, you probably did but if you didn't, would you please stop moving your mouth like a cow chewing grass? You know, Lisa, it amazes me that your mouth can be moving so much in this class and yet it moves so little in chorus!'

Later, Lisa told me that she was not chewing gum, just pretending to do so.

'You were faking it?' I asked.

'Oh, me and Karen like to bug him because he gets so uptight. I always do it because I know he hates it so much. Doing things like mocking them and chewing gum embarrasses them, like if you pretend to chew gum he'll say, "Lisa, spit out your gum," and I'll say, "I don't have any" and then open my mouth and shake my head and nothing comes out. That really embarrasses them.'

Gum chewing as well as many of the other categories in Table 6.4 illustrates the importance of group solidarity, participation, and support in 'bugging the teacher,' even for activities that were done individually without much conscious regard for the involvement of others. Bugging the teacher was far more than one student pitted against one teacher, but rather an act that cemented those involved in or supportive of the act into a common framework or bond. There was nothing more exhilarating to the group than to act in unison on a bug started by one or a few other students. Consequently things such as 'tapping pencils' or 'tapping feet' were euphoric activities when picked up by a large number in the class. These were activities that united the group in one of the few ways it could be united, in an alliance against a commonly perceived force – the teacher.

We bug them 'cause there's nothing else to do. Why did students bug teachers? Such activities were not always initiated for reasons of social solidarity, though that certainly was a consequence. Other more basic issues undergirded the initiation of bugging the teacher.

As may be obvious by now, there are certain teachers who were bugged almost incessantly, others who were bugged less. Whether a teacher was the target of this particular form of goofing off was, at least from the point of view of the students, dependent on two things: whether they thought they could get away with bugging them (or more accurately, the degree of bugging they could get away with) and the personal relationship they had with that particular teacher. Very often, complex factors affected these two reasons.

For example, the teachers who were most bugged were not liked for various reasons. Some, such as Hackett, 'are not nice to us,' which meant that 'they talk down to us' or 'treat us like babies.' Most teachers who were bugged seemed, to the students, to be distant from them and to have a sense of superiority. Additionally, they were 'mean' because they had lots of 'stupid rules' which did not make any sense: rules like having to print instead of write your names and if you didn't you had to do your paper again, or rules like writing your name in the right-hand corner of your paper rather than in the left-hand corner, or rules like doing 'stupid exercises' in grammar books. When this existed, Karen and Delilah told me that a teacher 'deserves' to get bugged.

'Why do you bug the teacher?'

'To get them mad.'

'Why would you want to get them mad?'

'Because they are really mean to us.'

'Because there is nothing else to do,' said Lisa.

'Because they are mean to us, and they deserve it.'

Conversely, teachers who were liked were bugged infrequently. Again, this did not mean that students did not goof off in their class, simply that they did not do it to bug the teacher as frequently. Usually, if a teacher was considered 'good,' he/she was not bugged as much. To be a good teacher in the eyes of most students meant to be 'understanding' or 'to know a little about what kids are like today.' A good teacher (and/or good class) was one in which they did not do 'just the same old thing,' all the time. For example, those students who had Crealey for science (and this was only a total of about fifty 'B' or better students), said they did not bug him much because they did 'a lot of fun stuff' (experiments, played chess, developed computer programs and the like). Mr Welch in art was seen equally as positively because students were permitted to sit together, talk while working on projects, and 'he doesn't get uptight if we walk around a little.' These classes, with the exception of a few of the math teachers, the PE teachers, and a few English teachers were the only classes where students said they did not goof off to bug the teachers. In all other classes they either did – or wanted to.

Yet, just because students did not goof off to bug the teacher did not necessarily mean that they liked the class or the teacher; it often meant that the teacher was too strict or observant to allow much of anything to go on. Mr Richards probably had the most efficiently run classes in the school. Papers were turned in in a uniform manner; books were stacked in a consistent way; he could leave the room for five minutes and rarely would there be a peep from anyone (some students always suspected that he was waiting around the corner to 'catch us'). But Richards was also one of the more disliked teachers in the school and that made students want to goof off far more than they did. Yet, it was difficult because he watched the class very carefully, gave out detention with some liberality, and besides he often had an aide with him to help supervise. This made it doubly hard to bug him, and bugs were restricted to individually initiated bugs; as Dave said, 'Just to piss him off,' things like smiling at him, purposefully piling the books the wrong way on the counter, tapping feet and so on. On one occasion I asked Dave and Steve about Richards's class:

'It's boring all right.'

Dave responded, 'You just can't get away with doing that much.'

Steve provided an illustration. 'He'll sit back in the room and fake like he's watching a movie, looking around at the other kids to see what they are doing. Then if you go to sleep he'll find a book or a yardstick and just slam it right, practically in their face, right on the desk.'

'He'll give you detention if you pick your nose. One day I fell asleep in geography.'

Steve laughed knowing full well what Dave was talking about,

'Everyone falls asleep in social studies. One time I fell asleep holding my book. Pow, right on the floor.'

From the comments of most students, there were more teachers whose classes were 'boring' than not, and 'bugging the teacher' had to take a subtle form because many of these teachers were fairly strict and had 'good control' over their classes. Consequently, the bugging had to be phased in at opportune moments, between events, intermittently so as not to draw too much attention, subtly so as not to indicate conspiracy. Yet this did not seem to alter too significantly the comment made by Steve about almost all his classes: 'Class is so boring and you wanna have something to do that is fun, so you bug them as much as you can.'

Bugging the teacher then had a dimension to it that reflected the collective nature in which it was defined, and the consequences that grew out of it for the students who engaged in it. Seen to be involved in 'boring classes' in which 'there is nothing else to do,' students viewed the nature of goofing off as an oppositional strategy to demonstrate symbolically their resistance to estranged labor which they experienced in much of their daily life within the classroom. While this separation from control may have been differentially experienced by individual students as to time and place, it appeared to be a universal experience that, when experienced in those places and times where individual experiences coalesced into collective realization, would result in bugging the teacher. It is this collective realization that made bugging the teacher largely socially initiated or sustained.

Time and space

If interactional factors predominated in the patterns of goofing off, two other characteristics helped define the parameters of goofing off, although admittedly to a lesser extent. These characteristics – those of time and space – were so omnipresent and pervasive that on first consideration they seemed barely worthy of mention. But like other aspects of the student world, it is a mistake to take too much for granted, and time and space proved to be important determinants of goofing off.

Time – timing and tempo. I reported earlier in this chapter how Dave once told me that goofing off to bug the teacher involved a sense of timing. His exact words were, 'You have to know the right time.' *That* seemed to be universally understood, as an earlier conversation with Dave and Steve revealed.

'Really, there's quite a technique in bugging a teacher.'

Dave agreed, nodding his head.

Steve continued, 'You have to know what to say at the right time, and when to do certain things. If the teacher is in a bad mood you don't say too much, you know, you give her a little room. But if he's in a good mood, you ruin it, you make their day lousy so they don't want to teach anymore.'

Randy, a friend of Dave's, agreed that 'you have to know just how much you can push a teacher if you don't want to get sent to the office.' Knowing the sequencing of events, the timing, and the tempo was very important in maintaining the delicate equilibrium between not doing anything and continually being in Pall's office. Students recognized that there were certain definite times during a class when goofing off was more effectively carried out than other times; there were also types of goofing off that were better suited to different times.

There were, for example, times to talk to your friends. Karen said that, 'When Hackett is working with a group is a good time to talk, but if you're laughing too loud and he hears you he really gets pissed.' In Von Hoffman's class, John told me that a good time to talk was when he was passing out an assignment or worksheet because he never seemed to do much if you talked then. Likewise, during films provided opportune times to talk in social studies because the room was so dark and so big, but you had to be careful that you knew where Richards was or else he would sneak up behind you and slap you with a ruler. Marcy's class was a particularly good class in which to talk because she always gave two or three different assignments in a class, and she was too busy collecting papers or sorting materials to keep close tabs on the entire class. She did not seem to mind too much if people talked as long as you did not start throwing things.

Any time an activity changed provided the potential for throwing or shooting things with friends and talking. Don, Dave, and Steve quite often took advantage of these interstitial areas in time to lob paper wads, rubber bands, and other assorted missiles.

Seatwork was another good time to goof off in a variety of ways, particularly talking, bugging students, shooting and throwing things. That was why sharpening pencils, throwing paper in the wastebasket, borrowing paper and such other activities were so important. These activities provided a rationale to be out of the seat, something necessary if you had a friend, 'you just have to talk to.' Lisa and Karen explained to me the strategy they had in operation whenever they were working on 'projects' or assignments.

'Like Karen will go up and sharpen her pencil and I'll break off my pencil point and go up to sharpen it and then talk to Karen.'

'Which class is this in?' I asked.

'Social studies.'

'Social studies *and* English,' Karen added emphatically.

'And every day you'll see her wad up a piece of paper and then go up and throw it in the wastebasket.'

'That's so I can go up and see Don. That's how I get detention. She told me I was out of my seat too often, but all I wanted to do was ask him if he was walking by my house after school. What's wrong with that?'

Most teachers tolerated goofing off to a certain degree but then took measures to stop it once that limit had been crossed. The secret for the student was to know the limit and then be able to switch to another form of goofing off once the limit had been reached or exceeded. Thus, strategies of bugging the teacher often changed because of an almost subconscious realization by the students that there was a need to move into a new form of bugging. The timing of such moves was partially dependent on the student awareness that timing of acts was correlated with the probabilities of being caught and the resulting consequences. For example, Terri frequently arrived late to chorus without an 'admit slip' because it provided her with an excuse to get a smoke in the girl's can in the middle of the morning. It was relatively easy to do this because she said, 'All they do in the office is give me an admit slip and tell me not to do it again.' In other classes, she said she'd never try that, because 'the first thing you get is thirty minutes from some guy like Jenkins.' Similarly, 'group stares' (where everyone stared at the teacher to make him nervous) or laughing at them was not attempted in some places because the consequences were too severe – for example, more work. According to Chris and John, they rarely did it in Richards's class because, 'He's so sensitive, he gets so flustered then really piles it on.' But the word was that everyone did it in Franks's class and that he was really 'too dumb to know the difference.'

Bugging the teacher, then, was a learned activity that changed to some degree every time the student went to a new class. There was a folklore among the students about what kind of bugs worked with which teachers and the times to use them. This folklore spread among the students and was acted upon and tested daily. It was known to be fairly easy to get away with nearly everything in Von Hoffman's class, and even students who never had him for classes would lean their head in the room and yell 'Hi Buzzard,' mocking his nose and thatchy haircut. Similar activities were not attempted in math or social studies, nor were they tried if things got 'hot,' that is, if there was a crackdown on particular actions. In such cases the students merely moved on to another form of activity, one that was calculated to bug the teacher.

To some extent, the belief system about time was uniquely indicative of the students' relationship to the general productive process as described throughout this volume. If students were, in fact, estranged from relevant control over what they spent so much of their time doing in terms of the requirements of the school – that is, 'working' – and if that work was seen to be something done mostly for others, then it makes sense that activities that involved 'work' would be seen to 'go slow.' Conversely, it should come as no surprise to know that students would find vehicles for making their mandatory time in such activities 'go faster.'

Such perceptual aspects of time also affected the patterns of goofing off. For example, students perceived time in terms of their consciousness of how fast it went. I asked Robin and Terri if some classes went faster than others.

'Social studies drags.'

'How does it drag?' I inquired.

Robin answered, 'Sixth period. Are you kidding, you've been in there.'

'The reading program, those reading machines' (referring to teaching machines where reading tapes were flashed on a screen and the student was tested for speed and comprehension). Terri said she had that third period.

'You mean that drags?'

'Oh, God man, does it drag,' Robin said. 'If I had a choice between kissing Bob Boyd, who is the "dog" of the school and doing reading . . .'

Barry indicated that he too saw time 'dragging' in some of his classes. I asked which classes dragged. He looked around and said:

'This one [English]. We sit here and we do the same thing over and over, prepositional phrases, prepositional phrases, and we just do it over and over and over and every day it gets boring. We sit there and do assignments three and four times. This class really drags because I know we are going to do the same thing again and again.'

'Is that what makes the classes go slow?'

'Yeah, doing the same thing all the time.'

Students with whom I associated attempted to adapt to subjectively different lengths of time by creating their own agenda to make the time pass more rapidly. I asked Phil what he did to make time go faster.

'Shoot paper wads, shoot people with paper clips, get everybody riled up because then you're all ready for battle anytime. Everybody is sitting there all cocked back and ready to go. Then all of a sudden time is over.'

'So that makes the time go fast?'

'Yeah, sure does help.'

'Do you ever get bored goofing off?'

'Sometimes, if nobody is paying attention.'

'Nobody is paying attention; what do you mean?'

'Like we're always cracking jokes in Von Hoffman's class and you know sometimes people will stop laughing or won't join in and then it starts to get boring.'

As Phil indicated, the key to making time go by in a boring class was to keep the momentum going, to anticipate things in the future that provided something to look forward to. But especially important was to involve one's peers in the process, for then the collectivity of goofing off made time go by even faster. Little wonder, then, that goofing off with friends was so highly valued, for it removed, to some extent, the alienative dimensions of student labor in the school.

Space – a lot of it depends on where you are. The physical arrangement of the classroom and the effect on student interaction never appeared influential in the amount and type of goofing off until one day I overheard Dave talking to Chris, mentioning how math was so boring because he was not located near any friends that were 'fun.' After this, I began to look more closely at how varying spatial arrangements affected the patterns of goofing off, and learned that the physical layout of the school and the location of the students within it was important as a factor affecting patterns of goofing off.

With few exceptions, classrooms at Harold Spencer were arranged in a standard physical arrangement – rows of movable desks lined up facing the teacher at the front of the room. Some rooms had tables lined up across the room with seats at each table, again facing the front. Two notable exceptions were the math 'lab,' into which about 40 per cent of the students were scheduled, and the 'big room' that housed some of the social studies and science classes. The math lab consisted of individual 'study carrels' along the perimeter of the room against the walls together with individual tables seating three or four students in the middle of the room. In the 'big room,' which was in reality a large college-style lecture room, students sat in long somewhat concave rows of tables with permanently fixed seats at the table. This room held about eighty students, the math lab about sixty.

Perhaps most important in any one spatial area as to the pattern of goofing off was where the student sat in any class. Obviously, the further removed the student was from the teacher's line of vision, the greater the probability that goofing off could occur with minimal intrusion from the teacher. Accordingly, at the beginning of the year, there usually was a jockeying for seats to the rear of the room and on the outside perimeter – those areas most marginal to the teacher's line of vision. Soon, however, seating charts altered these arrangements of peers.

Despite the implementation of seating charts, goofing off was used as a way to mediate the effect of seat location. Marcy once mentioned in the teachers' lounge that Karen and Lisa seemed to pass a lot of notes, but Mr Miller, the math teacher, said he never had a problem with that, just the fact that every time he turned around they were talking. Similarly, Marcy mentioned once that Don, Steve, and Dave were always 'throwing stuff' in her class, but Crealey told me he never had those problems with them in science. Marcy said that she could never figure out why Don, Steve, and Dave always 'acted up' in class and why she had trouble getting them to take their work seriously.

The answer to this paradox was quite simple. Don, Steve, and

Dave had learned to work around the structure of the school in order to carry out their agenda. Marcy continually remade the seating chart in order to prevent what was so important to these three – their social interaction about issues important to them and their group. While she attempted to disperse the boys in order to preclude that interaction, minimization of their not talking simply led to other forms of goofing – 'shooting things,' 'throwing things,' and 'bugging the teacher.' Often, attempts to discourage one form of social interaction resulted in other forms of interaction as represented by the various categories of goofing off.

This does not explain precisely why the actions of Don, Steve, and Dave did not frustrate Crealey in science. Part of the answer is found in how the classes were arranged and the way students were dispersed throughout them. In fact, if we compare where the students sat in two classes – the math lab and social studies – we can better understand the patterns of goofing off.

Students in the math lab told me they goofed off a lot, but almost always in the form of talking among each other. Either they talked at the tables where they sat in groups or they left their seats to meet at the pencil sharpener, on the way to the wastebasket, while checking answers at the table where the answer keys were kept. All of these were 'legitimate' forms of behavior, that is, were forms of activity sanctioned by the organization of the class. Students arranged to sit at tables or carrels were supposed to get up and move around to check answers, get new math packages, take tests, and so on. Because this was a permissible activity, students did not have to use as many circuitous ways to communicate; interpersonal communication was built into the instructional process itself.

The social studies class was completely different from the math lab. Students were not permitted to walk around during class; they were not permitted to talk during class; they were not granted the luxury of discussing informally among themselves during the time in which the class was in session. In addition, Richards was known for his propensity to give out large proportions of detention notices. John told me that 'he's got enough paper in there [meaning detention notices] that he'd write out a detention notice for everybody if he thought he had a reason. I saw him give five of them out in one day in ten minutes – just for chewing gum.'

But the fact that Richards 'watches us like a hawk' did not deter goofing off in social studies. It was just a different kind of goofing off. Most of the girls told me that they passed more notes in social studies than in any other class, and from my time spent in the class I would say they were right. Another type of goofing off in social studies was a form of shuffleboard along the tables, using wads of paper with pencils as the 'pusher,' a practice especially popular during films (of which there were many). And activities to 'bug the teacher' were more obvious in this class – tapping pencils, slamming books shut, laying heads on desks during films, and sleeping, tapping feet, and the like. Such activities were easy to disguise in a large room with between seventy and eighty students (as one person said, 'they can't really pay attention to every single person') and students took advantage of the anonymity provided by the spatial arrangement.

Summary and conclusions

Goofing off symbolizes the very essence of regenerative knowledge among students at Spencer. The activity itself is under the control of students and, more specifically, certain clusters of students from whom the behaviors are generated out of the bonds of friendship and collegiality. Knowledge about goofing off – that is, the parameters of meaning that circumscribe its reality – is generated through interpretation as students live out everyday reality in the school. A special communication system grows and evolves as students come into contact with an ongoing system of social relations defined out of a somewhat predefined but still developing material world.

The dynamics, the actual constitutive processes whereby goofing off takes on particular and bounded meaning in the school, is graphically described in this chapter. Even if we trace only the relatively benign events leading from Richards's class, to lunch, and then on to Von Hoffman's class, we see clearly the defining thread of collectivity weaving its way through these events, culminating in John's report about raising rabbits and the 'understanding' that friends backed each other in situations where teachers challenged the 'credentials' of a fellow colleague. Furthermore, the activities in which students were engaged to goof off were viewed by students to be qualitatively different, with some particularly well suited to cementing forms of direct social interaction (Table 6.2) that bound groups together while, at the same time, serving to exclude others from group interaction. In this sense, then, goofing off took on a particular meaning and constituted a very special form of contextually based communication – that is, one that grew out of a special relationship of students to the material world of the school.

Goofing off, in the form of 'bugging the teacher,' took on a special meaning because it was a strategy that could be initiated either collectively or individually, but still with results that served a collective function. Students clearly indicated that the potential for bugging the teacher was always there, and that it could take on different forms depending on the composition of the class, the approach of the teacher, and factors of time and space. Thus that mosaic of resources that might affect the character of 'bugging the teacher' was chosen selectively through an interpretive framework of knowledge that students had constructed, which they shared, and that they were able to describe to others like myself. Indeed, one of the more remarkable observations is that the system of regenerative knowledge is so effectively understood, not through intentional codification as in a handbook of organizational procedures, but through the common interface between human actors and a definite world of material experience. That it so showed reiterates the class-based existence of student knowledge systems, emerging from a common relationship to the core productive process within the school.

Here, then, are the basic building blocks of regenerative knowledge, of a system of understanding that is the essential process that makes for the collective nature of groups such as Don's and Chris's. Strikingly present in the goofing off and the activities of Don and Chris and their friends, as described in the previous two chapters, is the great extent of initiatory behavior, the extent to which students attempt to define relevant spheres of influence and to control the activities within those spheres. This initiatory behavior becomes important because it arises specifically from and to considerable degree in opposition to the formalized emphasis on reified knowledge and its attendant forms within the school.

How does this occur? Reified knowledge, as we remember, is that circumscribed knowledge system defined categorically and absolutely, and is knowledge over which students exercise little control as to its form and consequence. What is more, reified knowledge tends to be applied to individuals in isolation from other individuals, thus mastery of it by students does not require collaboration or dialog with others. In the fundamental conditions of reified knowledge, labor from students, in the form of 'work' (Chapter 3), is exchanged to the school in order for 'success' in the activities that the school defines as legitimate, that is, good grades. This is an 'unnatural' exchange in the sense that it takes away from students something that is part of the very means of life – control over labor and the consequences of that labor. Therefore, to the degree that, through the labor process, work becomes primarily a *means* to existence rather than the *objectivation* of existence, then the work is separated from the person who performs it. It is in this manner that the very nature of human consciousness is transformed through the process of estranged labor. If we accept the premise of Marx that the whole character of a species 'is in the character of its life activity;' and free, conscious activity 'is man's species activity,'[1] then we can see how uncritical requirements for reified knowledge can create the oppositional forms of regenerative knowledge such as 'goofing off.'

Regenerative knowledge thus emerges through such forms as 'goofing off' as a reappropriation of labor from its estranged (alienated) state under which it exists within the framework of reified knowledge. Yet such activities and the regenerative knowledge systems generated do not, in fact, actually reappropriate that labor, for the relationship of the student to forms of reified knowledge remains the same – estranged. But to compensate for, as it is a 'natural' state for humans to wish to control their labor and the products of that labor, and in opposition to the domination of reified knowledge, regenerative knowledge emerges in those organizational hiatuses that exist through the inefficiencies of mass education – inefficiencies in the manner by which schooling occupies students' time, the amount of time that formal education 'takes up,' and the standardization of tasks that 'fits' so few students at any one point in time.

We arrive then at the foundation of a remarkable paradox: that the very system of schooling as it is hierarchically arranged, and its fostering of social relations leading to estranged labor, creates those very conditions that give rise to the accentuation of regenerative knowledge and the forms on which it is based – forms that serve as oppositional to the organization and its manifest purposes. The school as an organization within capitalist/technological institutions comes to arrange knowledge in such a manner that the labor power of students is exchanged for products over which they have had little control. Herein, meaning is not only remote but is possible only to the extent that abstractions like grades are reinforced and said to be meaningful. Through such activities as 'goofing off,' and through the daily activities such as those we have seen Don and Chris and their friends participate in, the organization of reified knowledge is constantly challenged. The source of this challenge is not only forces outside of school, such as the media, the home (or as the result of the absence of a supportive home); it is also precipitated by the very contradictions that are an inherent part of reified knowledge itself – that it creates an oppositional form of interpretivity, community and appropriation of control where one is not present.

We then are faced with the fact that characteristics of junior high students, such a goofing off, are not naturally inherent to youth but rather are created forms in opposition to the very materialist world that breeds them.

7
Student 'power'

> In every social establishment, there are official expectations as to what the participant owes the establishment . . . whenever we look at a social establishment, we find a counter to this first theme; we find that participants decline in some way to accept the official view of what they should be putting into and getting out of the organization and, behind this, of what sort of self they would accept for themselves. Where enthusiasm is expected, there will be apathy; where loyalty, there will be disaffection; where attendance, absenteeism; where robustness, some kind of illness; where deeds are a multitude of homely little histories, each in its way a movement of liberty. Whenever worlds are laid on, underlives develop (Erving Goffman, *Asylums: Essays on the Social Situation of Mental Patients and Other Inmates*, Chicago, Aldine, 1961).

The supposition that forms of regenerative knowledge such as goofing off are borne out of the basic systematic modes of production of our society and its institutions (schools in this case) raises the question of exactly how such forms and the knowledge systems associated with them serve those who create them. Are they truly oppositional forms, exemplars of the downtrodden 'rising up' against the arrangements of capitalist educational organizations? To what degree is it a sign of 'psychic health,' as the poet Roethke put it, that the young are aware (although possibly not consciously) of the effects of the 'order' of institutions and thereby generate such oppositional forms? More pointedly, what is it that youth 'learns' through the creation of such forms and the meaning attached to them that prepares them (as we discussed in Chapter 1) 'to participate in the life of the civic community?'

The topic of student power, then, is certainly central to an understanding of student culture, and is the subject of this chapter; here I shall illustrate the vagaries of student power by dealing with a number of topics. First, I will describe a number of strategies used by students within the classroom environment in order to give students a sense of 'fate control.' These include strategies meant to change the agenda imposed by a person of greater authority; student communication through notes, being a 'pet,' and the use of humor in the classroom – all topics touched upon in previous chapters. Next, we will discuss some of the ways of circumventing formal rules as exemplified by smoking in school and ways of cheating. Finally, we will look at the phenomenon of 'skipping,' and learn about the dynamics of skipping, some of which are illegal but a great preponderance of which permit students to skip legally.

Classroom strategies

Changing agendas

Already we have noted that the ongoing structure of the classroom world led to a significant portion of the student's time being spent waiting for events to happen. Rather than do nothing, however, the students adopted a host of strategies that further allowed the alteration of classroom events to suit their purposes. In that the student's agenda was often superimposed upon the agenda that the teacher had established, the pacing and movement of instructional activities could be altered whenever a student or group of students used these strategies. The student was not simply a pawn in the classroom environment created by the teacher, but rather was an active participant in the dynamic interaction which made any one class what it was on any given day.

Instructional alterations. In my two years at Harold Spencer, I noted numerous occasions where students delayed classroom procedures, or at least moved the focus of those procedures away from themselves and to other students. Some of these procedures were quite simple and obvious. For example, the ongoing pacing of instructional procedures in any lesson involving student–teacher interaction (such as discussion or question and answer sessions) required student participation and student acceptance of the forum as legitimate. Yet often individual students tuned out of instructional procedures by simply refusing to be involved. Another common tactic for altering instructional procedures was to offer irrelevant answers to questions, a process that made the student the center of attention in the class for some portion of time as other students within the class chuckled at the response. In history, one day, Mrs Ronald was attempting to spark a conversation relative to the 'great man' theory of history, using the example of Franklin Roosevelt as a 'great man' who radically changed events. Suddenly, Don raised his hand and volunteered: 'Speaking of great men and events, did you see *Airport* on last night? Man, that was really exciting, they put this bomb in the restroom of the plane and . . .' He continued while the teacher patiently waited for him to get to the point. He never did.

Still another way of altering classroom procedures and causing delays was to state, when called upon, that an assignment had not been completed or, far better, to state that the wrong assignment had been done. Many students typically used the excuse that 'I did the wrong assignment' or 'I did exercise A instead of B, were we supposed to do A?' when called upon in class to provide an answer to a problem. Such reasons were used whenever the occasion demanded it, and these occasions were more than just not having the assignment completed. These rationales were often invoked by students if and when they decided that they did not wish to participate in either a classroom discussion or a question–answer session with the teacher. Again, since the teacher relied on students for the ongoing participation with instruction, no sanctions were invoked on those who chose not to participate, as long as this activity did not become a habit. Other delays could be invoked by not having materials available for class. Roger, for example, constantly 'forgot' to bring a pencil to at least one class a day, and John and Chris frequently left their assignment for Von Hoffman's class in their lockers, leading to, of course, an excuse to leave the class in order to get the materials. Gordon seemed unable to find his folder in math class more than could occur by chance alone. I finally learned that he sometimes filed his folder under the name of a person who was absent, just so that he could say he could not find it.

If it was somehow discovered to be misfiled, he wondered with amazement how it could have ever been found where it was. All of these delays, when put together within any one class, added to the length of time that the student could structure, and reduced the amount of time wherein students were totally at the beck and call of the teacher's agenda.

One of the most effective and pervasive manners by which students influenced the teacher's setting of the schedule (and hence reduced the amount of time wherein he was a passive member of the instructional setting) was through various but common negotiations with the teacher. These negotiations symbolized the degree to which students had some degree of power over the teacher, owing in part to the dependency of teachers on students for the fulfillment of the instructional process. Student negotiation as a device to change or alter a decision previously made by a teacher was not infrequent. Negotiation was particularly noticeable when tests were graded within class, and when a teacher could not present a good case why the acceptable answer was the only possible answer. In many instances, this resulted in the acceptability of a wider range of answers than the teacher had envisioned. The better students such as Chris, John, and Barry often placed pressure on Richards, who was a great stickler for detail, and met him on his own terms. They loved to catch him by indicating that answers, as found in the book, were singular rather than plural (for example, mountain instead of mountains) or that certain words were not capitalized in the book, even though his answer key had them as being capitalized. When they were attentive to such detail, the students often forced a change in the acceptability of the answer.

Most common, however, were students simply delaying the instructional sequence. If students took their time finishing assignments or tests, the teacher had to wait for all to finish before collecting the papers and moving on to the next activity. When the teacher asked if students were ready to take a test or if they wished more time for review, review always won out and, while it only delayed the inevitable, it still symbolized a modicum of activism and an ability to control some aspect of one's fate. When placed together, these various strategies of altering the classroom agenda illustrated the fact that, rather than simply being pawns, the students were able to carve out areas in which they too had power and in which their voice could be heard. Many students used such delaying tactics when they could, and these strategies were a natural part of life in the classroom.

Substitutes. Changes in agendas were even more predominant when substitutes filled in for the regular teachers. More often than not, students looked forward to those days when substitutes were present, as they were able to take advantage of the substitute's relatively weak knowledge base of classroom operations. The following incident was typical of days when substitutes were present.

One day, while heading toward Marcy's fifth-period English class, I met Art going to the same class. As we approached the room we noticed a substitute teacher enter the room, indicating that Marcy was not there that day. Art's face beamed and he said, 'Oh good, substitute's coming.'

We entered the room and it was evident that the class was not ready to settle down, despite the substitute's pleas. As the bell rang, signaling the beginning of the period, groups of students remained clustered at various locations, busily talking with one another. Finally, everyone moved into a seat. The substitute stood at the front of the room, arms folded, and finally said, 'I'm still waiting for you people to settle down.'

'That will be the day,' came a voice from the back of the room.

'Good luck,' said someone else.

'Long wait, honey,' said Don, although in a somewhat low and cautious voice.

Finally, the substitute, after consulting the lesson plans left for her, asked the class to take their grammar books and turn to page 327. 'We're going to do exercise C on that page,' she announced.

'We did that yesterday,' Art offered.

'We already turned that in,' someone else stated defiantly. The substitute however, had the lesson plan before her and she was not about to deviate from it. The assignment went on as planned.

But of course few could pay strict attention to doing a grammar lesson, especially Don, Steve, Gary, and Art. They were busy shooting paper wads among each other, despite warnings from the substitute that they stop it. Finally, she caught Gary in a position where he was just ready to launch a paper wad. He could not deny it; the substitute looked at her seating chart.

'You, uh [checking her chart] Frank Dennis, take your grammar book out in the hall.' Gary looked up and realized she was talking to him. Yet, as often happened when a substitute came, many students had taken different seats and the substitute called the name of Frank Dennis (who was absent and in whose seat Gary was sitting). 'I'm going to leave a note for Mrs Marcy about your behavior today.'

'Yeah, OK,' said Gary, gathering his materials and desk and moving toward the hall.

'That's not Frank Dennis,' a girl from the back of the room said, 'he's absent today.'

'Shut up!' someone said nearby. Apparently, the substitute had not heard any of this as she was busy scrawling out a note to Mrs Marcy. Gary moved out into the hall, and smiled in the knowledge that Frank Dennis would be reprimanded by Mrs Marcy when she returned.

The class proceeded to the exercise. About half-way through Art raised his hand. 'Are we supposed to turn these in?' he asked.

'Yes, I already told you we were turning them in,' the substitute answered without looking up from her desk where she was sitting.

'Did you say we were supposed to turn them in?' another person inquired. The teacher nodded her head. From the rear of the room, I heard another voice: 'I wonder if we're supposed to turn these in.' This question was asked repeatedly in the space of a few minutes.

Such was life when a substitute entered the scene, as students took advantage of the fact that they had greater knowledge about the proceedings within the classroom than did the teacher. Students frequently attempted to convince the substitute that some lesson had already been done, that they did not need to repeat something, that the teacher never made them hand in exercises finished in class, or that they were allowed certain privileges, such as leaving one minute early for lunch so as to beat the lunch line. The fact that substitutes rarely knew students' names often worked to the students' advantage, as chair switching and the like were common when substitutes came.

Yet, students could not dominate the substitute too much, for the substitute might leave a negative report about the class for the returning teacher. However, neither could the substitute not listen to student inputs, for in such cases students reported that the regular teacher was aware of how much they disliked a certain substitute, and too many reports could lead to a school 'scratching' that substitute from their list. This actually happened during the seventh grade, when Gary and a group presented a petition to Mrs Ronald in support of their position that a substitute handed out detention notices with far too much regularity. Mrs Ronald sympathized with the students' concerns, and requested from the office for that particular substitute not to be used in her classes. Thus, even with substitutes, the dynamics of classroom life resembled the delicate balance between aspects of power held by students as well as teacher.

Discipline. Supposedly, teachers had the upper hand in discipline. More often than not, their decision held and if there was a disagreement between the teacher's and student's side of a story, it was the teacher who was believed. This statement is, however, an oversimplification of reality, for students did exercise some aspects of power by virtue of their ability to control elements important to the issue of discipline.

A case in point: I was surprised that Von Hoffman did not reprimand students more than he did, at least in the form of sending students to the office or assigning them detention after school. But as Chris and I were walking from class one day, he mentioned something that helped me to realize why.

'Lucky for me that Von Hoffman doesn't knock you down for goofing off in class,' he said. 'If he did, I'd be flunking in there.'

'Why doesn't he?' I asked.

'Are you kidding? If he did, he'd have people in the office all day, then they'd really find out what was happening in that class.'

Chris's comment made considerable sense, and I then realized that students had power over not only Von Hoffman but any other teacher who might have a tendency to send their discipline problems to the office for resolution. Too much public disclosure of excessive discipline problems or of being unable to control a classroom effectively was a negative mark on any teacher, and especially so if the administration was looking critically for any flaws so as to institute termination procedures. So Chris was right; if Von Hoffman sent as many students to the office as he threatened, he, not the students, would suffer the most severe consequences. In fact, John once said that he, Chris, and Barry had the least chance of being sent to the office for goofing off, because all the teachers and the administration knew them to be relatively well behaved students, not the kind who were likely to be sent to the office once a week for discipline problems. Therefore, so their reasoning went, Von Hoffman was unlikely to send them to the office, because other teachers and Pall would have additional evidence that the problem lay more in Von Hoffman's conduct in the class rather than with the recalcitrant students themselves. John said that he felt that even the few times he was sent to the office by Von Hoffman, Von Hoffman softpeddled John's transgressions relative to those of others in the class (as he did with Chris's, as noted in Chapter 5); he also indicated that the only reason he was sent to the office was so that Von Hoffman could symbolize to the class that John could not get away with everything. Barry, certainly a well-behaved student, affirmed the students' perceptions that teachers had to know their limits. 'They [teachers] try to be as nice as they can to students and build up a reputation without students doing anything really bad; that way, nothing spreads around and the teachers don't get in trouble. See, that's what they're really worried about.'

Students developed various strategies to ward off more severe forms of discipline and punishment. These strategies often involved a knowledge of the teacher or administrator's mode of operation and, when desired, accommodation to that mode. For example, students knew that if Von Hoffman became irate and appeared, as Barry put it, 'as if he might do something irrational,' then it was time to appear contrite and sorry, in which case he would probably settle down. Joking was a workable manner by which to disarm Mr Charles and Mr Dennis if they became upset; this sometimes worked with Marcy, although it was not as predictable a strategy. Other teachers, like Richards and Mr Michael, threatened severe punishment if something were not done or if something were not stopped, and the most frequent strategy was for students to nod their heads as if to say that the teacher's bark was far worse than his bite.

Writing notes

Thus far I have discussed how students attempt to change the agenda in classroom situations. These classroom strategies reflect the somewhat overt use of student power in the classroom setting. Yet student power can often take very subtle forms, such as in the writing of notes. As I will now illustrate, communication via the note system represented another dimension of the power that students, by virtue of their place in the structure of the classroom, had over teachers who attempted to prevent such clandestine forms of communication among students.

Karen and her friend Terri, both of whom I knew quite well, were masters at passing notes, and unabashed practiced their art to the extent of advising the teacher of such in advance. While in English one day, Marcy moved the seat assignments of the two girls because they had been talking in class. 'That's OK,' announced Karen as she moved her books to an assigned seat at the side of the room, 'we'll write notes.' Marcy ignored this statement, or at least placed little credence in it, and the lesson continued. Yet, within two minutes of having been moved, Karen was busy scrawling a note on a piece of paper, after which she folded it, wrote Terri's name on the front and, after Marcy turned her back, placed it on an empty desk beside her in the adjoining row. A girl in the next row, checking first to be sure Marcy's back was still turned, picked up the note and passed it to Terri who was in the row adjacent to her, a little forward. The some procedure happened again, only in reverse, and their communication system went undaunted for the remainder of the period.

A variety of strategies were used to keep the note system active, even under the most adverse of circumstances. In Chapter 6, we discussed how individuals left their seats to sharpen pencils or throw paper in the wastebasket in order to carry on discussions of interest. Karen and Terri went one step further. One day, while paying special attention to their system of communication, I noted Terri (who was sitting beside me) busily writing a note. After she finished, she crumpled it up into a little ball and headed for the wastebasket and the pencil sharpener, both located in the corner near the front of the room. She carefully dumped the ball of paper on the floor near the wastebasket and then commenced to sharpen her pencil, after which she returned to her desk. A few moments later, Karen left her seat and headed for the pencil sharpener. After sharpening her pencil and checking to be sure Marcy was not watching, she leaned over, picked up the ball of paper, and returned to her seat to read the note that Terri had prepared.

Amazing cooperation existed when notes were passed between students. Students accepted that notes were the private business of the parties, initiated within and supported by their self-generated culture to maintain the interpretive structure through which members came to understand schooling and their role in it. Also, it was a form symbolic of the pervasive nature of reified knowledge that itself did not encourage the maintenance of communicative–interpretive systems relevant to the formalized purposes of the school. Thus, when faced with the realization that such communicative competence was not a requirement of schooling, but rather was discouraged except when produced on the terms of reified knowledge that demanded an acceptance rather than critique of the basis of knowledge, students created channels over which they had control and used them within the framework of their understanding of how to achieve power when it was not legitimately possible.

Being a pet

Pets were students who tried to 'butter up' the teacher or who complied excessively with the teacher's directions. In such cases, according to most students, special favors were subtly and indirectly passed to those students. Yet it made a difference whether the student was a pet because the teacher sought out the student or because the student actively cultivated the relationship, and this difference illustrates again the extent to which student-exercised power has to be understood within the context of the students' cultural patterns and regenerative belief systems.

The first group of pets were sometimes known as 'goody-goodies' and were not highly respected by other students; the latter were more esteemed. The goody-goodies were students who were called upon to grade papers, run errands, or take notes to the office. They often served as the teacher's student assistant, a factor that in itself made that person suspect with other members of the student body. Usually, goody-goodies were girls, and they served as pets in every class rather than in only a few.

The distinguishing factor, though, was that the goody-goody types became pets through the teachers' designation of them as 'good'; that is, doing their work all the time, not causing trouble, volunteering answers more than anyone else, and asking for help when it was needed. All students complied to some degree, but goody-goodies overdid it, thus the enmity sometimes incurred from other students. Teachers often played favorites and allowed these students special favors because they trusted them more. Often, goody-goodies were considered 'narcs' by other students, and if a teacher discovered something about students that he or she never could have known unless informed by a student, then the goody-goody pet was automatically suspect. Few students wanted to be a goody-goody pet because it led to considerable harassment from other students; often, those students so designated were isolated from the remainder of the student body.

But there was another, more finely tuned definition of a pet, one that symbolized a sense of control that a student had over a teacher. Students did not have a specific name for this type of pet but the distinguishing factor is best characterized by the fact that students referred to themselves or others as 'his pet' or 'her pet,' indicating the pet of a specific teacher rather than being a pet in general. To be a 'pet' of a specific teacher meant that the student had 'psyched' the teacher out, found his or her weakness, and then was able to exploit that weakness to their own advantage. It was not just doing what one was told that brought special privileges. It did mean, however, that rather than passively waiting for the teacher to select the student as a pet (in which case the student was still dependent upon the teacher for the honor) the student actively sought out the teacher in order to be so designated as a pet. Yet there was an obvious ulterior motive in being designated as this type of pet, and that was to extract special privileges.

Perhaps this type of pet is best illustrated in a conversation I had with two girls, Rachael and Tommi, girls whom I knew fairly well and whom I had occasion to talk with at length, but whose daily activities I did not follow since I was preoccupied with Don and Chris and their group of friends. I asked them what one did to become a teacher's pet.

'Act nice,' said Rachael.

'Goody-goody pets,' Tommi added, 'do all their work and get good grades and everything; they help the teacher to correct papers and they just start getting friendsy-friendsy with the teacher.'

'Like me,' said Rachael, ''cept I'm not a goody pet, I'm choosy about who I'm a pet with. Like I'm OK with Mrs Cossa.'

'Yeah, but Von Hoffman's your worst enemy,' Tommi said emphatically.

'For sure, and Richards too – and Mr Glenn; in fact most of them 'cept Mrs Cossa.'

'What kinds of things does Cossa let you do?' I asked.

'I don't have to do all the work,' Rachael replied, 'and I still get B's.'

'Why don't you have to turn it in?'

''Cause I'm her pet.'

'How'd you get to be her pet?'

'She talks back to her,' Tommi interjected.

'It's true,' Rachael said seriously, 'She likes competition. She likes people to challenge her once in a while and I do it, so I get special favors.'

'You mean because you challenge her, she likes you more?'

'Well,' Rachael said, 'it's not quite that simple. You can't challenge her on everything, you just have to know the right time to say stuff, and I do.'

I first found it confusing for the actions of pets to be highly regarded in some instances but not so in others, yet students told me that, from their way of looking at it, this was not strange at all. 'Every teacher has a pet or two, it might as well be you,' went the logic. I asked Tommi if other students were jealous if she was a teacher's pet in a particular room.

'They're not jealous, they just wish they could be the pet in that room.'

'They look up to you,' Rachael added, ''cause they know you have something that they haven't been able to get. They know you're crafty, that's important.

Humor

In our journey with Don and Chris and their friends, we have seen that their daily lives are filled with the construction of humor – ongoing and pervasive. Up to this point, humor has been discussed as part of the fabric linking friends together. Yet the place of humor in another context of the student's world illustrates the student's capacity to take advantage of classroom interaction and to channel it into momentary diversions suitable to their own agenda. In this sense, their ability to play off actions of teachers and other students provided brief points of control in situations ostensibly controlled by adults.

In a dialog between students and the teacher over a particular lesson, humorous quips were constant and often unending, so much so that the undercurrent of humor within the class went virtually unnoticed. But by becoming swept up in the ebb and flow, a rich and complex underlife was apparent.

One day, while in English class in seventh grade, Marcy was questioning the class on a story they had just completed reading in a literature book. Marcy asked the class to locate the name of the publisher of the story. After a few moments of perusing the pages, Roger finally raised his hand.

'Winston,' he answered.

'Cigarettes,' a voice behind him stated.

Marcy ignored that statement and proceeded to tell Roger that the publisher was Holt, Rinehart & Winston. 'And who was the hero of the story?' she asked.

'Maude,' a student replied.

'Did you see *Maude* last night?' I overheard another student near the front of the room ask in a fairly loud voice. 'It was really good this time.' Marcy ignored that statement but, looking at the student who uttered it, said in a matter of fact way, 'Throw your gum out, will you? I'm tired of seeing it.'

'I'm just chewing my cud,' the student replied on his way to the wastebasket to deposit the gum.

'The way you chew sounds like my sister,' added Roger. Marcy grew impatient with the bantering occurring among class members. 'OK,' she said, 'just in the way of review, in this story there is a scene where Maude rides in a biplane. What is a biplane? Dave?'

'It has two wings,' Dave replied.

'OK, then what does the prefix "bi" mean?'

'Two,' Dave replied.

'Two?' Steve questioned from the side of the room. 'Two, two, two, this is Darby Dog [from an Alka-Seltzer commercial].' So, on it went for the remainder of the period, with Marcy occasionally keeping the class on the subject-matter but with the constant undertone of plays on words continuing. Such a dialogue between students was often only noticeable if one took the role of the students themselves and had the time to trace the development of such humor. For the teacher, the scope of such humor went unnoticed (and undoubtedly unappreciated) as he or she was preoccupied with other classroom activities.

Using humor to embarrass a teacher was considered a real feat, but words were not always necessary to invoke the embarrassment of a teacher through humor; sounds sometimes served the same purpose. In Richards's class, for example, students often took advantage of the multitude of films and slide shows that were used in social studies class to provide diversion and ultimately embarrass the teacher. Both Richards and Mr Bruce like to use slides that were accompanied by a recording serving to narrate the slides. The signal for advancing the slide was provided on the record itself in the form of a high pitched 'beep' at the end of a section of monolog. As would be expected, a few students (Dave and Gary among them) had perfected the 'beep' sound so that they could cause Richards to advance the slide prematurely. At first, Richards was confused, thinking that the error was in the record but, noting the underlying laughter by many in the class, he soon realized that some mysterious source within the classroom itself was the cause of the problem.

Humor in the classroom was at its best and was most effective when the social composition of the class encouraged and supported it. Perhaps there was no class in my two years at Spencer that fit this criterion better than Mrs Paul's class in the eighth grade. The class was small, the students all knew each other well, and Chris, Marty, Pete, and a few other close friends were in the class daily. Humor as used in this class helps illustrate an interesting phenomenon in the daily lives of students within the classroom. While the teacher was talking or attempting to carry on a discussion based on some sequence of instruction, certain students were engaged in a secondary communication system, keyed to the sequence of instruction and legitimated through a reliance on humor.

One day in Paul's class there was a class discussion on a story from a social studies book. The story centered on the right of a social worker to make unannounced visits to a recipient's home in order to check on whether they (being women in this case, the social worker being a man) were living with a man while claiming, at the same time, the lack of an external source of income. This story was used as a vehicle to discuss the right of the British to demand certain taxes and obligations of the American colonists without their consent. Mrs Paul opened the discussion by asking the class if the social worker had the right to make these visits.

'Maybe he was jealous,' replied Pete.

'Yes, I think he did; sometimes these people cheat like mad,' Susan volunteered.

'He was a naughty social worker,' said Chris, continuing the underlying comments begun by Paul.

'How about the rest of you?' Mrs Paul commented, 'do you agree with Susan?'

'No,' a girl replied, 'They should get a search warrant.'

'It was show and tell time,' Marty said, after which he turned to Tom and said something that caused both of them to laugh. Melvin, the only black student in the class, asked 'Was he black or white?'

'What difference does that make?' Paul stated in a loud voice.

'I don't know, just thought I'd ask,' Melvin responded.

'He was horny,' stated Chris after Curt had given a somewhat serious answer.

'He wanted some free munchies.'

'He wanted to get his hands on her, ho ho!' By now, Chris, Paul, and Marty, with a few others, were carrying on their own line of discussion.

'OK,' said Mrs Paul, 'what has all this to do with the colonists' decision to boycott British goods? First of all, who knows what a boycott is? Curt?'

'It's when you don't buy things, like when people didn't buy sugar last year 'cause it was so expensive.'

'What did that prove?' Mrs Paul asked of Curt.

'So prices wouldn't go up.'

'Up, up, up in a puff of smoke . . .' began Paul, singing the lyrics of a song which was currently popular.

'Boys, let's pay attention,' Mrs Paul finally said.

The next day, however, was like all the others. The humor-oriented communication between Chris, Pete, and Marty was as natural as sitting at their desks, and stopping it was out of the question. Take, for example, the discussion of the colonists' rejection of the tight control of the British over the daily affairs of the colonies. Across the front of the room on the bulletin board were the pictures of all the presidents, from Washington through to Nixon. Mrs Paul had asked the class which of these presidents favored strong central governments and which favored relatively weak central governments. After a few moments' discussion, Pete raised his hand. 'How come,' he asked, 'none of the presidents in those pictures ever smiled?' (It was true, all had very serious looks.) We perused the pictures for a few moments, then Chris said, 'Ah, ha! One of them is smiling!'

'Yeah, it's the one on the end,' Marty said, and all eyes turned to the picture of Richard Nixon who, indeed, was smiling.

'I know,' Paul replied, answering his own question. 'It was

probably taken when he said "I am not a crook" for the very first time.' Everyone clapped.

Classroom strategies were important mechanisms in and of themselves, as each provided the student or groups of students with defensible and legitimate ways (and often accepted) of exacting some control over the direction of classroom activities. Such acts were significant as they were visible to other class members and thus part of a collective demonstration and recognition of both the act and the actor. They would have also been relatively meaningless had they been acted out singly and in a social vacuum.

Yet the strategies were even more important when considered as part of an ongoing system, forming a mosaic or a 'power grid,' which gave students a feeling of initiatory direction. Certain classroom strategies were less operable in some instructional settings than others, and some could be continued for longer periods, while still others had to be initiated and discontinued over time. Some were more explicit and obvious while others such as writing notes, being a pet, and uses of humor, were more subtle and indirect. Perhaps such lack of structure was what gave an aura of creativity to these classroom strategies, for many were utilized by students in somewhat of an extemporaneous manner, dependent upon their assessment of the climate at the time.

Beating the system

Thus far, I have pointed to some of the classroom strategies that students invoked. These strategies were characterized by the student attempts to challenge the authority of the teacher in a 'legitimate manner,' thus their use was unlikely to invoke negative sanctions. Not all student attempts to invoke power over those in authority were, however, 'legitimate.' Some were clearly illegal and, if discovered, could bring serious consequences to those students who were caught. Illegal activities were engaged in none the less, and students often developed complex and sophisticated ways to minimize the risk of being discovered. Two such activities, smoking and cheating, will be reviewed briefly in this section. I have chosen these activities for discussion because I was privy to detailed information about the underlife surrounding them.

Smoking

The prohibition against smoking in the school grounds was one of the most rigorously enforced regulations at Harold Spencer, and to be caught smoking often resulted in expulsion for three days. Faculty members and the administration patrolled the school relentlessly, between classes and especially during lunchtime, ever on the move to catch students smoking in their favorite spots. Staff members had identified those students who were most likely to be smoking in school and were prone to track those students during breaks and especially at lunch. Because smoking regulations were so rigidly enforced, and as the penalties for smoking could be severe, categories such as 'places to smoke without getting caught' and 'ways to smoke without getting caught' were the two most important aspects of smoking discussed by students who smoked. A well-developed knowledge system existed about these two subjects, and this knowledge was passed around and compared frequently among those students to whom it was important.

Smoking took place in two main areas of school property. Locations within the building were restricted to the rest-rooms, for those were the only places used almost exclusively by students and which were relatively invisible to the school faculty. Even there, though, they were not totally safe as faculty members checked on rest-rooms between classes and during lunch, and their use for smoking required considerable planning and knowledge of a number of factors.

The traffic pattern of teachers who might check the rest-rooms (or 'cans,') was one critical piece of information used by students. Teachers were supposed to check a 'can' near their home-rooms during the five-minute passing time between classes. In practice, such checking was done either at the very beginning of the passing period when a teacher was on his or her way to the teachers' lounge for planning period (and often, for some, to smoke) or at the very end of the passing period when they were returning. Thus the short 2–3-minute period in the middle was somewhat safe for smoking. Here, then, timing was critical.

Timing was also critical for knowing those periods of the day safest for smoking in the cans. For example, many teachers were about the halls immediately before first period and after school, so those were not regarded as 'safe' times to be smoking in the cans.

Similarly, at least during the eighth grade, Hawkeye and Christie Love often made rounds of the rest-rooms during lunchtime, thus it was risky to sneak a smoke if and when they were prowling around.

Students possessed additional knowledge about which of the cans were better for smoking than others. For example, the best can for the girls was the one in the A building, while the best one for the boys was that in the B building. The reasons behind this were quite simple. Don told me that the boys' can had a cold air return vent that students gathered around while grabbing a quick smoke, and that use of it effectively dissipated the smoke through the vents rather than remaining in the rest-room and billowing out into the halls whenever the door was opened. For girls, the A building rest-room was equally useful as there was a vent at shoulder's height that also removed much of the smoke. The use by girls of the C building rest-room required a little more finesse, but was still usable. Rachael told me that the vent in the C building was on the ceiling in the corner. The trick there was for the girls to stand in the corner with one girl stationed at the door to the hall watching out for teachers and keeping the door ajar just enough to create a draft into the rest-room itself. With the smokers all in the corner near the vent, the smoke rose to the ceiling vent and flowed out of the rest-room. Use of this room was more risky, however, for, as Rachael indicated, 'It's bad if a teacher comes in because the person who is way in the corner gets stuck because everyone is piled around her.' Thus, that person might have a more difficult time getting rid of the evidence should a teacher enter.

The ideal way to smoke in the cans was to use the toilets inside the stalls, an approach that could be used only if one was fortunate enough to get out of class and into the cans when they were not crowded. The smoker went into the stall, closed the door, and stood on the seat of the toilet, being careful not to stand too high so as to be seen over the top of the door. Thus, the closed door shielded them completely. Then, if a teacher entered to make a spot check on the cans, she would see nobody in the stalls and make a quick exit while the smoker was, all the while, puffing away. In the event that she did check more carefully, the smoker simply dropped the butt into the toilet and the teacher could not prove a thing.[1]

Strangely enough, however, some of the best places to smoke were not the clandestine out-of-the-way spots, but obvious places where teachers would not normally expect kids to smoke. Roger explained one reason for this. 'This sounds dumb,' he said, 'but the safest place is right out in the open, behind a building or even at the end of the sidewalk. You can cup your hand over your cigarette and pretty much hide it if you're careful. This way, you can see a teacher coming from far away and you have time to throw away your cigarette.' 'Rat,' a boy known by everyone to smoke joints at school, told me the same thing when I asked him where he and his friends went to smoke marijuana. He responded, 'We don't hide anymore, they always catch you. Best place is out in the open. One place we go is at the front of the school where the buses come in. We can see people coming from all sides. Besides, it's actually better to smoke a joint than a cigarette out there. Joints smell too much in the cans, and they don't make much smoke so you can smoke them in the open and nobody will see you.'

Another favorite spot was in the fields adjoining the school. These grassy fields had small ravines in which a number of smokers (mostly boys) were found during lunchtime and immediately before school. Such areas were difficult for the staff to patrol and thus students, utilizing some discretion, found the fields to be relatively safe spots as long as someone did not 'narc' on them.

Cheating

Cheating refers to strategies that students used to complete academic work through 'illegal' means. An examination of cheating provides further illustration of the power that students, by virtue of their location in the social and organizational structure, were able to operationalize *vis-à-vis* teachers.

Cheating meant obtaining answers from someone else or completing work based upon assistance from another person – both contrary to the goals of most teachers to assess students individually rather than on the basis of what they could do with a peer's help. Yet these standards were not always subscribed to by students. There was, of course, always the problem of the roving eye or the whispered 'what's the answer to question 3?'; other forms of cheating were more subtle and matter of fact.

In Marcy's seventh-grade English class, for example, I noted early in the year that both Don and Steve rarely used the time designated in class for completing assignments, but still they usually submitted the completed assignment the next day. I wondered how that could be, since they rarely had time, what with their 'extra-curricular' activities, to work at home. Soon, however, I noted a common pattern. Upon entering class, both Karen and Terri walked by Don's and Steve's chairs and dropped off their home-work assignments. Don and Steve then quickly copied the answers and returned the papers to the girls before Marcy collected them. Art used the same system, only he had a girl named Carri do his work for him. (Sometimes, Art simply wrote his name at the top of a paper, gave it to Carri, and let her write in the answers for him in a slightly scrawled manner to resemble his handwriting.) I once asked Don why Karen did so many of his assignments for him in English class. His response was that 'She's hot for me,' which was an accurate perception at the time. I also knew that Carri was 'hot' for Art; Terri was a friend of Karen's, but I never heard anything about her being interested in Steve.

Don, Steve, Karen, and Terri regularly used other strategies to cheat when they were in the same class together. Quite often, for example, they received each other's papers when papers were exchanged for correcting (usually Karen got Don's and Terri got Steve's by having other students pass those papers to them). The girls simply penciled in the correct answers, if necessary, when answers were read by the teacher. Occasionally, Don and Steve even went as far as to leave all the answers blank, in which case Karen and Terri wrote in the answers. In other instances, Karen and Terri traded answers by writing them on a piece of paper, crumpling the paper in a ball as if it were waste paper, and then conveniently dropping it on the floor whereupon the other party leaned over and picked it up.

Cheating was not as difficult nor as clandestine in such classes as in science, where there was considerable group work on laboratory experiments. In fact, cheating was more open and, in some ways, tolerated by teachers because they felt that such activities would catch up with students when tests had to be taken. I noted, both in the seventh- and eighth-grade science classes, considerable group work on lab exercises as a way of getting through the material as rapidly as possible and still having time to talk and share con-versation. One girl, Susan, told me that she and her friends worked together on workbook exercises in order to get the material finished as quickly as possible 'because we have better things to do.' When I asked her what these 'better things' were, she simply replied that talking with her friends was more important to her.

Thus far, I have talked about cheating as a way of accomplishing work between two or more people. In this respect, cheating might appear to be a procedure involving only a few people at any one time. In general, this was true, but there were instances of cheating on a larger level, involving greater segments of the student population at any one time. The use of the electronic test equipment is illustrative of this process.

The electronic test equipment was installed a few years before I came to Spencer, and was used in a number of classes: social studies, science, and health among them. It was located in a large room which held about ninety students who sat at long concave tables arranged in tiers. Each tier (of which there were eight) had ten to twelve seats or 'stations,' and each station had a small raised dial that could be turned to five different positions ('A' through 'E'). All dials were, in turn, connected to an electronic board at the front of the room. This board indicated the responses at each seat, and also calculated the composite responses in percentage terms. Thus the teacher could ask the entire class a series of multiple-choice questions, have the class turn to the appropriate answer on the dial, and record the answers from the electronic reader board at the front. In this way, a multiple-choice test could be administered to an entire class at once, and the success of each student could be determined and recorded immediately.

Use of the dials presented a challenge to many students as a way to beat the system. Whereas one could not look at an adjacent dial to get an answer (the options themselves, located on the dial, were recessed), students developed a number of strategies for trading answers. One of the more common ways to cheat was for a number of students sitting near each other to all agree to begin the dial from one point ('A' for instance) and then to turn the dial a given direction (usually to the right). A distinguishing 'click' was heard if the dial was turned slowly enough, and students could tell the correct answer by counting the number of clicks on the informant's dial. The use of a finger flashing system, where one finger represented an 'A,' two 'B,' and so forth was another useful system. Because the table had a three-inch 'lip' along the edge, flashing answers could be done with relative ease as long as a teacher or aide was not patrolling the room or was immediately behind the desk.

Perhaps most interesting, however, was the length to which

students went to prevent other students from getting the answers being transmitted. There seemed to be nothing worse than sitting nearby someone not liked and having that person sponge answers by tapping into the agreed-upon code system. Consequently, sometimes it was necessary to take steps to confuse those persons. This could be done in a number of ways. One boy who was a good student and did not mind sharing answers with some of his less fortunate friends, said, 'If there is somebody nearby whom I don't want to get the answer, I'll fuck them up a little by twirling the dial three or four times while flashing a few fingers at the same time. Pretty soon the person gets confused and he doesn't know which system is being used.' Gary told me that he and some of his friends used prearranged 'audibles' like football teams do. For example, if they wanted to confuse a person whom they did not want to get answers, they simultaneously flashed hand signals and used the dial, but two coughs by Gary meant that the finger flashing was the true system while the dial was being used as a decoy. In these and other ways, the transmittal of answers could be restricted to those with a need to know.

We can see then that both smoking and cheating were possible to the degree that students outnumbered teachers and that teachers could not be everywhere to supervise what students were doing. Such a numerical imbalance permitted some students greater opportunity to place into action their continual movements to resist the dominant instrumental knowledge system of the school and, instead, to move toward self-initiative in whatever areas they felt symbolized their own self-determination. For students who smoked (certainly the vast minority), creation of a specific knowledge system as to time, place, and context of smoking came to consume much of their time and thereby to represent a dominant strand within their belief system. Cheating, while not universal, still was widespread, even among the 'better' students such as Chris and his group, depending again on context and the student's interpretation of their role within that context. The cheating was an act of defiance in the sense that the knowledge meant to be learned was seen to be reified and mostly separate from the cultural system of the adolescents in the school. Because it was so separate, it often was not taken 'seriously' and in many cases was 'learned' as a way of fulfilling instrumental requirements that themselves were often of a vague nature.

It is in this sense, then, that even activities such as smoking and cheating can be seen as indicative of the basic labor process in the school. Both clearly represent the extent to which students would go in order to manifest their own beliefs about their role in the schooling process. Both are symbolic of opposition to the dominant technology of schooling, and symbolic of the regeneratively based culture of the group, derived from the relation of the group to the basic productive process of the school.

Skipping

Supposedly, students were to attend class from the duration of the period for each day unless they had an excused reason to be absent. To be absent from all or part of a school day was referred to as 'skipping,' of which there were two forms: illegal and legal. To examine skipping is to note the process as another illustration of the power that accrued to certain students because of their place in the organization and their relation to adults in authority.

Illegal skipping

'Illegal skipping' consisted of student-initiated absence from school activities for school-defined illegitimate reasons. Generally speaking, illegal skips involved not attending school for a given day(s) and then attempting to provide some evidence to indicate that the absence was 'legal.'

Such absences usually were in concert – that is, with other students of the same friendship group. For example, Don and Steve frequently skipped together as did Don and some of his older friends. Usually, this entailed going to the local park (if the weather was good), to one of two local shopping centers, or just hanging around home if the parents were not there. Some of the girls skipped illegally too, girls like Karen, Terri, and Rachael – and some of Rachael's friends. Their activities tended to be less daring, remaining at home, listening to records, watching television – activities of a more sedate nature. Rarely did I hear about junior high girls running around in cars or drinking beer while they were skipping.

Yet both boys and girls had the same problems while they were skipping – that of legitimating their absence from the school. To avoid being called into the office for having an unexcused absence (of which two were allowed per year), the absent student had to have a note from home, documenting the reason for the absence. Since it was difficult to obtain such a note from one's parents, other forms of legitimation were sought. Don said he used the 'sister routine,' having his sister write notes for him, signing his mother's signature. Karen too used her older sister as a source of notes, since her sister lived nearby and had skipped occasionally when she was in junior high. Friends were sometimes used in those cases where relatives were not available. If friends were not available, the student might risk signing his own excuse.

The latter two procedures were, however, risky. The office kept excuses on file and checked signatures for those like Don who skipped fairly regularly. Inconsistency in signatures could lead to a parental conference, with the attendant revelation to the parents that the student had not been in school. Thus, it was much better to use other strategies to skip illegally, and these strategies were much more frequent.

For example, often students did not skip for the entire day but instead for one or more periods within a day. Such action required some advance planning, because attendance was supposed to be taken at the beginning of each period and the list of absentees sent to the office, where it was compared against the master list of those absent first period. Consequently, if students were absent during a later period and not absent first period, they were supposed to report to the office the next day in order to resolve the difference. Such absences were, nevertheless, possible. One tactic was to find a reason to go to the office, then spend time lounging around the office waiting to see the person there.

The guidance counselors (and sometimes Mr Pall) were the obvious people to visit. The student would contrive a reason, not show up for class, then appear at the guidance office. Roger was good at this, as he told me one day.

'Sometimes I'll just not show up for a class and go down to the office and say I want to see Mr Nickles. I'll wait around there, give some shit to guys who have been sent to the office for smoking or something and then talk to Nickles about some "personal problem," you know, like some teacher is harassing me or something. When I'm through, I just get a pass from him and go back to the class. It's all legal.' Students often used visits to the nurse's office in a similar manner.

Don and others like Steve, who skipped portions of days, usually had calculated which classes were easiest to miss. This calculation involved knowing the attendance-taking procedures in each of the classes and using this information to the best advantage. Despite the constant pleas from the office for teachers to be diligent in taking attendance each period, some teachers were not so diligent, and very often the task simply slipped the teacher's mind. Yet, something had to be handed in, as student helpers collected the attendance slips posted outside each room. If the teacher had overlooked attendance for that class, it was not uncommon for students to 'volunteer' the names of those absent while the teacher looked for the absentee forms on their usually cluttered desk. This was where friends in the class came in handy, as they would make sure that those who had skipped that period were not included on the list. There was, of course, a risk here, as some 'goody-goody' or pet might break the cover and reveal that somebody indeed was skipping. Yet here too the almost universal norm against 'narcing' on another student favored the student who skipped. It was difficult even for the 'goody-goodies' to risk the wrath of other class members who generally admired those students able to complete illegal acts such as skipping successfully without bringing negative sanctions on to themselves.

The so-called 'individualized classes,' math and shop, provided a different way to skip for a period via the manner by which attendance was taken. Here, classes were large (sixty or more) and students, rather than sitting in rows, were either at tables or stations; thus visual attendance procedures were impossible. Given the size of the class, an oral calling of the roll took excessively long. Thus, each student had a manila folder in which his worksheets were kept and when he arrived at the class each day, he took his folder from a shelf on which the files were arranged alphabetically by class. After the class began, an aide or student assistant (usually from the high school) simply checked the folders still in the file and made the absentee list from the remaining folders.

While it was certain that everyone whose folders remained was absent, it was not as certain that those whose folders had been pulled were present. It was relatively easy, if one wished to skip either of these classes, to have a friend 'pull' a folder so that the absent student was counted as present. Of course, a system such as this could exist only if it was accompanied by considerable discretion. Large blocks of missing students would be noticed and the reasons why they had been counted 'present' would be investigated. Similarly, if any one student used this system to excess, then surely a teacher would catch on or some student might 'narc.' Amazingly, these excesses rarely appeared and I was surprised by the self-control practiced by students such as Don and Marty. Like those who smoked, they seemed to know how to manipulate the system to make it work for and not against them.

Legal skipping

A relatively small number of students skipped illegally, usually those who, while not always deviants, were at least somewhat 'less respectable' in the eyes of some teachers and administrators. There were other ways to skip too, ways that were perfectly legal and in fact encouraged by the school. An examination of the legitimate strategies of skipping illustrates how some other students used and created other vehicles for creating their own structure within the system of reified knowledge created by the school.

To understand these skipping strategies, it is useful to examine the context of the daily bulletin at Spencer:

> The Thespians will be excused at 10.00 a.m. today to go to a special performance of a play in Port City. Those students who are to be excused are noted on the enclosed list.
>
> Students listed below shall be excused at 9.30 a.m. to attend a science seminar at the high school. They should be back by 11.30.
>
> Pep Club members will be excused at 2.00 p.m. today to attend the football game with Edgewood. Students to be excused are the following:
>
> Honor Society members please report to the cafeteria at 10.15 tomorrow morning for group pictures.

While clubs were not as integral a part of student life at Spencer as they were at the high school level, they still existed and membership in a club permitted certain fringe benefits. Club activities could not always be scheduled after school, and members were often able to skip the normal school routine through participation in formally sanctioned club activities. Attendance at special events held at other locations, club photographs, and preparation for club activities were some of the common legitimate reasons for getting out of class.

Club activities provided a small segment of the legal skips. More frequent ways of legally skipping were available if one belonged to some school-wide music, drama, or art organization. Again, selected announcements in the daily bulletin reveal this:

> Members of the Pep Band will be excused at 2.00 p.m. to prepare for the Pep Assembly.
>
> Eighth- and ninth-grade chorus members are to be excused during fifth and sixth period today to prepare for the Spring Concert.
>
> The cast of the Interim play is to be excused sixth period today to rehearse for the play which opens tomorrow night.
>
> All play and production personnel are to be excused first period to get ready for the assembly today. Teachers – see the list which is in your box.
>
> All brass members are to report to the band room fifth period today for a special rehearsal.

Sometimes, such intrusions into the daily schedule became so numerous that teachers felt they had to make special pleas to get students released:

> Teachers. Could I have the following ten people during first period. We are behind in costuming for the play and time is getting short. I know I have asked that a lot of students be released in the past, but I promise this will decrease after today. Thanks.

Those who were members of the various athletic teams had the most available activities for legally skipping. Students who were members of two or three teams over the year (such as John and Dave in the eighth grade) often missed parts of at least two days a week.

> The eighth-grade football team will be excused at 2.00 today for the game at Edgewood.
>
> Please excuse the following boys who will be going to the baseball game at West. The bus is to leave at 1.30, so they should be excused at 1.15.

Girls had similar advantages, especially as a result of the ruling that schools had to fund girls' athletics to the same degree that they funded boys'.

> Girls' volleyball away at Edgewood today. The following team members should be excused at 2.00.

Lettermen often had additional privileges.

> All boys who lettered in football, wrestling, or basketball please report to the gym this morning at noon. We will talk to a representative about the possible purchase of jackets.

And, of course, there were always photographs to be taken.

> Would the following members of the football team please report to the stage this morning at 11.00. These boys missed the last picture session and they cannot be included in the annual unless they have their pictures taken at this time.

Members of the student council were able to skip legally.

> There will be a student council meeting this morning at 8.35 in room B-16. Everyone please attend. This is an important meeting.

Sometimes, special student council meetings had separate meetings.

> There will be a special meeting of the 9th grade room representatives today at 8.35 to discuss plans for the graduation dance. Meet in the library conference room.

Yet student body representatives had other duties requiring periodic absence from class. For example, they were responsible for collecting money for the school newspaper. In addition, they collected monies from the magazine drive, for school pictures, and for the school annual. Monies collected then had to be handed in to the office, a procedure that took about half of the first period.

There were also school-wide tasks of management and scheduling that took students from classes.

> Please excuse the following students to take the aptitude tests during the first period. They should report to the cafeteria immediately after attendance has been taken first period.

> The following students are to report to the cafeteria during first and second period to take make-up standardized tests.
>
> The following schedule indicates the periods which will be devoted to seventh- and eighth-grade registration for next year's classes. All students should bring a pencil and paper to the registration meetings.

Often, students had to be taken from classes in order to resolve other scheduling or managerial problems.

> The following students should report to the library during first period to clear up overdue library books.
>
> Please have the following students report to Mr Nickles to clear up scheduling problems.
>
> The following students have not turned in a federal data card. This information was due yesterday. They should report to Mr Pall during the beginning of second period.
>
> We have had to change the combination on some of the lockers. Students with the following locker numbers should report to Hansen sixth period to get the combination to their lockers.

A variety of circumstances existed that permitted legally skipping many of the instructional procedures within the school. Yet, it is important to understand how students perceive the availability of these opportunities. Let us turn to some discussions I had with Chris over his legitimate forms of skipping.

In the eighth grade, Chris, Marty, Jack and I were eating lunch together when Chris began talking about his involvement in the school drama activities. Marty listened very patiently, then finally asked Chris, 'You really like that stuff, don't you?'

Chris answered immediately, 'Sure I do, it's great. Not only is it fun but I get out of lots of classes. I can get out of almost any class I want.'

'Shit,' Jack laughed, 'the only way I can get out of a class is to get kicked out; the bastards don't trust me at all.'

'Me either,' said Marty. 'The only thing I get out for is wrestling.'

After this conversation, I realized that what Chris, Jack, and Marty said was true; some students had an easier time getting out of classes than others. While Chris and some of the students who were involved in sports and drama activities seemed out of classes more than they were in them, others did not have these built-in excuses. I asked Chris about this one day after he had been excused for two periods to work on play costumes.

'How do you get out of so many classes?'

'Well,' he replied, 'I guess the main thing is that it's an honor system kind of thing. If Mrs Mackle wants me out for rehearsals or to get pictures taken or to work on costumes or something, she just writes me a note and I take it to the teacher. I have a pretty good relationship with most teachers so they will let me go. Oh, she'll usually ask what class I have during a certain period and I'll tell her if I can get out of it.'

'Do other kids get out of class as easy as you do?'

'Well, some do, but like I said they [teachers] know they can trust me so they're more willing to let me out. They know I won't be behind the B building smoking dope.'

It seems that the trusted students were more likely to skip legally than were the students whom teachers could not trust. Chris could be absent from many classes when a play or musical production was being scheduled, as he had access to a *carte blanche* pass. Athletes were often excused from classes during football and track seasons in order to help line the track or football field. Girls who were good students had their avenues too, as some teachers enlisted the help of the trusted girls to assist in putting up bulletin boards and to make other last-minute preparations for school-wide open house.

Legal skips, then, were possible because many students offered more to the school than was required and, by so doing, received certain privileges in return. Participating in athletics, drama events, student body functions and other such 'extra-curricular' activities meant that the students, while they were taking on more responsibility, were also provided with a broader power base to utilize in their role as students. And by conforming more to the expectations required of those in extra-curricular activities (putting forth effort, being reliable, not taking excessive advantage of liberties), students were, as Chris indicated, bound to be trusted more as they, through their participation in school-organized activities, demonstrated acceptance of school-sanctioned norms. Thus, students who were trusted did not have to resort to skipping illegally because of the many opportunities they had to skip legally.

Other students, however – those such as Don, Steve, and Roger – did not take advantage of such legal skips because of their more obvious opposition to the fundamentals of reified knowledge and its requirements. They did not participate in the activities sponsored by the school because in order to do so would signify a tacit approval of their subservient role in the school and an acceptance of the right of the school to permit privileged deviancy. Such was not acceptable to them, as they were coming to see the requirements of school-based knowledge as a restriction of their communicative network determined and controlled by them. They then turned to illegal skipping, which was more consonant with their perceived beliefs about control of the labor process. Their actions point out that, while we can see that students as a whole can be considered a class because of their generalized relationship to the productive process, important differences did exist, and these differences were indicative of the manner in which class-based cognitive structures became operative in the daily dynamics of student life within the school.

Summary and conclusions

The material we have reviewed illustrates that the extent to which students exercise power over certain regularities of school life affects how students (or groups of students) view their role in bureaucratic organizations. Quite simply, the exercise of power by students at Spencer depends both upon the structural location and role of the student within an organizational matrix as well as certain personal attributes – some achieved, others ascribed. The actual manifestation of power, differentiated as it was, was constitutive of the total student cultural system as it was maintained, created, and redefined by students. Yet, the consequences of student processes of control, the control itself serving as a form of regenerative knowledge, were somewhat uniform.

As a form of knowledge, the exercise of power in this manner indicates how cultural processes are reproductive and how participants, through their opposition to the imperatives of schooling, actually participate in that reproductive process. Let us examine each of these conclusions in turn.

First, noting that students had some degree of power built into their very position within the organization does not diminish the importance of the personal attributes of power. As we saw, positions offered the potential for power, but students had to work their way into them and use them to their best advantage. Thus, one had to work at being a pet, work out strategies of going to see the counselors at the right intervals and for the right reasons, and one needed to sense the timing and tempo for using various classroom strategies in order to change the pace of instruction. The successful exercise of power by students often was an inventive process, one requiring considerable calculation, discretion, and a sense of being able to weigh the consequences. Nothing could guarantee success, and estimations sometimes went awry. Yet, the inability to know in advance the consequences of every instance in no way detracted from the dynamic aspects of working for increased power in situations that ostensibly left students powerless.

The very dynamic process by which students actively created dimensions of their own culture is brought into sharp focus through understanding student power as a constitutive social process creating specific and *different* 'ways of life' through interaction with a material world. Students who were best able to utilize attributes of personal power together with aspects of positional power were those who exercised the most power within the school. Students like Chris and John, who gained power through their ability to exert their will or beliefs over other people, and who occupied varied student roles such as in drama and music productions, athletics, or student body positions, were the students to whom the most power accrued. They interacted mostly with authority figures in the school, had the greatest opportunities for legally skipping, and were best able to enact various classroom strategies. This was the case largely because they were conceived of 'differently' and thus were afforded more opportunities to combine the structural and personal elements of power. Chris, for example, was able to get away with a much greater use of humor in the classroom setting than were others who were not 'good students,' because his intrusions were believed and believable, while the outbreaks of others often were seen as purposeful intrusions. Additionally, the good students were perceived as valuable both within and outside of the classroom, and more opportunities for power flowed in their direction.

The distribution of power among students also illustrates the existence of a system of stratification based upon status and prestige. Certain students were able to negotiate a wider variety of legitimate statuses or positions within the school; these statuses, in turn, carried with them higher prestige ratings in so far as they were judged by those in authority within the school. Because students who were involved in those activities offered, through their labor, 'commodities' (mostly in the form of prestige) that the school deemed useful, the exchange value of the student labor in activities such as athletics, drama, and clubs was in the form of legal skipping. Indeed, the exchange-value also often translated into intangibles such as the ability to use classroom strategies such as humor or 'being a pet' more successfully than might otherwise be possible. Less highly regarded students (at least in the eyes of most of the adults in the school) could not or chose not to provide that labor in those desirable areas, had no 'commodity' to exchange, and thus were not provided those opportunities for legal skips; these students relied on their own self-created acts to maximize their self-determination. The more highly regarded students, however, being permitted forms of legitimated deviancy, resorted less frequently to illegal acts.

If power is a form of regenerative knowledge, then we can see more clearly how the understanding about reified knowledge exacts an uneven toll on the students. We can also see how the analysis of student labor and its use-value comes to play a critical role in how this toll is affected and in what forms for which students. A vicious circle is formed, one wherein the degree of student acceptance of reified knowledge affects forms of regenerative knowledge (such as power), the presence of which in turn feeds the very interpretive world of the student – one wherein the student comes again to accept to various degrees the official life of the school. The basic labor process and the manner in which that labor creates and reinforces regenerative knowledge, then, has long-term consequences, the beginnings of which are first worked out in schools.[2]

A second major conclusion relates to the limits within which student power operates and the reproductive nature of cultural forms associated with regenerative knowledge. The material in this chapter has documented some of the strategies used and avenues open for students to exercise power within a situation where they are accorded little formal participation in the ongoing life within the school. Yet, we should not be deluded into thinking that students, by their definition of the situation and the activities that followed, had created or were offered a major role in decisions about their place in the school, for such was not the case. Clearly, students acted where and when they could, some more successfully, more inventively than others. Yet, the range of their activities did have major limitations.

It is within these limitations that the avenues of power must be understood. I believe that the student underlife, characterized by goofing off and the exercise of power, is important. Life in school is the student's first (and perhaps most influential) experience within the confines of a complex organizational system where many events are beyond their ability to control and where they must act on the basis of how other people tell or expect them to act. Once in the school, they no longer have the degree of fate control that they had with their play group, neighbourhood friends, or even family. Relations in school are more distant, less under their control, and they must work out their own role and create the kind of self they themselves will accept.

But it is important to realize that it is the student who creates that self – indeed, even through oppositional forms such as goofing off and the exercise of power. This self-creation is more than mere resistance that is created through an interpretive framework, for the resistance has certain enduring consequences as well. In the case of oppositional forms as they existed at Spencer and the meaning that oppositional forms take, the very system of reified knowledge and its attendant forms remains intact and, in fact, is further reproduced. This is so because resistance to school-based knowledge through regenerative knowledge does not oppose as much as it forms a separate reality. Regenerative knowledge and the attendant forms such as goofing off, smoking, skipping, while they do rise out of the extant system of social relations within the school and to some extent resist those social relations, do not directly challenge them because any collective self-consciousness of how reified knowledge ultimately leads to estranged labor is absent. Students know something is 'wrong' but they cannot easily articulate what is to be done. Consequently, we see forms of resistance arise, interpreted selectively by students and contingent upon their degree of affiliation to reified knowledge, and reinforced in part through cultural capital outside of the school. But the meaning attached to such forms is more a reaction to, not conscious opposition of, basic social relations.[3]

Opposition forms may have a greater effect on anti-schoolers like Don and his group than 'mainstream' groups such as Chris and his friends because these forms take on so much of a meaning (both qualitatively and quantitatively) for anti-schoolers in the school. The significance of these forms continues on into adulthood, serving to doom to a great extent the student to a life of the hands rather than of the mind. This, then, is how regenerative knowledge itself selects out and affects students differentially, often on a class basis. Yet, forms of regenerative knowledge tend also to affect all students equally in that their creation and emergence serves to reinforce the interpretation that systems of social relations are not meant to be confronted and critically analyzed, but rather resisted through these opposition forms. And in the rise of the forms themselves, indeed the meaning attached to them, the basic precepts of the system of social relations as they exist in the school remain unaffected, unexamined. The more activities such as goofing off persist, the more they act as a release from the system of estranged labor in the school and the more that system continues. It seems then that systems of regenerative knowledge, while they are present in the form of resistance, are also present as reproductive of that very system they oppose. As participants, as creators of those cultural forms, students are reproducing forms that will damn them to expressions of reaction but will not foster critical opposition. In this building of culture, students participate in the building of reproductive processes that make it likely they will suffer the same fate elsewhere, especially in the workplace and through that 'civic responsibility' that is the purpose of the junior high school. It is, it appears, very much as Marx said:

> Thus through estranged labour man not only engenders his relationship to the object and to the act of production as to powers that are alien and hostile to him; he also engenders the relationship in which other men stand to his production and to his product, and the relationship in which he stands to these other men. Just as he begets his own production as the loss of his reality, as his punishment; just as he begets his own product as a loss, as a product not belonging to him; so he begets the dominion of the one who does not produce over production and over the product. Just as he estranges from himself his own activity, so he confers to the stranger activity which is not his own.[4]

8
Summary and conclusions

> Man is an animal suspended in webs of significance which he himself has spun. I take culture to be those webs, and the analysis of it to be therefore not an experimental science in search of law but an interpretive one in search of meaning (Clifford Geertz, *The Interpretation of Cultures*, New York, Basic Books, 1973).

In this story, written as a result of two years of fieldwork, I have attempted to describe the culture of a small group of early adolescents in a junior high school. I learned that junior high students do many things in the course of their careers as students. They attend classes, participate in athletic events, sing in the school chorus, attend student council meetings, eat lunch together, talk before, during, and after class, and engage in a wide range of behavior, all while part of the environment of the school. Through it all, students have a propensity to coalesce into friendship groups that provide, for many, the real meaning of their daily life in the school. Yet, student associational patterns are important beyond the mere fact that they exist. In the first place, even though students actually spend far more of their time in class under the guise of instruction than in any other activity, the students themselves indicate that they spend most of their time hanging around together or engaging in group-centered activities, either during or outside the context of the class. In this sense, the students' perspective of time spent in school differs quite dramatically from that held by an external 'objective' observer who can clock student activities throughout a normal operating day. Second, and related to this first point, students – no matter what their level of academic performance – de-emphasized the academic side of school in their interactions together. Rarely did I hear students discussing grades, assignments, or what subject-matter had been covered in class. Instead, they spent most of their time discussing after-school activities or the activities of friends in and out of school. Finally, group-oriented behavior was so important and pervasive that it was expressed in a variety of ways and affected significant portions of the daily routine of the school.

Group-initiated social forms generated what I have called regenerative knowledge, a knowledge that is interpretive in nature and the meaning for which depends largely on the contextual nature of the social setting in which it is based – the material world from which it arises. As such, regenerative knowledge emerges from the interactive processes between the formalized, explicit purposes of the school and the life that students create for themselves within the organizational boundaries established by the school.

The focus on regenerative knowledge places the school in a different perspective than that adhered to by most educators. If we were to examine the reality described in many teacher-training courses or that presented about curriculum, we would expect to find students preoccupied with the academic side of school; indeed this academic side would most specifically be characterized by versions of what we saw at Spencer – reified knowledge. The assumptions are clear in most curricula, no matter what the approach: students attend school to learn the subject-matter at hand and the favored curriculum – be it individualized, tutorialized, group centered, teacher centered, inductive, deductive, programmed or whatever – will do that best. School, then, according to the conventional wisdom of educators, is congruent with learning and formal learning is what school is all about. Charters speaks to this issue in this discussion about the relationship between social psychology and education and, while our focus is social and cultural, the point is no less relevant for our purposes:

> Probably nowhere are the thoughtways of educators (many of them) and of social psychologists more disparate than in their views regarding the importance of the immediate interpersonal environment in affecting behavior. As the instructional process has been formulated, especially in educational psychology, the student's personal ties to his peers, his location in a system of

> informal social relationships, the personal meanings he attaches to being in class and in school, the views of the teacher and the instructional devices imposed on him – all these are regarded as error items, to be controlled by randomization, in pursuit of the real determinants of academic performance. In effect, the student is conceived of as an isolated atom, removed from its social molecule, responsive only to impersonal, technical events arrayed before it.[1]

Challenging the traditional perspective on schooling permits us to begin to question both the manner in which our formal educational system is structured, as well as to examine the complex construction of the lives of those people who pass through schools, thereby changing, sustaining, and defining them. We see, for example, that there is more to the process of schooling than the correspondence between the intentions of educators and educational outputs as registered by exposure to, as Charters notes, the 'technical events' arranged before the student.

In examining this facet of student life at Spencer, I have proposed that this regenerative knowledge is important in and of itself, but also as it pertains to a knowledge form equal to the knowledge on which the formalized curriculum was based. By 'equal' I mean explicitly that the student 'learns' as much if not more from the knowledge derived from strategies such as goofing off, joking behavior, and other comparable activities as he or she might learn in math or English class. *What* it is they learn and the ultimate consequences of this knowledge constitutes the basis of our discussion in this chapter.

Three fundamental issues grow from our inquiry into the lives of students at Harold Spencer and warrant examination here. First we must examine the structural regularities of the school to understand how that structure, exemplified through the reified knowledge transmitted by way of its forms, serves as *a productive force* with the potential to transform the raw material of human will and behavior toward an entity ready to participate in labor exchange. Second, we need to address more fully another equally critical productive force – that 'web of significance' as Geertz terms it, that is the world-view generated through the student interpretive structure. These two forces both oppose and reinforce each other as they are contextually interpreted and acted upon by the students in the school. To the degree that such an interaction produces knowledge about school and learning, and eventually comes to enter the world of commodity exchange (Figure 1.1 on p. 22), then a culture of early adolescence has import for its relevance to the society in which it exists. Finally, then, we need to place the concept of 'culture' into a perspective that is broad but at the same time focused. We can do this by probing into the fundamental meaning of the term 'adolescence' as that concept is translated into educational practice in the junior high school. In so doing, we return ultimately to a fundamental issue posed at the beginning of the book – the purposes of junior high schools in our society today.

Structural attributes of the student role

The question of why it is that students play a relatively passive role in the academic life within the school, and what they come to know as a direct result of this role, is directly related to the manner in which the education of students is organized. Schools, like any other organization, have distinct means by which the products or clients are processed. Understanding this production process helps us to understand what the objects of that process experience – as human beings and in human terms.

The basis of structure

First the school is hierarchically arranged in such a manner that the principal is at the apex of authority and students are at the bottom.[2] In between are the teachers who maintain certain prerogatives not held by the principal. In Spencer's operation, the principal was the final arbitrator of all matters pertaining to the implementation of district policy in the school. As we saw, his authority covered both teachers and students when it came to issues that might impair his decision-making abilities, although he did leave the operation of specific classes to the teachers. The teachers, for the most part subject-matter specialists, controlled activities in their own classroom and arranged activities in which students were to be engaged. The students themselves had virtually no formal power or authority and were not included in any significant way in discussions pertinent to the daily operations of the school.

Connected with the hierarchical authority arrangements is a second distinguishing factor of the structure of the school, that of student separateness. Students were seen and treated as something distinct from adults – as entities removed from the world of adults. In this sense, students were viewed largely as empty vessels only partially imbued with the abilities and maturity to hold responsible positions in student government or to make decisions about the nature of the instructional process. Their formal educative process was viewed much like a car moving down an assembly line, with components being progressively added until such time that the product was recognizable and believed to be complete.

If the structure of the school was ordered so that students' knowledge was 'added to' as they proceeded through the educational system, then we would expect the presence of an instructional style congruent with that characteristic. At Spencer, that style was largely one of information giving, with the teacher either providing the information for students to learn or establishing a curriculum that guided the student into standardized and known ends. This characteristic, well documented in Chapter 3, was viewed by teachers as the predominant mode of instruction. Instruction at Spencer was so ordered that students received information, and teacher assessment of students was dependent upon student indications of how well they could demonstrate their grasp of the knowledge disseminated.

To facilitate the education of students in masses, two other structural modes were present. First, students were processed in large groups to classes where they were provided essentially the same treatment. Students proceeded to and from almost all classes in groups of twenty-five to thirty-five where they were exposed to similar substantive areas presented in a common code. (The math lab may appear as an exception to this, but it isn't. All students were subject to the same material and it was presented in the same fashion; only the rate at which the students completed the material differed.) Second, activity within classes tended to be routinized so that predictability could be built-in. Classes began and ended at set times, attendance was taken and turned into the office, and classroom procedures were standardized so that students and teachers basically knew what to expect in any given class.

All of these structural factors support each other and facilitate the orderly process of mass education in the school. The hierarchical arrangement facilitates the decision-making process; if people do not agree with the decisions being made (or not being made), then at least they know who is making them. Because students are treated as products and only minimally involved in decisions relative to their formal life in the school, the complexity of decision-making is reduced. The instructional style of information giving operates much more effectively when routines are standardized and when students are processed in large units rather than by individuals or smaller units. The organization of the school then makes the type of education as exists at Spencer much more manageable and less complicated. Teachers can get on with their task of information promulgation and students can adapt readily to their role of information receivers.

School structure and its unintended consequences

While these conditions facilitate the processing of large numbers of students through their junior high career, the very presence of this efficient organizational arrangement produces unintended consequences. First, because of the flow of students throughout the school day to and from classes and within the classes themselves is done *en masse*, significant portions of time are spent on organizational maintenance activities. In Chapter 3, I proposed that a full 45 per cent of every day was spent in non-instructional tasks – going to and from class, eating lunch, giving directions, passing out materials, collecting papers, waiting for the class to finish an assignment, and other such activities. Thus, in the typical six-and-a-half-hour school day, students were free from instructional duties requiring their immediate attention for two to three of those hours per day. Teachers continually impressed upon students that they should not 'waste time' in class, but few teachers realized that the entire school day contained a large amount of what was 'wasted' in so far as the manifest purposes of the school were concerned.[3] Yet, had they been aware of the large block of time in which students were free from the constraints of instructional activities, teachers could have done little about it. The problem was not as much in the teachers' ineffective use of time as much as it was in the structure of activities endemic to the organizational arrangement itself.

A second unintended consequence of the organizational form of Harold Spencer was that of minimal demands by the school for involvement of students in school-sponsored instructional as well as non-instructional activities. The main requirements made of students while in class were that they do what they were told to do – participate in class when called upon, hand in papers when required, take tests, and maintain themselves in an orderly and obedient fashion. It made little difference if a student did more than required, as the only 'reward' was the possibility of a higher grade, a future reward salient to only the minority of students, and a norm not important within the friendship groups. Indeed, so little was required that a student like Don could skip school an average of one day a week and still get mostly A's and B's. Even involvement in extra-curricular affairs was at a minimum and, with the exception of athletics and some music-drama activities, such involvement was often of a ritualistic nature.

This structural arrangement thus leads to an emphasis on students' interaction with reified knowledge primarily through the manipulation of rules in order to ensure relatively successful action. Here, students are concerned with the activities as outlined in Chapter 3 – getting by, getting the right answer, and in ascertaining a level of expectation and doing little more than is required to complete a unit or course. It is this type of activity that schools require most of students, as the formal curriculum and the manner of its implementation demands that students adopt a largely 'confrontive' knowledge style. By confrontive I mean that dispositions, information, and facts are arranged for interface with students by those in authority to arrange them; these dispositions and information are then presented to students who are told, in essence, to absorb it. In anthropological terms, then, the school is engaged largely in enculturative functions, bringing the young into the larger society much as Plato said 'like putting sight into blind eyes.'

The assumptions reflective in school structure – the technical interest

To examine the varied aspects of the school and its effects on student experiences, the conceptual framework of the German social philosopher Jürgen Habermas is helpful.[4] In fact, his ideas have served as the basis of our discussion of reified and regenerative knowledge found throughout the study. Habermas's 'critical theory' centers around the concept of 'knowledge' and the attendant determinants of what counts as knowledge as well as how such knowledge is used. Since the assumptions about knowledge pervade schools and are reflective in its daily routines, it is useful for us to examine briefly each of these dimensions.

First, Habermas sees knowledge being differentiated by what he terms '*cognitive interests*' or the orientations and basic assumptions about what constitutes knowledge. Such cognitive interests serve as basic discriminators between types of knowledge, and help to define knowledge and the nature of the assumptions about the cognitive processes that are part of coming to 'know' something. In this sense, then, the acceptance of 'facts' on an *a priori* basis, to be used as part of a deductive argument, may be said to be part of a knowledge paradigm of the highest quality, given a presence of consensus about the 'truth' of those facts. On the other hand, facts that are not universally accepted but which exist owing to their acceptance by a restricted group of individuals (such as a subculture) and which have come to be known, not empirically but contextually (as though sharing an experience), may be said to be a knowledge paradigm of a different order and one less acceptable to a majority because of its restricted nature. Each of these paradigms and their attendant assumptions constitutes then a different 'cognitive interest.' Each may be reflective of different structural arrangements.

Given the presence of a cognitive interest, there exist related modes of inquiry or *knowledge systems* that establish the procedures by which one comes to 'know' within the boundaries of any one cognitive interest. The focus on such 'knowledge systems' pertains to the specific procedures by which one comes to 'know.' In the first case noted above, the manner by which one comes to know deductively may involve the ordering of facts in such a manner so as to arrive at a conclusion given the standards that determine how one arrives at conclusions. The procedures of laboratory science would be such an example for, if one accepts the assumptions of what is 'real' in the physical sciences, then there exists a fairly well prescribed set of procedures for arriving at conclusions. Alternatively, one may come to know not through predefined procedures agreed upon by all, but through a process of 'building' knowledge much as children may do in games or religious communities may do as they make sense of experiences through the creation of spiritual explanations.

The final dimension referred to by Habermas is the type of *human activity* engaged in as a result of the acceptance of certain cognitive interests and modes of inquiry. Here the important focus is upon the use to which knowledge is put – that is, how the knowledge is applied and for what purpose. Returning again to the examples noted before, knowledge in the area of scientific inquiry, depending as it does upon empirical modes of inquiry, typically is used for specified problem-solving purposes – that is, to accomplish a specified end. On the other hand, knowledge that is generated (rather than applied), while it may be used for similar purposes, is more likely to be used as a form of communication and understanding, the basis of which *could* lead to problem-solving.

Generally speaking, then, what 'counts' as knowledge affects the process by which knowledge comes to be 'known' which in turn affects the type of activity engaged in as a result of the knowledge existing. Habermas's scheme is useful because it delineates the basis of what is known, how it comes to be known, and how that knowledge is used. This tri-part framework seems particularly useful for our purposes because it focuses directly upon those situations and phenomena wherein competing knowledge systems may exist, thereby permitting a clearer explanation of the *basis* of competing knowledge systems. It should be clear by now that any institution wherein socialization is a prime function (as it is with schools) is one wherein such competing knowledge systems will be present. The fact that knowledge is defined, maintained, and altered within collective (rather than individual) contexts makes the origins, processes and uses of knowledge in schools even more important to understand.

The dominant cognitive interest reinforced in most schools is what Habermas would call a *technical interest*. The assumption of technical interests pertains to the manipulation of a given environment so as to control that environment in the terms that the environment defines. It involves gaining control over reality as that reality is assumed by others to exist, thus the term 'technical' so as to emphasize 'how' rather than 'what.' Technical interests, as manifested in the curriculum at Spencer, focused on the 'how' more than the 'what' issues. Specifically, the orientation of knowledge at Spencer was for students to confront the curriculum in such a way that they successfully met it on the terms in which it was presented. There was little space for a dialog with the information presented, and the assumptions underlying knowledge were less important than the manipulation of knowledge as presented.

The pre-eminence of technical interest in turn leads to a mode of knowledge – a way of understanding – based largely upon establishing a relationship between elements of reality in a linear/deductive fashion. Said differently, it is the understanding that comes from coalescing 'facts' into a series of means–ends relationships. This knowledge mode is what we have termed *reified knowledge* (what Habermas calls *empirical–analytic*) because it is the knowledge of the empirical sciences. In this mode of knowledge the emphasis is upon causal relationships, the component parts of which are 'facts.' Acceptance of these facts is part of the definition of what is 'known' to exist. Consequently, 'facts' are not treated as abstractions that are problematic but rather as givens that are 'real,' and the origin of which is not questioned. This particular form of knowledge specifically led to the emphasis in math of arranging numbers in a particular fashion to produce the answer–conclusion. Similarly, playing 'Home on the Range' in Hackett's music class produced the concept of 'melody,' and with it the consequent association that musical arrangements produced 'melodies.' The ordering of information into relatively static explanatory systems of this nature is a characteristic of empirical–analytical modes of inquiry, and was the preferred and established mode of inquiry sought by most teachers at Spencer.

Finally, in a technical cognitive interest and an empirical–analytical mode of inquiry (reified knowledge), the dominant social action is *instrumental*, or purposive–rational action governed by technical orientations and empirical–analytical knowledge. The use of technical interests is in the application of information to the solving of predefined problems. This knowledge is to be used for defined purposes, and conclusions are drawn not for their own sake but as they can be applied to the solution of specified problems. At Spencer, the ordering of technical interests to instrumental action is best typified by the required action of students to solve dilemmas posed for them in advance by teachers, and for the purposes of 'succeeding,' 'passing,' 'getting by,' etc.

Now if technical interests and their attendant knowledge systems and social action dominate the formal structure of the school, what does involvement in such interests on the part of students teach them? It is interesting to note here that there is a close association between the assumptions of technical interests and the basis of the labor process in modern bureaucratic–capitalist societies. Labor or work is itself based upon technical interests because it emphasizes the manipulation of available information for predefined ends, normally the production of some 'product.' That this product is produced, not for its own sake, but as the labor used to make it is exchanged for an intermediate commodity (wages) which in turn is exchanged for other products (food, shelter, etc.) means that work, for most of us today, is a process regulated by the assumptions of technical interests and instrumental action. This is especially true because the manipulation of information inherent in the labor process is not normally regulated by those producing the product but rather is controlled by those controlling the capital used to make the product.

Such was no less true at Harold Spencer where the passive forms of student involvement in work activities, student proclivity to view the assumptions about work as emanating from those in authority (the controllers of capital), and the fundamental role of students in exchanging their labor power for intermediate products (evaluations) which in turn were used for other purposes, all bear a remarkable similarity to basic assumptions about work in capitalist societies. Thus it is reasonable to conclude that the emphasis upon technical cognitive interests in the school is remarkably reproductive of a cultural process found in the workplace. Thus it is for this reason that, through reified knowledge, students enter the earliest stages of capitalist labor formation wherein the fundamental assumptions of the appropriation of labor from those producing labor power are present.

The discussion thus far should not be construed as a denigration of technical interest, reified knowledge, or instrumental action. Indeed, the function of the school and formalized educational systems in so enculturating students has long been recognized, and there is no doubt that students must be equipped with factual apparatus, the origin and nature of which cannot always be addressed. There is, as Dreeben has pointed out, a demand by society that students learn principles of universality, or the categorization of knowledge on the basis of rational–specific criteria rather than on the basis of the characteristics of persons exhibiting the criteria.[5] Such makes for a more smoothly functioning, cohesive, and predictable society, certainly necessary in any complex culture. Others such as Cohen have stated that, in any society, the purpose of education is to 'shape men's minds' in such a manner that they respond to a set of symbols and stimuli in a roughly predictable fashion, thus ensuring the survivability of the state.[6]

The issue for discussion then is not so much the presence of cognitive interests of the genre described herein, but rather the claim, implicitly if not explicitly argued at Harold Spencer as in other schools, that this is the *only* type of legitimate knowledge that students need, or indeed that it is the relevant standard against which all other knowledge is measured. It is this claim that predominates in a society based on the prerogatives of hierarchy for in such a system the traditions of position and the privileges of class often determine the legitimacy of knowledge. Consequently, in state societies wherein education serves the purpose primarily of fostering allegiances among the young to the state and wherein the young are prepared for life in that society as that society has defined it, we would expect reified knowledge – transmitted through hierarchical organizational structures – to predominate, involving rather superficially the active collective involvement of the young in the creation of possibly divergent cognitive interests, modes of knowledge, and social action.

Apparently, students think otherwise. Given the presence of large amounts of time and the relatively minimal demands made of students while they are in school, they have time to involve themselves in what to them are rewarding activities that provide degrees of prestige and power – those social activities that they engage in with their friends. For as long as students comply with the demands made upon them and do not incur the wrath of Edwards or Pall or any one teacher, then they are free to be in the school to talk about and work out activities that have meaning to them. If students are only minimally involved in the classroom setting, if little allocation is made for a student like this who, despite being a good student, must participate in the same activities at the same rate as the slowest student, and if students have little control over their destiny in an institution in which they spend such a great portion of their waking hours, then they will perceive themselves to exist in a separate reality, one that, while unclear to adults, constitutes the students' making sense out of their world as they experience it.

The derivation of meaning within structure

The theme of this book suggests that student labor is mostly estranged, and because of this students attempt to reappropriate relevant portions of their lives in school so that they, rather than others, control it. The knowledge that grows from such reappropriative strategies is regenerative in nature, as it is based on the context of action and the collective interpretations generated by students sharing similar experiences.

The assumptions of student meaning – the practical interest

The involvement of students in creating such an interactional network is reflective of a practical cognitive interest in Habermas's critical theory. By practical, he means that the assumptions of such knowledge are not related directly to instrumental action as defined by the assumptions of knowledge, but rather are focused upon the creation and clarification of meaning, the attainment of communication, and the resultant production of collective and mutual ties between individuals into a community of individuals sharing common belief systems. Practical interests concern knowledge that grows out of collective interaction, not knowledge that precedes and is the basis of collective interaction. Accordingly, under a practical interest, the parameters of knowledge are not predefined, but rather are generated contextually by individuals sharing interpretations of the material world. That knowledge so generated comes to be 'accepted' by participants leads to its categorical separation from the knowledge of technical interests, which is dependent on the legitimacy furnished through 'objective' criteria.

Such practical interests are related to what we have termed *regenerative* knowledge systems – what Habermas calls a hermeneutic mode of knowledge, or one that is largely interpretive and symbolic in nature. In regenerative knowledge, the validity of propositions and actions is not to be found in their technical or external basis, but rather through the internal understanding of these propositions and actions and the meaning attached to them. Regenerative knowledge is particularly important because it is based on a cognitive interest stressing the attainment of collectivity and interdependence between individuals sharing similar experiences within a social or organizational structure. In the student world of Harold Spencer this dimension was all important for, as the students themselves made clear, the 'real' knowledge of school (for them) was not found in the empirical–analytical mode of knowledge, but rather through the interaction with friends and the fabric of meaning generated within.

Such practical cognitive interests and modes of knowledge result in a particular form of human action, known as *communicative* action in Habermas's critical theory. In communicative action, we find as its intent the emphasis upon reciprocity and mutuality of social interaction, such that the norms and agreements that rise from such mutuality become understood by actors and become binding. This type of action is exactly that found in Don's and Chris's world, through goofing off, and in the exercise of student power – all governed by variously binding consensual norms defining reciprocal expectations about behavior. In this sense, then, while instrumental action is governed by empirical rules and strategies, communicative action is governed by symbolically understood rules and strategies.

If technical interest and reified knowledge is the basis of 'work' in modern societies, then practical interests and regenerative knowledge is the basis of another fundamental human activity – the existence of meaning and understanding that grows from social interaction. Such meaning and understanding comes about not through the arrangement of predefined facts in order to produce a given product, but rather through relatively free social interaction wherein understanding arises through the manipulation of information controlled by those involved in creating the meaning. It is through practical interests that we find the antithesis of technical interests, for decisions about the basis of knowledge lie with those who produce the knowledge rather than through some outside criteria created and managed by those in control of the labor process. Technical interests in capitalist societies serve as the basis of labor and contribute to the estranged nature of labor; to the extent that the premises of estranged labor are resisted, that resistance is generated through the assumptions of practical interests.

The practical interest and student action: some contradictions

This framework proposed by Habermas permits us to examine the significance of the student world in a broader context, for behaviors such as those that students refer to as 'goofing off' are not just isolated cases of student misbehavior, exhibited in a random fashion over time. Rather, they are part of a complex and interdependent rite of friendship and associational patterns, all part of communicative action. Goofing off, as well, is a boundary-maintaining activity, with activities being inclusive of friends and exclusive of those whom the participants do not wish to include. Student humor in the classroom served a similar function, particularly the wise-cracking, plays on words, joke telling, and the series of anecdotes that often were ongoing between students like Chris, Paul, and Marty. Humor, like goofing off, often established or reaffirmed group membership in a symbolic but pervasive manner. Humor also provided students who engaged in it a sense of fate control, an ability to establish their own agenda of activities and to attempt to control aspects of the classroom environment normally not under their control.

Classroom activities such as goofing off and joking relationships rarely have been examined in terms of the meaning behind the acts and the purpose they serve for the students who engage in them. Most often these acts are seen to result from a lack of student interest in the instructional program. While they may, in part, be the result of this, such activities serve other purposes as well. They provide meaning to the students' daily existence in the school and solidify group interactions. Additionally, such activities are rarely engaged in independently but rather collectively, giving them a social meaning greater than the scope of the act itself. They provide the important mode of knowledge noted by Habermas – that of the establishment of community and mutuality. In this sense, then, such acts of student 'brinkmanship'[7] are not the isolated acts of individual students, but more often are the forms out of which grows regenerative knowledge.

Practical cognitive interests and the consequent regenerative knowledge growing from it is important for a number of reasons. First, as I already have pointed out, regenerative knowledge and its consequent social action – communicative action – grows out of the constant movement by students to reappropriate control in a setting where formal control is appropriated from them. In the labor process, students are separated from influencing both the means of production as well as the ends, and consequently are involved in what Marx termed estranged or alienated labor – labor in which 'as soon as no physical or other compulsion exists . . . is shunned like the plague.'[8] Appropriating control, then, and the emergence of understanding, interpretations and agreements as to the process by which that control is to be instituted and maintained, is a constitutive social process that cannot be understood outside the context in which it exists – herein a context within which the elements of the labor process are the fundamental determinants of subsequent communicative action.

Appropriating control is also deeply and closely attached to class cultures, as outlined earlier in the book. The 'identity of interests' noted by Thompson provides the potential for class-based appropriative processes to emerge, and these processes become particularly conditioned through the labor that constitutes the basis of the 'essential life activity' into which people are born and which helps shape those interests. It is for this reason that the practical interests and regenerative knowledge that predominate the working-class life of so many Spencer students is important, for it represents at least a partial reproduction of the class culture that predominates the estranged labor so typical of the adults in their families.

Accordingly, we need to understand (as Habermas makes clear) the fundamental ties between work and labor on the one hand and symbolic interaction on the other. Certain materialistic conditions (the predominance of hierarchy, the nature of the labor process) associated with, for example, technical cognitive interests, while they may breed knowledge that can serve as a productive force (reified knowledge within the context of bureaucratic organization) also influence, to a large extent, the shape of communicative action engaged in by students. In the same respect, practical cognitive interests that influence communicative action may mediate somewhat the instrumental action fostered by the school. A fundamental contradiction exists here, as noted by Waller some fifty years ago, and this contradiction is endemic to schooling wherein control is appropriated from those educated:

> From the fact that situations may be defined in different ways and by different groups arises a conflict of definitions of situations, and we may see the whole process of personal and group conflict which centers about the school as a conflict of contradictory definitions of situations. The fundamental problem of school discipline may be stated as the struggle of students and teachers to establish their own definitions of situations in the life of the school.[9]

It is in this sense that schooling that is based on the fundamental appropriation of control over labor in the productive process, as in work in any bureaucratic organization, is contradictory. For while it so appropriates that control from students, thereby achieving to some extent the instrumental action desired by the school, such schooling also creates, at the same time, the very conditions that give rise to communicative action. It is this communicative action that may serve as the very foundation for eventual labor-based opposition to the school-based cognitive interests and attendant organizational dynamics that gave it birth.

The student world and what is learned in school

The meaning of the student world

I have noted throughout that most students at Harold Spencer proceeded from day to day in rather a routine fashion in so far as 'success' in completing their academic requirements went. Some, like Roger, did not do as well as others, but the majority of students 'passed' their courses with average grades or better and the overwhelming majority moved on to the next level or grade. If seventh grade in 1973–4 was representative of the district at large, then 30 per cent of the high school class of 1979 enrolled in an institute of higher learning while the remaining 70 per cent worked, joined a branch of the military, traveled, or took up other activities. These students will be variously successful in whatever career they have chosen to follow. What is more, they will continue their educational and work career, complete with joys and frustrations they experienced at Spencer.

Student experiences in the school can be seen as preparation for life – not only through the acquisition of such specific skills as reading, mathematics and writing – but also in terms of the behaviors and modes of knowledge students came to accept and re-create. These behaviors include the recognition of authority, the ability to follow directions, the requisites of attendance and punctuality, and the acceptance of a limited role wherein they are restricted in the use of their abilities. The reified knowledge form that the school stresses is a knowledge that is rational, relatively preordained, and one in which students play a passive role in the process of knowledge acquisition, these parameters of knowledge acquisition stressing knowledge handed down rather than knowledge explored and tested. Such behaviors and patterns of knowledge are not unlike those that will be required of students when they enter the world of work.

The role of 'student,' then, is preparatory for roles that adolescents will occupy later in life. To adapt successfully to the student role facilitates later adaptations to roles as office workers, salespersons, assembly line workers, taxpayers, parents, church members and all other positions that open up as youth proceed through the life cycle. That the student, while in school, learns much that is necessary for later life, then, is no accident, for schools as organizations serve as 'boot camps' for teaching this role behavior. As we noted earlier, it is common knowledge that schools do in fact socialize, and one can reasonably expect that schools will socialize students in ways that reflect the larger society of which schools are an important part.

However, all is not so simple, for, as we have seen, there is no one-to-one correspondence between the cognitive interests stressed within the school and the social action engaged in by students. Student-initiated social action is primarily communicative action, not instrumental action, which is to say that students do not spend large portions of their time engaged in the realm of action as stressed in the school's organization of knowledge. Rather, we find the nascent forms of what amounts to resistance to reified knowledge and the commensurate action demanded, that resistance serving both to oppose and grow out of the manner in which knowledge is organized in the school.

Student role-taking and 'learning'

If we accept this view, then, we cannot help but speculate as to what students 'learn' through their participation in, indeed through, the very generation of such contradictory knowledge modes and social actions. The fact is that students must live in two somewhat distinct worlds of knowledge. The first is declared legitimate for the purpose of education but is characterized by the appropriation of control of student labor in return for commodities with an exchange-value. On the other hand, in the realm of regenerative knowledge, forms of action often are not officially sanctioned by the school, but the reappropriation of control through communicative action requires considerable effort on the part of students and serves as a form of resistance to school-based knowledge. In crossing and re-crossing between these two dimensions of knowledge – indeed in adapting successfully so as to proceed through the school curriculum – students learn behaviors and predispositions that help them, both directly and indirectly, with their school career. In examining what it is they have learned, two particularly important matters come to mind.

The ability to act out a role is one behaviour learned. I have spoken about how the students' definition of the situation is, in part, affected by the environment as experienced. They adopt strategies that, when acted out, make that environment more sensible. Yet these strategies do not occur in a behavioristic cause–effect relationship where certain structural conditions demand a certain role. While there may be general patterns, students still choose how they will interact with friends during the school day, when to use humor in the context of the classroom, with what teachers a joking relationship is possible, how to beat the system to catch a fast smoke, or how to talk a teacher out of an assignment or a grade. To this degree, students decide what part of themselves will play a particular role at a point in time and what role will be played at other times. The discussion of student power in Chapter 7 amply illustrates this point.

Additionally, as students have the prerogative to take on a role, they also have the flexibility of refuting what appears to be a normative role. For example, much of the use of humor and goofing off is in the form of challenges to teacher authority in such a way as to avoid incurring negative sanctions. While the student role generally required passivity, obedience, and respect for authority, students often challenged that role by actions which were vague or which were so obviously humorous that teachers did not feel threatened. In other cases, where a teacher knew a student to be defiant and prone to 'resist authority,' the student might, like Roger, go on a streak where they said 'yes, sir' or 'yes, ma'am' and be a model student, all to be what others did not expect them to be.

In learning to play at roles that are an outgrowth of less desirable situations, one might say that students are learning to be adaptive. They are learning to face a variety of environments, assess their role in that environment, and then to adapt to it by taking from it what they can on their own terms and to ignore or disregard the rest. We all do this in a variety of contexts – we keep the job we don't like because it pays well, we avoid conflict with our peers by stressing conviviability, we are good providers in the home but not very respectful of our spouses.

Some may see such adaptation as a positive sign, certainly necessary to the stability in any institution. Adaptation as resistance may be evidence of the pliability of the human will and the tendency for human beings to oppose, in whatever form they are able, curtailments of human freedom. Such 'resistance,' then, may be championed because it is symbolic of the attempts by students to own the assumptions of their own knowledge systems, thereby rejecting, to some extent, the assumptions of school-based knowledge. Such role playing and the commensurate focus of students on the assumptions of regenerative knowledge can, however, turn on itself, and therein further bind students to the very technical interests which class-based practical interests often serve to resist.

I have come to believe that much student 'resistance,' rather than constituting a revolt against the perceived unfairness or lack of significant regard which the school structure generates, merely is an escape from its anxieties. It gives the impression of power while ignoring the conditions under which relative powerlessness exists. It represents the beginning stages of what Slater has called being 'alone together' in which individuals and groups retreat and escape, leaving the structure still intact to enact its toll on others.[10] We do this as adults for example, when we tolerate our jobs while getting our 'kicks' from leisure-time activities, those activities serving to 'put off' our discontent about work. Our relaxation through leisure does not change the monotony of work, rather it makes it qualitatively less important in the life of the worker. Also too, as we increasingly subjugate ourselves to consumptive patterns that often delude us with a false sense of happiness, we turn our attention from the political, economic, and cultural realities that make never-ending consumption a way of life in advanced technological states. Thus the fundamental problem with the forms of resistance that are adaptations *to* school-wide emphasis on technical cognitive interests is that these forms too often continue on and ultimately leave unaddressed the structural regularities of estranged labor.

We arrive, then, at the rather striking conclusion that it is not just the process of schooling as organized through technical cognitive interests that serves as a productive force. Quite simply, the school does not have that extent of a domination over students – their time or attention – to serve in a fashion so as to grind out stamped pieces of machinery that conveniently fit into some societal assemblage. Rather, it is the very student culture itself – the totality of action and beliefs about those actions – that serves as a productive force. Through cultural processes that are constitutive of regenerative knowledge systems, the raw material of daily life in the school is transformed into a way of understanding life – a world-view. Such a world-view – including as it does an understanding about organizational life, authority, labor, and power – is transformed into a commodity or a product that comes to be exchanged in the dominant system of economic and cultural exchange, state capitalism in our case.[11] Even regenerative knowledge production must therefore be seen in a materialist sense, for it grows out of an interpretive process wherein people do in fact make themselves within that structural world in which they live.

Toward rethinking schooling and youth

Through the conceptual scheme suggested by Habermas, I have attempted to show the relationship between knowledge orientations (or cognitive interests), knowledge systems (the process by which knowledge is considered to be 'legitimate'), and subsequent social action engaged in as a result of what is 'known.' This framework is useful because it permits us to describe, in comparative terms, the fundamental knowledge orientations of schools as educative agencies within a state society as well as those that grow from the activities of the students whose labor power is exchanged within the school.

Technical and practical cognitive interests appear to be contradictory, and we need to understand whether the opposition of knowledge is a natural state of affairs or if such different interests can be compatible. Is a synthesis possible between the legitimate purpose of education – the presentation of basic factual knowledge – and claims by human actors that their labor power is to be controlled by them? Will productive processes of schooling that appropriate that labor lead to the creation of a separate cognitive interest whose nature will be to reappropriate control where possible? The basic productive processes of schooling are critical here, and, to address this issue, we need first return to our discussion in Chapter 3 of teaching and its organization, and examine more closely the organizational correlates of technical interests and reified knowledge.

Teachers, teaching, and technical interests

We have noted throughout how the cognitive interests assumed by schools such as Spencer result in patterns of estranged labor for many students, such that they have but a modicum of control over defining the means and ends of educational work. Such a need for human actors to engage in free forms of man's 'essential life activity' results in the intense peer interactions of many students and strengthens the norms and ideational systems extant within those groups. Yet the material and productive process also limits the role of teachers and influences *their* perspectives and beliefs about students and the learning process. Living, working in and making sense of the environment in which they operate influences the propensity for teachers to view students through 'variety reducing' outlooks (those limiting the number and scope of relevant characteristics), thus enabling teachers to handle the range of inputs and variability present throughout the day. This in turn leads toward standardization as an important aspect of the school's emphasis on technical interests, reified knowledge and instrumental action.

The manner by which teachers differentiated between students at Harold Spencer illustrates how we can understand the effects of organizational constraints on teachers and the resultant standardization of student characteristics. Teacher differentiation of students was based upon somewhat visible but often sketchy criteria.

Teachers usually mentioned *effort*, *ability*, and *personal criteria* as important factors. The importance of *effort* was especially strong and teachers placed considerable faith in students who tried hard and persevered, even though they might not accomplish much in the way of visible 'learning.' To teachers, student 'effort' provided a relevant and meaningful subjective factor whereby students could readily be assessed and by which discrepancies between actual and potential performance could be mediated.

The premium that teachers placed on effort appeared somewhat excessive, for effort was as much an index of conduct as it was an indication that a student who was trying hard was not likely to be goofing off in class. Yet, consider that during any given day, between 150 and 180 students passed through the teachers' room. While the teacher was able to learn each child's name and recognize their most visible traits and behaviors, often there was little other opportunity to know the student's more subtle abilities, interests, or assets. 'Effort' was a criterion those behaviors of which were visible and which could be applied to all students. It was deemed relevant because it facilitated both the learning of skills as well as 'proper' behaviors necessary for adaptation in the larger world. What is more, teachers viewed effort as something that, while not measurable, required their collective professional judgment. Using this judgment enabled teachers to make relatively quick and (to them) meaningful decisions about students on terms that had considerable applicability to the successful operation of their own role.

The teacher's designation of student *ability* as an important tool to differentiate among students was simplified by attributing ability either to factors present in the student's family/home life or to the experiences of the student in elementary school. In either case, both contributing factors were external to the junior high school and largely beyond the control of the junior high teacher. Such a facile explanation of the origins of student ability, while it may seem to be a form of 'buck passing,' still makes some sense when considering the confusion that exists about the origins of ability and the effects of schooling versus the influence of the family and other environmental factors. Teachers had neither the time, inclination, nor the resources to make sophisticated demarcations between students in so far as why some seemed more able than others. The attribution of ability to some outside power, while incomplete, still is somewhat understandable as a manner by which teachers could make sense of their environment.

Finally, teachers commonly used *personal criteria* related to such background knowledge as family conditions and the performance of older brothers and sisters in school to explain the results of standardized tests as well as to assess general ability levels. Not all teachers used these tests in their classes and not all teachers referred to the standardized achievement tests given each year. Yet I found those teachers who did use such information embellished it with their own information gathered over time. Thus a student who did well on such tests but poorly in class was said to be an 'underachiever,' while one who performed better in class than the test scores indicated was often dubbed an 'overachiever.' The use of this background information served to explain test results, something the tests did not provide. While the scores themselves may have provided an 'objective' definition of the student's level, they did not explain *why* the scores came out in the manner in which they did. Only the teacher, through his or her knowledge of the student, could provide this information. Such background information served to provide simplistic (if somewhat simplified) explanations of scores, and reduced the uncertainty over discrepancies between test and classroom performance.[12]

The beliefs about differences between students and the instructional procedures as practiced in schools like Spencer are outcomes one would expect in the general education of over 1000 students in one building in a space of six hours a day and for 180 days a year. Standardized procedures such as the massing of students, the establishment of routines to facilitate handling of a large number of students over short periods of time, and the organization of knowledge in such a way that learning is seen to be the dissemination of technical information that students are expected to know – all give rise to the propensity of teachers to assume variety-reducing belief systems. These standardized procedures, in turn, are buttressed further by the existence of hierarchical lines of authority, the separation of students from decisions affecting their life in school, the passing of information from teacher to student, and the routtinization of maintenance procedures. Mass education that is predicted on the assumption that technical cognitive interests determined by the school are the primary objective of learning can do little but perpetuate standardized organizational processes which, in the end, contribute to superficial assumptions about student characteristics relevant to knowledge.

To the extent, then, that teachers come to view the schooling of students through the assumptions of reified knowledge, the ideology of teachers regarding students reflects a materialist-based cultural form. *It* too grows out of the ways by which teachers create their own history as they make and are made by that materialist world. The manner in which schools are organized to distribute that knowledge is part of that material world, for that organization has associated with it the assumptions that are ingrained in the history of the capitalist state.[13]

Schooling, adolescence, and state hegemony

Life at Harold Spencer illustrates that the schooling of junior high youth in our society is based on providing a somewhat standardized array of experiences predetermined for everyone. This homogeneity is accomplished, in part, by conceptualizing students in a predefined manner and then handling most learning situations uniformly and routinely. The typical instructional modalities exist in a manner so that student homogeneity is demanded, else the system becomes discordant by generating more variety than it can handle. Still, it is not that students are overtly coerced into this standardization of treatment, but simply that they must learn to react to appropriate institutional definitions when necessary, and to learn those to be given – beyond question. The school, then, as Jules Henry once said, 'metamorphoses the child, giving it the kind of Self the school can manage, and then proceeds to minister unto the Self it has made.'[14]

In so ministering unto the kind of self it has made, education as it is formally legitimated and controlled in schools such as Spencer, exists as a hegemonic system for those youths involved in it. By hegemonic I refer, as do Gramsci and Williams, to those formal meanings, values, and beliefs that a dominant group or class develops and propagates.[15] In the process of schooling at Spencer, such domination takes place through those dynamics of schooling that limit the variety of sanctioned cognitive interests, knowledge forms, and actions, and which operate so that students participate unknowingly in action that weds them further to domination. The resultant hegemony thus reinforces, to a considerable extent, the belief that most of what is 'known' is linear and reified, and that it is controlled, disseminated, and legitimated by those who have the authority to do it. In schools such as Spencer, however, the pervasiveness of technical interests (and accordingly, instrumental action) exists not out of the conscious manipulation or control by any person or group of persons, but rather emerged out of a constellation of values and beliefs that has emerged from the historical and contextual forces productive of an educational system, the nature of which is rarely questioned. To the extent that critical issues such as the domination of reified knowledge and the attendant separation of students from the control of their labor continue unexamined, the reproduction of such patterns constitutes a hegemony over the lives of students.

Yet the domination of knowledge forms through the schooling process does not, in and of itself, constitute hegemony. Rather, hegemony is any lived system of values and meanings which, as experienced, become mutually confirming in such a way that they dominate and subordinate the whole process of living. This domination saturates to such a depth that political and economic regularities are not questioned but rather infuse everyday life so as to become commonplace and commonsense. It is in this fashion, then, that forms of regenerative knowledge, themselves often resistant of the dominant technical interests of the school, serve also to accelerate domination of the existent productive process. This occurs through the proclivity of students to use communicative action for its own sake rather than as a forum for opposition against the domination of the political–economic framework that legitimates technical cognitive interests. A hegemony exists, then, through the percolation of the dominant productive forces into the very cultural processes spawned by and through the student culture, leading students to live out the very hegemony they resist.

Finally, hegemony becomes even more complete because the dominance of technical cognitive interests – translated through reified knowledge – turns knowledge and information from a raw state into a commodity, the presence of which serves the state in the terms the state has defined for itself and its members. Reified knowledge becomes a commodity because such knowledge is not entertained for its own sake but ultimately as the labor process transforms it from its natural state to something with 'exchange-value,' in Marx's terms.[16] Such exchange-value comes to mean that the commodities so created have an independent life of their own, so they can be transferred between buyers and sellers in such a fashion that the meaning of the commodities becomes detached from the labor that created them.

Of course, as I have discussed elsewhere, such hegemony is never complete and never subverts totally indigenous cultures. Rather, the 'good sense' (as Gramsci termed it) that is part of those local cultures infuses the very essence of the dominant productive forces, to such an extent that any hegemony is, to various degrees, resisted and contested. As those forces are contested, then, the extent of hegemony of those productive systems may be altered or strengthened, depending upon the extent of group consciousness present about those productive forces.

Having said this, I have argued that, at Spencer, penetrations into the essence of the labor process were infrequent, and thus capitalistic productive forces moved toward domination.

How does this work? Virtually all forms of reified knowledge fundamental to the basic productive forces at Harold Spencer exist to be used for some other purpose. The most obvious purpose is in the creation of 'grades,' which serve as symbols that are exchanged by other teachers and the students for future classes, experiences, and associations. Such knowledge, once transformed into grades, comes to be understood not for itself but as it can be translated into something of exchange-value, for example, the grade. Yet grades are not the only symbol for reified knowledge and its exchange-value. The whole issue of legal and illegal skipping is illustrative of another. In our discussion of that topic in the last chapter, we found that the acceptance of the conditions of reified knowledge – that is accepting the given nature of such knowledge and the right of teachers to proclaim it – could be exchanged for privilege in the form of legal skipping. Those individuals who consistently did not accept the premises of reified knowledge could not create commodities which they could use to buy 'legal skips' through the exchange system. Thus they had to resort to forms of illegal skipping.

The ultimate exchange-value of reified knowledge lies, of course, in the credentialing value of schooling. To the extent that school attendance contributes to later occupational position, then the credential is perhaps the single most important commodity created by the instrumental interests found in schools like Spencer. Here, too, we find that school experiences become variously understood by students to such an extent that interpretive structures have influenced the selection of those occupational possibilities. And it is here too where the hegemony of schooling remains most influential, for the exchange-value of the knowledge of schooling is certainly not equal, just as a ten-dollar bill is not equal to a one-dollar bill.[17] When reified knowledge is accepted and/or circumvented (as was the case with Chris and most of his friends), then the exchange-value of that knowledge is relatively high because the worth of reified knowledge in the society at large is relatively high. On the other hand, reified knowledge that is ignored or rejected (as it was for Don and most of his friends) leads students to place a much greater premium on regenerative knowledge, the exchange-value of which is judged to be relatively low in the larger society. The later emphasis on regenerative knowledge by many workers in the labor force, and their subsequent acceptance of reified knowledge only by 'protest,' signifies their placement in routine jobs that need supervision through hierarchy – not at all unlike similar social processes in schools where those who do not accept the assumptions of school knowledge are relegated to special classes where they receive 'special' (supervised) attention. Thus we see the class-based effect of hegemony, and the manner in which the school contributes to its continuance.

It is through the assumptions about early adolescents and serving them in that image that the contemporary junior high students have come to exist in the form they do. They exist in that image because both technical and practical interests order knowledge and experiences into productive forces that reinforce state hegemony in a mutually confirming way. Education, then, becomes a 'lived hegemony,' one that is created and re-created as a culture, not one that impacts man from without, but one that, as Williams notes:

> is always a process. It is not, except analytically, a system or a structure. It is a realized complex of experiences, relationships, and activities, with specific and changing pressures and limits. . . . Moreover . . . it does not just passively exist as a form of dominance. It has continually to be renewed, recreated, defended, and modified.[18]

The definitions of the adolescent and the manner by which schools process students according to the image they have created of them raises more fundamental issues that usually are ignored. Those issues revolve around the basic nature of early adolescents and the reasons why junior high schools have come to confirm them in the manner that they do. Educators rarely question these assumptions because they assume the answers not to be debatable, as early adolescents generally are classified as young people aged 12–16 who, in the process of maturing in our society, exhibit distinctive physiological, psychological, and social characteristics. After all, it is that concept that has undergirded junior high schools such as Harold Spencer. It is those schools which, as we reviewed in Chapter 1, are supposed to 'guide and counsel' youngsters in preparation for adulthood. But if this guidance and counsel, together with the process of instruction and indeed even the very forms of opposition engaged in by students through communicative action, serves a hegemony of state capitalism, then how did this come to be?

The 'development' of early adolescence

The assumed and distinctive characteristics of adolescence are based, in part, on the perspectives of G. Stanley Hall who, in 1904, conceptualized this stage of development as 'dualistic' – characterized by deep concern for self as well as development of a collective conscience, the presence of both hyperactivity and focused direction, and the coexistence of childhood folly and maturity. Hall thought that adolescence should develop in a protected environment where these dualistic conflicts could be resolved productively with the assistance of unique organizational forms and specialists in adolescent behavior. There is no doubt that the popularity of such an approach, influential in the increased specialization found in secondary education of junior high schools, was based on these organizations serving the particular needs of young people during this stage of their life – a stage of 'transition.' The junior high school was then to provide a moratorium of sorts from public life, and its creation validated the existence of early adolescence as a particular stage of development requiring specialized attention.

Such a tradition influences the fact that we continue to view adolescence, particularly the obsession of early adolescents with peer groups and their penchant for social approval and camaraderie with peers, as a function of psychological development – that is, as a 'natural' transitional stage that children go through (and which adults must tolerate) on their way to adulthood. It is almost as if there were a colony of genes existing in children, present at birth and which remain recessive until about age 12 when, like CONTAC time release capsules, they are slowly but inexorably released into the bloodstream, producing the erratic, hyperactive and peer-approval-seeking behavior we classify as typical of this age group. While this analogy may be a bit extreme, it reinforces the obvious point that the traits associated with early adolescence are viewed as rooted in the correlation between physiological and psychological changes.

Such a vision, however, has not always existed. Some few social historians have devoted considerable time to the study of children, youth, and related subjects, and they point out that the popular conception of the adolescent was invented more than having always been with us. How this came to be is an interesting phenomenon in itself, and is worthy of our attention.

Originating from the seventeenth-century middle-class belief that children, in order to grow up as free and mature organisms, needed to be sheltered from too early an association with the corrupting and disturbing influences of the adult world (such as work, sex, death), the modern notion of adolescence was proposed by Rousseau in *Emile* in 1762. Therein, he saw the child reaching a new state of early maturity wherein the experiences of the past could be put aside and a truly healthy nutritive process could begin anew. Rousseau referred to this stage of development as a 'second birth, when the true education of the child was to begin.' Rousseau signaled the moment of this second birth as the beginning of puberty, and visualized rampant physiological and psychological changes in children, as if they had awakened from a long sleep. While heretofore puberty had been viewed as a normal process of no tremendous physical importance, pubescent children were now viewed as something distinctly different. Soon medical texts and the emerging studies of the human mind were filled with references to the universality of exploding energy at the time of puberty, the awakening of sexual desires and the manner by which their release (as through masturbation) could deplete all other energies needed for growth and maturation, and the erratic behavior of the adolescent as s/he battled the conflicting currents of growing social ties and the residues of self-love left from childhood. After Rousseau, and partly as a result of his writings, learned people came to see that handling the traumas of adolescence could best be achieved through a prolongation of innocence – through a moratorium wherein the child was protected from adult duties and responsibilities – wherein maturity could be nurtured, controlled, and regulated by educated parents and, most of all, by the legion of professionals who were soon to follow.

The emerging capitalist state could not afford this modern concept of adolescence prior to the late eighteenth century because of the critical need for all young adults to be integral components of the family economic unit. It was, therefore, 'uneconomical' to prolong the innocence of children if that meant that those children could not contribute fully to family economic functions. But as family sizes began to decline, as families became integrated into a growing urban culture, and as the growing middle class increasingly prepared its children for work in bureaucratic organizations outside of rather than as part of the family, prolonged dependency of children became not only more possible, but also more functional. In the United States, American moralist reformers caught on to the need for a natural development of young people, free from the unhealthy forces of too early a contact with adult responsibilities, and the concept of adolescence as a distinct, critical, and incapacitating stage of life firmly took hold in the nineteenth century. This ideology, coupled with industrialization and an urban economic market place within which the employment of the young increasingly was becoming less automatic, 'demanded that families, eager for their children to rise in the world, take steps that would segregate their young people from the world of casual labor and the dead-end job.'[19]

What we see here, then, is the emergence of a concept of adolescence roughly paralleling a critical period in the development of state-corporate capitalism. The popularity over Hall's formalization of adolescent development theory (especially such aspects as identity and dependence) occurred at a period of time when the 'use' of people aged 12–18 was being severely questioned, and when the state increasingly was becoming involved in policy pertaining to that use. For it was about the end of the nineteenth century that those classified as adolescents emerged from centuries of integration in the economic sector, first as functional members of family economic units and then, more recently, as part of that large exploitable labor pool on which corporate capitalism emerged predominant. But, by the end of the nineteenth century, large numbers of youth were no longer necessary to fill the factories and mines, as that function could be served more efficiently through the labor of new immigrants from eastern and southern Europe. Accordingly, because they no longer were necessary to provide the exploitable labor that so many had provided at one time, adolescents became the new reserve army of unemployed, threatening to depress further salaries and disrupt the social order.[20] Because of this, adolescents were, in essence, declared 'surplus' and made into dependent, passive beings who had to rely on the state, through increased schooling, to make them into adults. And as corporate capitalism continually affected the lives of adolescents in this manner, the state responded with policies on adolescence that reinforced the images of youth that had grown out of the growing merger of the state and corporate capitalism.

Little wonder then that Hall came to conceive of adolescence as an era of dependence and confusion, as a period whereupon as awakening from a deep sleep, 'youth . . . understands neither it [the world] or himself.' The alleged immaturity, the dependence, the confusion had grown out of the dependent status accorded to youth through their assigned surplus condition, a situation into which Hall had never inquired. Also, he never imagined that the institutions arising as a result of his theories – institutions meant to serve the young – would only serve to make youth more dependent and ultimately appropriate the results of their labor.

Yet, while Rousseau, Hall, and their contemporaries may have created the adolescent, and while the economic forces of state capitalism propelled the adolescent into an increasingly marginal role, it remained for 'experts' within that state and society in a variety of settings to 'invent' adolescents in such a way that made them and/or their families dependent on those experts for guidance and advice as well as for the very life experiences to which the adolescent would be subjected. By the early twentieth century, the biological qualities of adolescence, together with the accompanying psychological characteristics, had become the basis for a loosely articulated social policy formed by a growing legion of child savers. Accordingly, experts arose in association with voluntary associations (settlement houses, boys clubs, the Boy Scouts), churches (youth groups and religious education for the young), public agencies for juvenile rehabilitation (juvenile homes, reform school), and in association with child-rearing guidance (in the form of the plethora of child-rearing and 'how to raise your adolescent' books).[21] Last but certainly not least, there was schooling.

The expanding army of professional educators and the organizations they represented were at the forefront in contributing to the ultimate invention of the adolescent we have today. Educators used the growing emphasis on adolescence as a distinctive class as further justification for the general increase in the age of compulsory attendance from age 14 to 16, for the expansion of schooling into secondary education, and for widening the scope of schooling into such fields as hygiene, sex education, and guidance – all of which were compatible with the popular view of the distinctiveness of adolescence and the philosophy that, like a chronic disease, it had to be continually treated. Similar too was the progressive philosophy that a major purpose of secondary education was to be 'socialization' and 'life adjustment' as young people were preparing for life in a more complex world. Central decisions made by the mid-nineteenth century – decisions that wedded schooling to the trajectory of the state and its political – economic structure – ensured that the form of schooling would move toward hegemony.[22] As the organizational structure of schooling evolved to include specialists whose sole function it was to define social problems in terms of how the school could be enlisted to solve those problems, educators helped create a *Weltanschift* about adolescence. Kett summarizes this well:

> The fact that a large number of individuals who started from different directions were able to converge on the adolescent made it easy for them to think of adolescent behavior as a universal behavior, lurking in the heart of every boy and waiting only for the opportunity to be discovered.[23]

Were they waiting to be discovered? History shows us they were not. For example, almost two decades ago Philippe Aries showed us that, at least for the concept of adolescence as a distinctly different phase of life from adulthood, the notion hardly existed until the seventeenth century and that, prior to that period, the young dressed, resembled, and in many ways acted like adults.[24] Likewise, as Gillis, Kett and Musgrove have indicated, the very idea of segregating children and subsequently adolescents in schools for extended periods of time scarcely existed in either Europe or the United States until the nineteenth century.[25] Instead, learning, training and the general life of the young person occurred within the context of the family and the larger community within which most young people assumed active roles. The purpose of schooling during this period of time was to supplement other sources of learning, not to usurp them, thus schooling was much less predominate as an elongated period of one's life. The critical role of peer groups as orienting forces in the life of the adolescent and as noted at Harold Spencer was virtually unheard of in pre-nineteenth-century society, and took on importance only as the young systematically became excluded from responsible life decisions and were made dependent for longer periods of time. As institutions advocating that dependency expanded, those who worked with the young successfully established what never had been before – a dependent and segregated class of young people called 'adolescents' to whom they applied professional expertise in preparing these youngsters for adulthood.

The in-between years – 1984

The structure of junior high schools, conceived of 75 years ago, is not congruent with the realities of early adolescence in society today. The very basis of state capitalism as translated through the organizational structure of secondary schools contributes to the environment within which separate youth societies arise and from which our social/psychological classification of early adolescence is maintained. The culture of adolescence, rather than being one of liberation, turns into a productive force of cultural reproduction. Accordingly, the very process of schooling helps to create adolescence, then turns to serve those persons in the image in which it has created them. Adolescence is not necessarily a time of storm and stress, a period during which youth need be treated as incomplete and dependent beings, but rather is part of an ideology – a system of signs, practices, and routines that conditions and structures the range of ideological messages. This ideology is in turn associated with a particular cultural–economic system – in this case a capitalistic/technological society whose dominance is both extended and contested within the very student culture in its schools.

We live with that legacy today. The idea that many of the attributes associated with junior high youth may not be 'real' so much as an idea to which we have grown accustomed must not escape us, and we need look critically at early adolescence as a belief as well as the organizations built to perpetuate that belief. To move students into a responsible and critical education might well be impossible as long as we channel those same young people into institutional settings structured on the premise that young adolescents are somehow naturally dependent, inferior, empty vessels that need to be treated as such.

It could be different. What if somehow we were able to treat early adolescents as responsible persons whose knowledge system was not inferior to that of adults, and instead just different? What if our formalized socialization procedures were not based solely on technical interests as in most modern societies, but toward a transcendent competence wherein individuals were better able to create history by learning critcally to examine their place in it? What if we could ritualize competencies such as the manipulation of basic skills by asking students to put these skills collectively to work in their community and to come to understand that process – much like the applied and ceremonial functions of the Australian 'walkabout' perhaps, or the *aumanga* and *aualuma* of Samoan villages where young adolescents of each village are formally integrated into the political structure of that village. Our schools, by maintaining adolescents in a dependent state for so long, are hardly an adequate preparation for the independent, assertive life that our culture romanticizes.

Supposing other institutions in our society could view the adolescent in other ways too; the results might be quite different than they are now. No starry-eyed idealism intended here, but simply a critical understanding of the modes of knowledge we use to make sense of our lives; after all, is this not an important first step in the understanding of the junior high student? It makes little sense in an era where demographic and social structural factors such as earlier menarche, lowered voting ages, and family situations where (because of the higher number of either single-parent families or those in which both parents work) the young, in many ways, have increased responsibilities, to treat adolescents as passive dependants in school while expecting active independence in many other walks of life.

The world of Don and Chris and their friends, then, is not so much the world they have created for themselves, but rather the world we have created for them. This conclusion has been reached before, for, as was said over fifty years ago about adolescence in a different culture,

> Whether or not we envy other peoples one of their solutions, our attitude towards our own solutions must be greatly broadened and deepened by a consideration of the way in which other peoples have met the same problems. Realizing that our ways are not humanly inevitable nor God-ordained, but are the fruit of a long and turbulent history, we may well examine in turn all of our institutions, thrown into strong relief against the history of other civilizations and weighing them in the balance, be not afraid to find them wanting.[26]

Such a call should serve well as the starting point for future policy deliberations affecting young adolescents. Certainly, such deliberations will need to focus intently on the daily life of Don, Chris, and others at schools such as Harold Spencer Junior High School; such deliberations will also need to consider strongly how those schools are an integral part of the larger social/political order.

Appendix A
Lesson Plans

> Each man . . . carries on some form of intellectual activity, that is, he is a 'philosopher', a man of taste, he participates in a particular conception of the world. . . . The problem of creating a new stratum of intellectuals consists therefore in the critical elaboration of the intellectual activity that exists in everyone at a certain degree of development (Antonio Gramsci, *Selections from the Prison Notebooks of Antonio Gramsci*, Quinton Hoare and Geoffrey Nowell Smith (eds), tr. from Italian, London, Lawrence & Wishart, 1971).

What are we to make of all this? Two years with junior high school boys can make one both resigned and dismayed. Resignation develops primarily because much of what is described herein 'is the way it always has been' and, indeed, such a realization is, in part, true. Yet, when any dimension of life is held before us as in a mirror, the perspective we take on that life, indeed the meaning and significance of it, often becomes evident where it was not so before. A purpose of this book has been to serve as that mirror, for, as the anthropologist Clyde Kluckholn once noted, it would not be the fish that first discovered the existence of water.[1] A state of dismay may be present because it seems that, short of major structural re-organization – one that significantly alters family, work and political institutions, as well as school – little can be done to alter the predominance of technical interests in the school and the amazingly consistent way by which practical action can turn to build hegemony by serving the very interests it opposes. The manner in which activities such as goofing off, humor, smoking, and skipping serve not just as opposition to the dominant structure but eventually incorporation into it shows that these forms are not just isolated activities. Rather they have meaning as they link up to the capitalist culture from the outside – as part of the labor process, of power and resistance, of knowledge. Changes, then, must also link up from the culture outside, else those changes are focused upon phenomena that are viewed as aberrant pathologies rather than focused upon phenomena that are part of a total and interdependent organism.

There are no facile solutions to these contradictions of technical and practical interests, particularly given the organizational configuration of the school and the purposes it represents. First, we must accept the fact that, almost by definition, schools serve to bring the young into the larger society and there will be contradictions between technical and practical cognitive interests.

Yet, the fact that schools socialize has never been a debatable question, and we should not look at that as 'bad' in and of itself. However, while some contradiction always is present in any educational setting, differences between the goals of teachers as socializing agents and students as those in the process of becoming socialized will be especially pervasive and ongoing. This is especially true as long as the state monopolizes formal education and if schools continue to be organized in a manner that treats knowledge in an instrumental fashion. If schools exist to bring students into the society as presently envisaged by society's gatekeepers (of whom educators are members), and if that socialization is to involve a process of 'pouring in,' with little involvement of those being treated, then increased contradictions are inevitable. Waller discusses this fundamental contradiction when he notes that:

> a . . . more universal conflict between students and teachers arises from the fact that teachers are adults and students are not, so that teachers are bearers of the culture of the society of adults, and try to impose that culture upon students whereas students represent the indigenous culture of the group of children.[2]

The central issue seems to be to provide students with the resources to make such contradictions productive, and to provide teachers with the frame of reference to understand that, through such conflict, students indeed can gain the capabilities to become active learners. This can occur only to the extent that knowledge which can free individuals and groups from the assumptions of the past – knowledge that calls into question the understanding of its origins and meanings and that which involves students collectively in discovering and reinterpreting that knowledge – becomes legitimated as part of the school curriculum. This, then, requires a different orientation, one that proposes liberation from, rather than total acceptance of, the constraints of history and culture.

Such knowledge requires a revised orientation, purpose, or (in the terms of Habermas), 'cognitive interest.' What is demanded is knowledge organized as an *emancipatory interest* – that is, knowledge whose purpose it is to liberate actors from historically contingent constraints through a process of self-reflection and critique. Such a cognitive interest or assumption is not separate from the technical and practical interests discussed earlier, but rather is synthetic, or one that realizes that systematic and comprehensive understanding of factual–empirical knowledge (characterized through technical interests) demands an open, self-critical community of inquirers whose knowledge base grows out of intersubjective relations that build toward mutuality (practical interests). Implicit, then, in the orientation of both technical and practical interests is the demand for the conditions of emancipation, that is, that ideal state of affairs where work–technical interests and interaction–practical interests can converge. In the case of schools, then, the orientation would be toward education as a process wherein students view themselves as active yet limited historical subjects.

The knowledge system (parameters of how one 'knows') that would constitute an emancipatory cognitive interest is *critical–dialectical*, or one that is philosophical and sociological at the same time. The purpose of critical–dialectical knowledge is to call into question the basis of knowledge (that is, the cognitive interests that establish the knowledge) and then to examine the ways by which knowledge has been and continues as a social phenomena, created by and determined in part by systems of social relations throughout history. Critical–dialectical knowledge strives for discovery of those forms of human knowledge that are said to be 'necessary,' contrasted with knowledge that is historically conditioned. In so doing, a critique of society and the individual's place in it can be generated.

The human action that will grow out of an emancipatory interest and critical–dialectical knowledge is what we call '*power*,' the ability of individuals to materialize the knowledge of emancipatory interests. This is not necessarily a power characterized by confrontation, or one of overt rebellion (although such is possible). It is, however, the beginnings of an action where individuals can materialize their understanding of themselves both as historical objects as well as determinates of history. In schools, this would mean adolescents as active rather than passive learners, as both independent and collective learners, integrated into the social world around them. Through relatively undistorted communication, they would have the power to alter that world, not in one fell swoop, but through learning to raise to a conscious level the contradictions that emerge in a liberal/capitalist system. In this manner, youth would be more conscious of the manner by which cultural hegemony is reproduced through forms that, on the surface, may appear liberating or at least oppositional.

Yet, we need question how possible it is to develop, nurture, and foster an emancipatory interest in a setting characterized by cultural hegemony. Indeed, we must ask if the hegemonic state of schooling is such that the cultural forces of the dominant social structure are so pervasive that emancipatory interests would be difficult to foster. For, as we have argued, a lived hegemony constitutes a sense of reality for most people, a sense of finality, because that reality soaks into actions and beliefs that appear often to resist ideological domination.

No hegemony, however, is complete and thus no hegemony is completely dominant. For a complete state of hegemony to exist, the self-identity of individuals (for example, through the acceptance of powerlessness) must be made through the conscious manipulation for control (as in the dominance of hierarchy in the school) as well as the development of a constitutive system of meaning and values (as exemplified in the student culture itself). Such total self-identification is difficult to achieve. Inevitably, contradictions will produce conscious movements or tendencies that resist the dominant social/political system. Further, oppositional practices will grow out of oppositional forms, counter-hegemonies will grow out of hegemonies, more contradictions will emerge from stability. In this sense, then, all forms of resistance contain in them both the seeds of incorporation back into the dominant structure (as we saw throughout much of Chapters 6 and 7) as well as the generation of counter-hegemonies, through such forms as skipping, defiance, and conviction. In this regard, Don's absences from school, his refusal to accept the inanity of the smoking school, and Chris's conviction that he could learn more in the library by himself than while putting up with Von Hoffman's class, are indications of the incipient stages of that resistance.

It is into these cracks, through these inconsistencies, and as a result of an acute understanding of the significance of contradictions, that educators can begin to consider an education characterized by an emancipatory interest. First, recognition of the world and the way it operates provides a context, a *Weltanschauung*, for action. Recognition of that context provides a perspective for specific plans for action. In the remainder of this section, I wish to outline a context for action as well as specific plans for educators to consider.

Context

By context I mean major premises concerning the setting in which schooling occurs. These premises help constitute a framework for practice around which educators can begin to move away from education as a technical interest and toward education as an emancipatory interest. The context discussed herein, not surprisingly, follows the cultural–materialist perspective evident throughout this study.

The role of individuals as change agents. First, educators must understand the appropriate role of individuals and collectives as agents for appropriate educational change. General information about and understanding of junior high students, for example, certainly is important and is an avenue that every educator can pursue directly. Understanding the interpretive world of students, the forms through which that interpretive world is acted out (through goofing off, for example), and the long-term consequences of that opposition is quite important. Similarly, teachers must come to know that they as teachers make a difference and that what they do does have a tremendous impact on students. Patently, there is a difference between a student's experiences in Von Hoffman's class and those of a student in Mrs Paul's class. A student in Mrs Paul's class, for example, might read and discuss Shakespeare, Malcolm X, Margaret Sanger, or William Faulkner while a student in Von Hoffman's class probably would not even know who those people were. To say that knowledge of such people in our history will 'make a difference' is, of course, a value statement with which some may disagree, but I know that exposure to such writings would be important to the education of my own children. Understanding the roots of such literature and its meaning could constitute the beginnings of a critical–dialectical form of knowledge.

Yet, if such individual efforts are recognized for what they are, it is also imperative to understand that there are long-term structural changes that need be considered in education. It is these changes – ones concerning issues such as curricular reform, governance of schools, the relationship between education and work – that cannot be taken on alone by individual teachers but rather must be considered collectively as a mode of political action. I will have more to say on this later, suffice it to say here that it is critical that educators demarcate between changes that can be accomplished in the short-term and those of a long-term nature.

Contradictions as catalysts of change. Particularly in modern capitalistic societies, schooling largely serves the state through the manner in which the patterns of culture are reproduced throughout. Such schooling also gives rise to contradictions and opposition, some of which is obvious, other less obvious. Typical of the range of contradictions generated by schooling are the high rates of truancy that indicate the extent of disregard that increasing numbers of students have for schools; an increasing credentialism wherein degrees are required for even the most menial jobs, despite the fact that most new employees must be retrained by employers; the pervasive presence of opposition through inattention, goofing off, and other forms of passive resistance; and the attempts of educators to 'manage' such resistance through 'scientific' means called 'classroom management.' These facts and others indicate that schooling in our society proceeds through patterns and cycles that appear to be increasingly accentuated as to extremities. These cycles give rise to the fact that schools, like other organizations in capitalist societies, create their own contradictions and thus sow the seeds of their own difficulties. Educators are in a unique position to recognize these difficulties for what they are, and to help guide students toward a critical–dialectical knowledge mode by utilizing these contradictions as tools for critical knowledge rather than as manifestations to be avoided or suppressed.

The importance of dialectics. Educators must come to understand the importance of the fact that adolescents, as all human actors, continually create that social world in which they live, both today and in the future. Although it is true that the world which students inhabit is made for them – and before them – teachers should strive to enhance student creative potential by making them more aware of their own role in re-creating and reproducing the world of social relations in which they exist. Teachers especially must come to see their clients not as passive dependent objects on whom the teacher performs a treatment, but rather as independent historical subjects who actively re-create a cultural reality.

The integration of context. Schooling occurs in a contextual world, and that context includes the systematic effects of class, race, sex, on the schooling process. Too few educators understand the infusion of such factors into the daily rhythm of educational practice; too few understand and recognize the effect of school practice on the perpetuation of those contextual dimensions. It seems that daily school life must be continually considered within such a framework, and indeed educators can so examine such practice. One of the fundamental issues uncovered in this study is the almost universal belief on the part of students that 'work' is what those in authority make one do. 'Work' then becomes synonymous with estranged labor, as it is separated from the control of the individual doing 'work.' The potential impact of such a belief on students of differential socioeconomic backgrounds is great, as we showed through the manners by which Chris and his group came to 'adapt' to school *vis à vis* the manner in which Don and his group 'adapted.'

Practice

We now suggest some specific practices for educators who wish to act on the premises just mentioned. These practices are but beginnings, and can be enhanced only through the ongoing praxis of educators as they build toward education that truly is emancipatory. These practices can be grouped, for convenience, into the focus on students, curricula, and teachers.

Students – Learn to recognize the assumptions behind labels and concepts typically given to students. What do terms such as 'underachiever,' 'overachiever,' 'trying hard,' 'smart,' 'slow' mean? On what criteria are they based? What is the nature of the social system that supports such criteria?

Question more regularly and intently the purposes of educational practice in which you routinely engage. Inquire not so much into whether educational objectives are met presently but what long-term consequences will result as a function of that practice. Learn to see educational practice as partially determinant of cultural reproduction, and question that which is being reproduced.

Work simultaneously toward student self-determination and responsibility. Once students have begun to understand their role as active creators of their own history, work toward giving them increased self-determination in that history. On the other hand, don't be duped by ostensibly radical programs that advocate students creating their own education. Rather, work toward student understanding of technical and practical interests through emancipatory interests.

Curriculum – Advocate a curriculum that not only exposes the young to knowledge of the social structural relations to be changed, but provides the tools necessary in that system of social relations that is to be changed as well. It is irresponsible for students to be equipped to function in collectively operated groups or organizations without being equally competent in the social relations of hierarchical organizations. Thus, if students are to be aware of the economic and political patterns that influence their plight, those students must be competent to operate the rules of that world that is to be overcome. Thus, it is crucial then for students to be well-read, articulate, and literate – to be well-schooled in the system of schooling.

In this regard, the 'relevancy' of curriculum has many dimensions. Information necessary to the development of critical–dialectical knowledge may be 'relevant,' but total *laissez-faire* techniques by which to achieve that knowledge may not be, for through such practices students can come to be dominated by forces and factors about which they are unaware. Consequently, there is nothing wrong with rote memorization, as long as students are critically aware of what is being memorized, and for what purposes.

Knowledge acquisition through emancipatory interests should be seen fundamentally as a collective, not an individual experience. In this regard, students should be given maximum opportunity to learn from each other and other adults as they come to understand themselves as historical creations and creators. Group work in schools typically is the sharing of ignorance; work toward the pooling and creation of understanding.

Work toward linking students with other relevant networks productive of critical understanding and perspective in order to maximize the potential for contradiction. Work with labor unions, social activist groups, welfare agencies, and minority organizations to develop a critical awareness of the assumptions behind social relations among and between groups, on the nature of hierarchy, on the relation between dependence and independence, indoctrination and dialog. Work to help disaffected students become more familiar with bourgeois interests, assist racial and cultural groups to understand those of opposite persuasion as well as their own.

Teachers – Strive for greater collective concern with educational issues in teacher organizations rather than only working conditions and salaries. If such a movement cannot be made successful, form a separate organization devoted to client emancipation through education.

Support and work for the design of systems that are counter-hegemonic to the current monolithic state-controlled educational system. Became informed about alternative schools, private schools, schools operated by disaffected groups; understand their strengths as well as liabilities. Support policies that have the potential for more flexible educational practice, such as certain voucher schemes. Above all, listen with skepticism to what professional interest groups say about such plans.

The purpose of education should be to strive for individual and collective capability and consciousness, and educators have a fundamental responsibility to assist in this task. To the degree they do not fulfill this responsibility, then they are part of the problem. To do less is to admit the hegemony of state capitalism in schooling and to view ourselves as little more than cogs in the flywheel.

We all create our own culture, our own history. What we create is our choice!

Appendix B
Methodology

> The genuine mark of an empirical science is to respect the nature of the empirical world – to fit its problems, its guiding conceptions, its procedures of inquiry, its techniques of study, its concepts, and its theories to that world (Herbert Blumer, *Symbolic Interactionism: Perspective and Method*, Englewood Cliffs, New Jersey, Prentice-Hall, 1969.)

This study began with no preconceived hypotheses to test and with but a general frame of reference to guide it. I knew from my own past experience as a junior high teacher that students would attend classes, do much of the work expected of them, and generally comply with the regulations that governed the operation of the school. I also knew that social interaction was important to junior high students, and I surmised that students would probably develop an interpretive structure by which they could make sense of their schooling experience. That students could act in a manner consonant with their beliefs about their role and setting was an especially important assumption I made.

Given these initial suppositions, I realized that I would have to chronicle more than just attitudes or opinions but also the process by which those views were constructed. how those views came to influence action, and how this action, in turn, affected subsequent views on schooling. I was interested in the entire aspect of what is variously referred to as 'world-view,' ideational systems, or the *Weltanschauung* of students, especially as evident in and applied to schooling. In this framework, human beings – individually and collectively – are viewed as active agents who constantly decide the kind of self they will accept for themselves. What they accept depends, in turn, on how they see themselves in relation to the material world from which they derive their cues. Equally important is the manner in which critical aspects of that material world help define that definition of self.

This process model, derived in part from the theory of symbolic interactionism, is in contradistinction to much of social theory that reduces human society to categories that do not act – social classes, occupational groups, 'cultures,' and the like. Symbolic interactionism presupposes that any acting unit – be it an individual, social group, or organization – takes action in the light of situations that exist and that become a basis for action. Herbert Blumer, one of the original spokesmen for this approach, states:

> The acting unit necessarily has to identify the things which it has to take into account – tasks, opportunities, obstacles, means, demands, discomforts, dangers, and the like. It has to assess them in some fashion and it has to make decisions on the basis of the assessment. Such interpretative behavior may take place in the individual guiding his own action, in a collectivity of individuals acting in concert, or in 'agents' acting on behalf of acting units developing acts to meet the situation in which they are placed.[1]

In this approach, then, the interpretive process that serves to mediate any given situation is of crucial importance.

In emphasizing the importance of interpretive behavior and the construction of a world-view, we must be careful to account not only for the constructive process, but the structural regularities that influence that process. Thus, we must ask the extent to which particular interpretive 'realities' are associated with certain organizational forms, and the degree to which those organizational forms themselves are constructed and are problematical rather than given. The symbolic interactionist approach justifiably has come under some fire of late for its naïveté on these organizational–institutional regularities and their relationship to the interpretive process, as Sharp and Green indicate:

> Simply to dwell on the surface structure of consciousness, as the phenomenologist seems to advocate, may mask the extent to which such consciousness may conceal and distort the underlying structure of relationships. . . . In the same way that

> Marx was against his analysis of society and history at the level of consciousness but rather sought for the basic social structures which regulate interindividual action, so we need to develop some conceptualization of the situations that individuals find themselves in, in terms of the structure of opportunities the situations make available to them and the kinds of constraints they impose.[2]

Accordingly, I needed to be aware as well of what factors are important in defining both the interpretive process as well as the consequences of that process, recognizing too that those consequences may be differential. If one is to understand how acting units interpret their environment and how these perspectives influence further action, then that individual must take the role of the acting unit to be studied rather than remaining outside the situation being studied and inferring what it is like to be (in our case) a student in a junior high school. This posture has the advantage of allowing the actors themselves to define what is important and meaningful rather than the observer making the determination for them, as Blumer comments:

> To try to catch the interpretive process by remaining aloof as a so-called 'objective' observer and refusing to take the role of subjectivism – the objective observer is likely to fill in the process of interpretation with his own surmises in place of catching the process as it occurs in the experience of the acting unit which uses it.[3]

The best manner by which this approach can be accomplished is for the observer to adopt strategies in the tradition of anthropological and sociological fieldwork wherein the observer attempts to become a part of the same fabric as those he is studying. The fieldworker attempts to be accepted by them, to become part of their everyday lives, to experience the things they do, and to better understand the values that affect what they do. The fieldworker attempts to become partly socialized by those to be studied so as to understand better their lives, all the while remaining the outsider who attempts constantly to call into question everything seen and heard. As a quasi-member of the groups studied, the fieldworker constantly asks 'what questions does what I am seeing or hearing answer?' as a way of understanding the interpretive process characterizing social groups, as well as the structural factors that influence such a process.

My opportunity to conduct this study in this fashion came the year I finished my doctoral studies when I accepted a position on a research team whose purpose it was to evaluate a five-year federally funded project in Jefferson. This project offered research promise, not only because of its unusual long-term nature, but also because of the commitment made by the funding agency to a documentation of the history of the project, the emphasis on examination of a variety of elements within the schooling process and, most particularly, the interest of the funding agency to support 'new' evaluative models, particularly those devoted to the study of the context of schooling through 'anthropological' techniques. The interest of the director of the evaluation team in my notions of studying students as part of this project encouraged me to believe that what seemed an unlikely opportunity might provide the resources I needed to follow a burning interest.

The reader has no doubt noted by now that there is very little mention of any kind of 'special project' within this study, and it is not the purpose of this book to report on that project.[4] To say at the outset that the purpose of the project was one of 'comprehensive change' wherein staffing, the role of the community, and instructional techniques emphasized individualized/personalized approaches to schooling – all these provide some flavor to project objectives. To go into more detail here would serve no useful purpose as student life was not significantly altered by the project (in fact, the project can aptly be described in a manner similar to that of most innovations, merely 'exchanging one set of books for another').[5] Yet, our evaluation of the project was not necessarily tied to the originally stated objectives, but rather as well to an understanding of what was transpiring in the community, the administrative component of the district, the world of the teachers, and that of the students as well. The emphasis of our evaluative effort quickly shifted from project objectives to as complete a documentation as possible of the schooling process in general. We felt that the project and the district as a social entity were unalterably bound together, and that we could only understand the life history of the project if we took this stance.

At the end of my first year as a member of the evaluation team, I proposed that I spend the majority of my time the next year studying student life in the junior high school as one way of better understanding schooling and its context in the district. My colleagues on the team were examining other phenomena – the interface between the school and the community, central office management and decision-making, broad-based instructional and curricular reforms, the district's means of self-assessment, and, of course, data from standardized testing. Yet, we needed to know in rather detailed fashion what it was that students were doing in the schools and how (or if) all of this rhetoric about 'change' reached students and in what fashion. It seemed more than appropriate to send somebody 'in' to a school or some schools to gain an understanding of the schooling process as those who experienced it understood it. My substantive interests and past fieldwork experiences seemed to point to my election to become a junior high student the next academic year.

The decision on Harold Spencer and seventh-grade students, while carefully considered, still had some elements of fortuity to it. During the last three months of my first year in Jefferson, I had been spending some time in three of the upper grades of the district elementary schools, working on a small project in which our team was attempting to study the relationship between instructional design and student cognitive outcomes, paying special attention to peer associations as an intervening variable in that process. We were particularly interested in this problem at three of the elementary schools that had adopted modifications of 'open concept' architectural design and corresponding instructional changes such as Individually Guided Education (IGE), which are individualized approaches to such subjects as mathematics and reading. In the process of doing this study, I had asked teachers at all three schools to nominate for me five students in each of three categories – superior or excellent students, average students, and below average students. I asked them to make these recommendations based upon the student's academic performance and not on behavior, and I also asked them to base their assessment on what the students did in class, not on what the teachers felt their 'potential' to be.

This is how I originally met most of the principal actors in this study – Chris, Don, Roger, Steve, Dave, Karen, Robin, and others. Chris had been nominated by his teachers as exceptionally able, probably one of the best students that they had in their classes over the past few years. In the same light, Don was characterized as an average student, but a 'high' average, meaning that he was not quite as able as Chris but certainly one who demonstrated quite a knack for doing well. In checking grades and examining papers at random, I found these assessments to be accurate – at least on a scale of A's, B's, etc. Chris had almost all A's with some B's while Don had a mixture of B's and C's with an occasional A. Many of the other students in this document also were noted by teachers – Roger as an average student and Bill as an excellent student, for example. But then, too, many of the students whom I met were not noted by any teacher but rather entered into my camera lens as a result of my knowing other students like Chris or Don.

I only spent 3–4 hours a week in each of the elementary schools, but it was sufficient time for students to become accustomed to my presence and to come to see me as a relatively natural (if somewhat strange) phenomenon. I maintained a very low profile at first, simply observing who associated with whom over what issues. My omnipresent note writing made students curious and, to allay their suspicions, I always allowed them to read the notes if they wanted (few did, but those who did found them 'boring'). As our research plans began to solidify, I became more intrigued about the possibilities of using these students as my 'guide' into seventh grade at Harold Spencer. Toward the end of the year, I approached a few of the students with this idea: I asked them if I could go to Spencer with them the next year and if they would show me around so that I could meet more of their friends and gain a better understanding of what it was like to attend school there. Since our sociometric instruments had confirmed what I had imagined – that Chris and Don were two of the most popular boys in the sixth grade (as indicated by the number of students who chose them as friends) and the fact that they were part of two somewhat distinct friendship groups (as indicated by number of mutual choices), they seemed likely individuals to serve as guides for me at Spencer. Their response to my proposition was positive but not particularly enthusiastic. Don simply shrugged his shoulders and said it was 'OK' with him, although he further indicated that 'it seems like a boring way to spend your time.' Chris's response was similar, although he appeared a little more enthused about the idea, wanting to know if I would make him 'famous.' This hurdle cleared, I still had one more major hurdle to clear: that of gaining the approval of the administration and faculty at Spencer.

Technically speaking, our presence in the district was a necessary condition for the district to receive funds for the project, but it was not sufficient to gain us access to any and all settings. Such access still had to be negotiated with principals and teachers. Edwards already had the reputation of disliking 'evaluators' owing in part to his confrontation with the district evaluation office over an incident where students had been asked to respond to a question stating 'school is like jail' (his statement to me about this was that the question was ridiculous because students had never been to jail). Thus, I knew it would be no easy task. A week before school opened in the Fall, I scheduled an appointment with Edwards during which time I told him what I had been doing at the elementary schools and expressed my desire to work with some of the same students at Spencer. To say that he was unenthusiastic would be an overstatement. I attempted to allay his fears of the study being an evaluation of his teachers, but the best I could extract from him was a promise that I could discuss my proposal with the staff the following week. Teachers at that meeting raised few questions; Edwards posed most of the questions himself as if attempting to prompt teacher questions on potentially sensitive areas (that students would 'act up' when I was in class, that even though I was studying students, information could be used to evaluate teachers, and the like). About a week after the staff meeting, I saw Edwards in the district office, at which point he told me that 'the staff' had given me clearance to begin. Later I learned that this image of uncooperativeness on his part was his 'way,' a way to which most teachers had long since become accustomed.

The next week I began my work at Spencer – work that involved most of my time in the field for one year and about a half of my time the subsequent year as 'my' seventh-graders moved into eighth grade. My approach throughout was quite simple: I dressed casually but not sloppily, and attempted to fit into the behaviors and discussions of those students whom I knew the previous years, students like Chris, Don, Roger, and John. In the earliest part of the first year, I spent the majority of my time in classes so as to learn the routine of the school. I also used the opportunity to become better acquainted with the teachers. As the year progressed, I spent increasing amounts of time hanging out in the hall before and after class, eating lunch with students, going with them on field trips and to extra-curricular events such as basketball games, and sometimes participating with them in after-school activities such as walking to Shakey's. Since I lived in the school district, I also had occasion to meet students in stores, hitchhiking, at sports events, movie theaters, and the like. Despite the fact that I was three times their age, students seemed to accept me much as one of them.

Once initial entrée issues were resolved, I settled into a routine of data collection, recording, analysis, and eventual writing that was to occupy me fully for the next three years. The first year in the school involved extensive observation of classes and situations wherein I attempted to 'map' the reality of the student world. I saw my first main task as one of understanding the world of formalized learning, so I began by attending all of the classes that students like Chris and Don attended. Obviously, I could not be everywhere at once, so I took as my focal point those classes attended by students in each of the friendship groups. I also attended other classes for purposes of cross-checking information, as well as to create a 'smoke screen' to prevent institutional identification of those students with whom I had become affiliated. My normal routine was to take a seat in the class (usually in the rear so I could see and hear better) and relatively close to someone like Don or Chris. I always had a notebook with me, and always wrote in it so as to preserve events as accurately as possible and to legitimate myself as a person who sought out and collected information. Yet, many times, extensive note-taking was either impossible (such as on field trips) or would, I felt, affect the natural flow of the situation (such as during lunch). In these situations, I would jot down key words or quotes as soon as practicable, and fill in the information at the end of the day. After school, and depending somewhat on my other responsibilities, I filled in and rewrote the notes I had collected during the day, an activity that consumed anywhere from one to three hours.

Much of the detail of this study was gained from interviews of two types. First were somewhat informal interviews normally considered to be part of the participation–observation process. A second and much more formalized and focused form of interviewing involved a concerted effort to generate student categories on topics that they used to describe their world-view of school. To understand such categories, two assumptions guided my interview strategy. First, in order to understand how students 'made sense' from their place in the school environment, I could not assume that I 'knew' what they knew but had to allow students to identify salient issues within the context of their daily life in the school. Second, I had to use student descriptors of this reality, and not 'translate' that reality into my own vocabulary. I thus made the assumption that the vocabulary a group uses to describe its world is used for a purpose, and represents a lexicon uniquely understood by those members of the social group sharing the same interpretation of the material world. Such an assumption led me to an approach based upon prior work in the field of cognitive anthropology.[6]

In this approach, sometimes referred to as 'cognitive mapping,' the investigator attempts to understand how it is informants define concepts, formulate propositions, and make decisions. Such understanding usually is accomplished in a five-step process that includes (1) determining the areas that are culturally significant to informants, (2) recording the statements in these areas in the language of informants, (3) examining these statements for domains that describe these areas, (4) eliciting categories relevant to each domain, and (5) determining the critiera used to describe or differentiate categories within a domain. Looking first at (1) above, I had determined, after a few months in the school, that much of the student conversation centered around two topics, (a) things they did in school, and (b) people in the school. Within each of these broad topics, a number of more specific topics were mentioned – topics like, in the case of (a), 'work,' 'skip,' 'goof off,' and so on (Table 6.1 on p. 166 illustrates the range of activities students said they did in school).

Using the term 'goof off' as an example of the cognitive mapping process, I had heard students discuss goofing off many times and had witnessed, indeed even participated in, activities that they considered to be goofing off. Goofing off was discussed variously in terms of who goofed off, where goofing off was done, and how it was done. In this sense, then, goofing off could be considered as a large organizing term, referred to as a *cover term*, with a variety of dimensions: for example, how, when, where and with whom. These dimensions are called *domains*, and represent a category system linked by a cover term or set of activities all occurring within some restricted environment.

Once having established the basic cover term of goofing off with its applicable domains, my next step was to have my student informants 'map' their world of goofing off for me. My informants were coalitions of friends, both boys and girls, who varied in their degree of academic ability, participation in school activities, and popularity with peers. To the extent that these factors are deemed important in describing students, the groups were representative of the student body at large.

I then scheduled both group and individual interviews with a total of twenty students. Three separate interview sessions were conducted with every student and each 45–60-minute session was tape recorded. In the first session I merely checked my earlier supposition about the saliency of goofing off to students by posing the question: 'Tell me some of the things you do in school.' The cover term 'goof off' was mentioned by every group and, because I had trouble restraining the students from going on about goofing off, I knew it to be qualitatively relevant.

In the second interview session, I tried to elicit the parameters within each different domain of goofing off by taking the student's statements about goofing off and posing them as questions, that is: 'What are the ways you goof off?'; 'With whom do you goof off?'; and 'Who doesn't goof off?' Each question elicited a number of responses, or *categories*, which indicated the range of activity within that domain.

While the students provided a large number of categories, I needed to take my inquiries one step further to ascertain the significance of any one category, its weighting, and the relationship between clusters of categories. To accomplish this I took the categories within a given domain, typed each on a small card, and during the third session asked the students to *group* similar cards and tell me why they grouped them in that manner.

I found this process to be particularly useful to explore in depth the student framework of reality within the school. It provided a rich and detailed description of student life in the school, and in a fashion that was student, rather than observer, generated. This enabled me to understand student life better and to make important and critical connections between words and deeds – between what students described to me and how I observed them to act in the school setting.

Use of a variety of records, files, official documents, and other anecdotal information helped supplement observational and interviewing techniques. I asked for and was assigned a mailbox in the school office, and received all announcements and material normally received by teachers. This gave me advance notice of such activities as field trips, assemblies, and other special events, and such information not only assisted me in scheduling my time but provided cues as to what I had to follow up on when I was absent. I also had access to student records and files, grades, evaluations, papers, and other comparable information kept in the main office or by individual teachers. The school staff was most cooperative in granting me such information. Finally, I had full use of curricular material and student assignments, as I too was treated as a student by others when teachers routinely included me when passing out worksheets, supplemental readings, and tests and when students routinely passed them out to me as they would to any other student.

The distribution of my time did not remain constant over the two years I spent collecting data for this study. When Chris, Don, and the others were in seventh grade, I spent the first semester conducting the bulk of the classroom observation work and expanding the network of students with whom I became acquainted. During the second semester of seventh grade, I validated observations by 'checking up' on selected classes and discovered that the basic patterns established the first semester continued into the second. I thus changed my focus during the second semester to more in-depth interviewing with informants and on the cognitive mapping process. Throughout the seventh grade, I continued to attend the school at least four complete days a week, but by the end of the second semester was much more selective about the classes and the extracurricular events I attended. During the second year, I attended even fewer classes, restricted my associations to Chris and Don and the people with whom they came in contact, and spent an increasingly greater amount of time in trying to understand the teachers and the ways they organized their system of understandings. (This latter information proved to make this book too lengthy and had to be eliminated.) By the second semester of eighth grade, I was spending only about 30–40 per cent of my time in the school, with the other project responsibilities occupying increasing energies.

My role in the study changed over time, from one of initial contacts and 'testing the water,' to one where I encouraged students to see me in the role in which I wanted to be seen, finally to one where official and non-official roles mixed. The first month or so was somewhat strained with most students except those few with whom I had made an agreement in elementary school. Students who did not know suspected that I was a teacher, a 'narc,' or just somebody strange, and I found them occasionally 'acting up' when the teacher was out of the room and then checking to see if I did anything about it. Once that stage was over, I encouraged the students to see me as a person writing a story about the school, and I complemented this role by becoming more proactive, initiating more conversations, asking students to describe the purpose of actions, and finally engaging in the in-depth interviews. After two to three months, informal roles became more predominant and students saw me as much one of them as a writer.

That students would treat me as one of them is hard for someone who has not had a similar experience to understand; but I found that students will treat anyone in relation to the capacity in which they act and not on the basis of age, size, or official role. Since students came to see me as another student, I found that they became bothered if I 'observed' too much and often I was gently but seriously chided if I did not participate in the work they did. Likewise, students seemed suspicious if I was absent too much, did not attend the classes they did, or did not hang around before or after school. I remember one instance in particular where Roger ignored me for two to three days after I had been absent while away at a professional meeting. He never said anything directly, but his comments to Don and Steve made it clear that he believed it less than fair that I had told them at the beginning of the year that I wanted to be treated like a student and be part of what they did, but then was able to exercise adult prerogatives by leaving when it was convenient for me. Thus I tried to avoid absences as much as possible, or at least to make them as inconspicuous as possible (by claiming illness, for example) because I felt that being a student only on adult terms and not 'putting up' with what a student had to do was not a very valid way of understanding junior high school as students experience it.

About half-way through the eighth grade, I began seriously to consider how these data should be organized and eventually written. One factor motivating me in this direction was that the federal agency sponsoring the evaluation study wanted to know what I had been doing for over a year. I was given a deadline for producing a brief 'report' of my progress to date. This document was sent to the agency and they, in turn, sent it to reviewers for criticism. The remarks of these reviewers encouraged me to think more seriously about a more analytical organizational framework for the entire monograph. Rereading the field-notes convinced me of the desirability to preserve the descriptive approach on which the study had been based, and it seemed natural to focus on the place of classroom instruction, the everyday life in Don's and Chris's groups, and their attempts to create a self-determinative existence within the formal structure of the school. These themes led to the descriptive basis of Chapters 3 through to 7. Constant dialog with the data and various literature convinced me, however, that I could not ignore the structural/institutional aspects of schooling as they influenced the small slice of reality I had experienced at Harold Spencer, and I realized that this case study data provided for interpretations of *why* students depended so much on regenerative knowledge structures and the consequences of that process. I had only the rudimentary aspects of that framework by the time I had completed a second draft of the study (which served as the 'final report' of this aspect of the evaluation project). The current framework, based in part on 'critical theory,' did not take shape until I had rethought the study after the project was completed. This conceptualization continued as I read a wide variety of literature and returned to the data I had collected. A rereading of Marx's earlier writings, especially *The Economic and Philosophical Manuscripts of 1844* and the *Grundrisse*, convinced me of the applicability of the cultural–materialist perspective, which I later coupled up with the Habermas's writings on cognitive interests. The fact that this framework emerged two to three years after the data were collected should allay any suspicions that the interpretive framework for the study was superimposed on the study while fieldwork was still ongoing.

As noted, I did finish a draft of the report before the project terminated. Portions of that draft were circulated to selected teachers at Spencer, and to a few of the principal actors (Chris, for one; Don expressed little interest in reading it). Their comments were helpful, and I made some small corrections based on those comments but, for the most part, preserved the substantive aspects of these chapters as students and teachers both confirmed the accuracy of what I had said.

I am more than aware of the many shortcomings of this study. It is a small slice of the total reality of schooling. Spencer may not be indicative of all junior high schools; indeed, the students explicitly mentioned in this study represent less than 10 per cent of the total student body at Spencer. Questions of generalizability run rampant, as they always do with studies such as this. It is impossible for me to say that the events described in this study are representative of all junior high schools although, being an ex-junior high teacher myself, I believe that most are. Yet for those who have some familiarity with the literature on youth and schooling in contemporary societies, I would ask them to recollect the works that stand out as the most influential. In my own mind, Waller's *The Sociology of Teaching*, written in 1932, is one of those; not too far behind are Henry's *Culture Against Man*, Cusick's *Inside High School*, and Paul Willis's recent book on working-class youth.[7] None of these studies used random samples, structured questionnaires, or tested the null hypothesis. All are case studies, and all still survive as excellent commentaries of student life in schools and the place of schools in the larger social order. In the meantime, the greatest number of studies that have followed the canons of positivism have fallen by the wayside, respected in their time for their methodological rigor but soon forgotten because of how little they said about so many. The accuracy of this study and the import of its conclusions, then, will have to be assessed by its readers, should they teach junior high school in rural North Dakota or urban San Francisco, should they be the parent of a junior high student (as I am), or should they teach about learning and/or adolescence on a college campus. To the degree that I have accurately represented the lives of the students at Spencer to those audiences and to the extent that my analysis of the meaning and purpose of the junior high school may lead to a reappraisal of that institution, then the study accomplishes its purpose.

Notes

Series editor's preface

1 Samuel Bowles and Herbert Gintis, *Schooling in Capitalist America* (New York: Basic Books, 1976).
2 See Michael W. Apple, *Education and Power* (Boston: Routledge & Kegan Paul, 1982).
3 This is discussed in much greater detail in Michael W. Apple (ed.), *Cultural and Economic Reproduction in Education* (Boston: Routledge & Kegan Paul, 1982).
4 Paul Willis, *Learning to Labour* (Westmead: Saxon House 1977).
5 See Philip Wexler, 'Structure, Text and Subject,' in Apple (ed.), *Cultural and Economic Reproduction in Education*, op. cit., pp. 275–303.
6 Goran Therborn, *The Ideology of Power and the Power of Ideology* (London: New Left Books, Verso Edition, 1980), p. viii.
7 Richard Johnson, 'Three Problematics: Elements of a Theory of Working-Class Culture,' in John Clarke, Chas Critcher, and Richard Johnson (eds), *Working Class Culture* (London: Hutchinson, 1979), p. 234.
8 Apple, *Education and Power*, op. cit., p. 25.
9 Paul Willis, 'Structures and Forms in Cultures of Resistance in the School,' Unit Thirty for Open University Course 'Popular Culture,' unpublished third draft, December 1981, p. 11.
10 Willis, *Learning to Labour*, op. cit.
11 Willis, 'Structures and Forms in Cultures of Resistance in the School,' op. cit., p. 7.
12 Paul Willis, 'Shop-floor Culture, Masculinity and the Wage Form,' in Clarke, Critcher, and Johnson (eds), *Working Class Culture*, op. cit., pp. 185–98.

1 Introduction

1 Leslie W. Kindred, *The Intermediate Schools* (Englewood Cliffs, New Jersey: Prentice-Hall, 1968), p. 24.
2 Nelson L. Bossing and Roscoe V. Cramer, *The Junior High School* (Boston: Houghton Mifflin, 1965), pp. 22–6.
3 Edward L. Thorndike, *The Elimination of Pupils from School*, Bulletin no. 4, US Bureau of Education, Washington, DC, 1907.
4 Leonard P. Ayres, *Laggards in Our Schools* (New York: Russell Sage, 1909).
5 G. Stanley Hall, *Adolescence* (New York: Appleton, 1904), p. xi.
6 William T. Gruhn and H. R. Douglass, *The Modern Junior High School* (New York: Ronald Press, 1971), pp. 61–8.
7 See, for example, Philip Jackson, *Life in Classrooms* (New York: Holt, Rinehart, & Winston, 1968), James S. Coleman, *The Adolescent Society* (New York: The Free Press, 1961), Ray Rist, *The Urban School: Factory for Failure* (Cambridge: MIT Press, 1973), Louis M. Smith and Pat Keith, *Anatomy of Educational Innovation* (New York: John Wiley, 1971).
8 The one exception to this is John Lounsbury and Jean Marani, *The Junior High School We Saw: One Day in the Eighth Grade* (Washington: ASCD, 1964). This study, as the title suggests, involved one day in the life of a sample of eighth-graders and was very heavily oriented toward instructional activities.
9 Joan Lipsitz, *Growing Up Forgotten* (Lexington: D. C. Heath, 1977), p. 10. See also Chad Gordon, 'Social Characteristics of Early Adolescents,' in Jerome Kagan and Robert Cole's, *12 to 16: Early Adolescence* (New York: W. W. Norton, 1972). A recent book that recognizes the importance of the emerging 'middle' years is Mauritz Johnson (ed.), *Toward Adolescence: The Middle School Years* (University of Chicago Press, 1980).
10 Jackson, op. cit.
11 Ibid.
12 Ibid.
13 C. Wayne Gordon, *The Social System of the High School* (Chicago: The Free Press, 1957).
14 Coleman, op. cit.
15 Willard Waller, *The Sociology of Teaching* (New York: John Wiley, 1965).
16 Philip Cusick, *Inside High School* (New York: Holt, Rinehart, & Winston, 1972).
17 Paul Willis, *Learning to Labour* (Westmead: Saxon House, 1977).
18 Ralph Larkin, *Suburban Youth in Cultural Crisis* (New York: Oxford, 1979).
19 This argument in its quintessential and best-known form is Marx's, found in his *Thesus on Feuerbach*. See also Raymond Williams, *Marxism and Literature* (Oxford University Press, 1977) for a clearer discussion of the Marxist perspective of culture.

20 Peter Berger and Thomas Luckmann, *The Social Construction of Reality* (Garden City: Doubleday, 1967), p. 3.
21 Karl Marx, *Capital*, vol. 3 (New York: Random House, 1977), p. 800.
22 Michael Taussig, *The Devil and Commodity Fetishism in South America* (Chapel Hill: University of North Carolina Press, 1980).
23 See, for example, Richard Edwards, *Contested Terrain* (New York: Harper & Row, 1979), Michael Burawoy, *Manufacturing Consent: Changes in the Labor Process Under Monopoly Capitalism* (University of Chicago Press, 1979).
24 Karl Marx, *Capital*, vol. 1 (New York: Random House, 1977), pp. 38–9.
25 A more extended discussion of methodology is found in Appendix B.

2 The community and the school

1 E. P. Thompson, *The Making of the English Working Class* (New York: Random House, 1963), p. 9.
2 Paul Willis, *Learning to Labour* (Westmead: Saxon House, 1977). For an excellent discussion of distinctions between the British and American 'working class,' see David Hogan, 'Education and Class Formation: The Peculiarities of the Americans', in Michael W. Apple (ed.), *Cultural and Economic Reproduction in Education* (London: Routledge & Kegan Paul, 1982), pp. 32–78.
3 A comprehensive analysis of the elements of working-class culture can be found in Richard Johnson, 'Three Problematics: Elements of a Theory of Working Class Culture,' in John Clarke, Chas Critcher and Richard Johnson (eds), *Working Class Culture* (London: Hutchinson, 1979), pp. 201–37.
4 Harry Braverman, *Labor and Monopoly Capital* (New York: Monthly Review Press, 1974), p. 25.

3 The classroom world

1 For additional perspectives on time in classrooms, see for example Philip Jackson's *Life in Classrooms* (New York: Holt, Rinehart, & Winston, 1968), Jules Henry's *Culture Against Man* (New York: Random House, 1963), and Philip Cusick's *Inside High School* (New York: Holt, Rinehart, & Winston, 1972).
2 On the basis of being with Don, Chris, John, and others throughout the two years, I was able to estimate that at least ten minutes of each class period were consumed by these more informal elements of time and its management. This, of course, is an average; during some days pacing and management activities were more frequent while there was little apparent time management on other days. This ten-minute estimate does not include the first and last five minutes of every class, previously discussed.

3 Philip Jackson, 'Reading and School Life,' in Malcolm P. Douglas (ed.), *Claremont Reading Conference: 34th Yearbook* (Claremont: Claremont Graduate School, 1970). Philip Jackson once commented that it seemed paradoxical that learning to read, a process that occurred as much informally and during times spurred by the exigencies of the moment, was a process rigidified and geared around the organizational maintenance activities of the school.

4 Waller described this most aptly when he said 'a second and more universal conflict between students and teachers arises from the fact that teachers are adults and students are not, so the teachers are the bearers of the culture of the society of adults and try to impose that culture upon students, whereas students represent the indigenous culture of the group of children.' Willard Waller, *The Sociology of Teaching* (New York: John Wiley, 1965), p. 104.

5 See James S. Coleman, *The Adolescent Society* (New York: The Free Press), and Philip Cusick, *Inside High School* (New York: Holt, Rinehart, & Winston).

6 Herbert Gintis and Samuel Bowles, *Schooling in Capitalist America* (New York: Basic Books, 1976), p. 39.

4 The world of Don's group

1 It may be useful here to discuss the nature of a 'group' as I have used the term, since the word may raise certain preconceived notions. Most of the studies of adolescents have been done at the high school level (Cusick, Gordon, Coleman, and Hollingshead) and even there they have been done with seniors in high school. These studies have pointed out the importance of peer groups within the social structure of the high school and have shown the groups to be pervasive and assumedly enduring. Hollingshead, Gordon, and Coleman talk about the gross level groupings of students, both as influenced by interest and values and the persistent influence of socioeconomic variables. Cusick refined this notion when he described the myriad of groupings that exist within the high school and pointed out that student groups are not so much large-scale differentiations as much as they are a constellation of smaller dyads and triads revolving around particular key perspectives. These studies all share the common focus on the groups as somewhat closed and permanent, staying essentially the same in membership over time.

This does not seem to be the case at the junior high level. It is true that students are very group conscious and that the constellation of smaller groups of students are as evident as at the senior high level. Yet, as Chapter 4 will point out, the groups were much more transitory at Harold Spencer than they were reported to be in the studies of the senior high school. Group membership was more subject to change over time as new constellations were often formed between the seventh and eighth grade. This was not something that was particularly noticeable on a day-to-day basis, but over the course of two years it became quite apparent that group allegiances were slowly shifting and altering, depending upon a set of important considerations. Some of these considerations were as simple as the class schedule of the student which placed him into contact with a different array of students. Yet, this is true at the senior high level, too, although I imagine that by this time the student's interests and perspectives have developed sufficiently (and rigidly) enough for vagaries to be overcome. While the dynamics of the group are of prime importance at the junior and senior high level, it is important to add, at the junior high level, the *dynamics of grouping* (or the process of group formation) as an important consideration when discussing what junior high students do. This should become more apparent as the narrative within this chapter continues. For purposes here, then, the term 'group' refers to a cluster of students who acknowledged close interaction based upon common interests and perspectives.

2 The program had originated in California; in fact, two of the district administrators had traveled there that year to see it in operation. Since this was a new program, and since Dave had been one of the earliest persons to be honored to go through it, his experiences generated considerable offtime conversation for a few days.

3 These were the situations that I always wanted to avoid. Breaking up fights could mark me as an adult with certain authority, and thus jeopardize my relationship with the students.

4 Two studies to which I will refer in more detail later bear out the manner by which regeneration systems 'take over' finally and completely by the time students have reached high school. See Philip Cusick, *Inside High School* (Holt, Rinehart, & Winston, 1973) and Paul Willis, *Learning to Learn* (Westmead: Saxon House, 1977).

5 Willis, *Learning to Labour* (Westmead: Saxon House, 1977), p. 128.

5 The world of Chris's group

1 Of the boys who were members of this group over the two years of the study, only one, Marty, had a GPA (Grade Point Average) below 3.0 (his was 2.74.) The remainder of the principals described in this chapter maintained cumulative GPA's of between 3.2 and 3.7.

6 'What did you *do* in English today?' 'Nothing, just goofed off'

1 Karl Marx, 'Economic and Philosophical Manuscripts of 1844,' in Karl Marx and Friedrich Engels, *Collected Works* (London: Lawrence & Wishart, 1975), p. 259.

7 Student 'power'

1 Some students, especially girls, regularly complained to teachers that they were not able to use the rest-rooms facilities because smokers would not let them in the stalls. Such complaints, when aired at faculty meetings, usually prompted increased teachers' surveillance of the cans.

2 The overdomination of regenerative knowledge among working-class boys prepares them, some argue, for class-based positions as manual laborers. See Paul Willis, *Learning to Labour* (Westmead: Saxon House, 1977), Chapter 5.

3 This is manifested in the industrial sabotage of Lordstown in the late 1960s. Perhaps most illustrative is the fact that upwards of 80 per cent of Americans would not work in the same job if they could make the choice again. See James O'Toole *et al.*, *Work in America* (Cambridge, Mass.: MIT, 1973).

4 Karl Marx, *Economic and Philosophical Manuscripts of 1844*, in Robert Tucker (ed.), *The Marx-Engels Reader* (New York: W. W. Norton, 1978), pp. 78–9.

8 Summary and conclusions

1 W. W. Charters, Jr, 'Social Psychology and Education,' *American Educational Research Journal*, vol. 10 (Winter, 1973), p. 77.

2 Some of the points made herein are also elaborated in Philip Cusick, *Inside High School* (New York: Holt, Rinehart, & Winston, 1973), Chapter 8.

3 I had a few teachers read drafts of this monograph to check it for accuracy. Most at first were surprised at the indication of such large amounts of time being used for maintenance activities, but all confirmed the accuracy of my figures.

4 Habermas's works are many, but most of the discussion herein is drawn from his *Knowledge and Human Interests* (Boston: Beacon Press, 1971).

5 Robert Dreeben, *On What Is Learned in School* (Reading, Mass.: Addison-Wesley, 1968).

6 Yehudi Cohen, 'The Shaping of Men's Minds,' in Murray Wax, Stanley Diamond, and Fred O. Gearing (eds), *Anthropological Perspectives on Education* (New York: Basic Books, 1971), pp. 19–50.

7 Joseph W. Licata and Donald J. Willower, 'Student Brinkmanship and the School as a Social System,' *Educational Administration Quarterly*, vol. II (Spring, 1975), pp. 1–14.

8 Karl Marx, *Economic and Philosophical Manuscripts of 1844*, in Robert Tucker (ed.), *The Marx-Engels Reader* (New York: W. W. Norton, 1978), p. 75.

9 Willard Waller, *The Sociology of Teaching* (New York: John Wiley, 1965), p. 297.

10 Philip Slater, *The Pursuit of Loneliness* (Boston: Beacon Press, 1970).

11 Marx felt that labor was the focus for understanding man, and any society could be examined on the basis of how it 'has developed its productive forces, the division of labor, and internal intercourse.' Karl Marx and Frederick Engels, *The German Ideology* as quoted in Jerrold Seigel, *Marx's Fate* (Princeton: Princeton University Press, 1978), p. 173.
12 For further information on teachers' interpretation of test scores, see Kenneth C. W. Leiter, 'Teachers' Use of Background Knowledge to Interpret Test Scores,' *Sociology of Education*, vol. 49 (January, 1976), pp. 50–65.
13 See Joel Spring, *Education and the Rise of the Corporate State* (Boston: Beacon Press, 1972), Chapter 5.
14 Jules Henry, *Culture Against Man* (New York: Random House, 1963), p. 292.
15 See Quinton Hoare and Geoffrey Powell-Smith (eds), *Selections from the Prison Notebooks of Antonio Gramsci* (London: Lawrence & Wishart, 1971) and Raymond Williams, *Marxism and Literature* (Oxford: Oxford University Press, 1977).
16 Karl Marx, *Capital*, vol. 1, Section 2.
17 See Basil Bernstein, 'Social Class, Language, and Socialization,' in Jerome Karabel and A. H. Halsey (eds), *Power and Ideology in Education* (New York: Oxford University Press, 1977), pp. 473–486, Pierre Bourdieu and Jean-Claude Passeron, *Reproduction in Education, Society, and Culture* (Beverly Hills, Calif.: Sage, 1977).
18 Raymond Williams, *Marxism and Literature* (Oxford: Oxford University Press, 1977), p. 112.
19 Joseph Kett, *Rites of Passage* (New York: Basic Books, 1977), p. 171.
20 The evidence surrounding economic factors that defined adolescence as a concept is most convincingly presented in Frank Musgrove, *Youth and the Social Order* (Bloomington, Ind.: University of Indiana Press, 1964) and Selwyn Troen, 'The Discovery of the Adolescent by American Educational Reformers, 1900–1920,' in Lawrence Stone (ed.), *Schooling and Society* (Baltimore, Md: Johns Hopkins University Press, 1976), pp. 239–51.
21 See, for example, David Nasaw, *Schooled to Order* (New York: Oxford University Press, 1979). For a discussion on the impact of such experts on the structure of families, see Christopher Lasch, *Haven in a Heartless World* (New York: Basic Books, 1977).
22 See Michael B. Katz, *Class Bureaucracy and Schools* (New York: Praeger, 1971).
23 Kett, op. cit., p. 243.
24 Philippe Aries, *Centuries of Childhood* (New York: Random House, 1962).
25 See John Gillis, *Youth and History* (New York: Academic Press, 1974), Kett, op. cit., and Frank Musgrove, *Youth and the Social Order* (Bloomington, Ind.: University of Indiana Press, 1964).
26 Margaret Mead, *Coming of Age in Samoa* (New York: William Morrow, 1928), p. 233.

Appendix A Lesson plans

1 Clyde Kluckholn, *Mirror for Man* (New York: Whittlesey House, 1949).
2 Willard Waller, *The Sociology of Teaching* (New York: John Wiley, 1965), p. 104.

Appendix B Methodology

1 Herbert Blumer, 'Society as Symbolic Interaction,' in Arnold Rose (ed.), *Human Behavior and Social Processes* (New York: Houghton Mifflin, 1962), p. 187.
2 Rachel Sharp and Anthony Green, *Education and Social Control: A Study in Progressive Primary Education* (London: Routledge & Kegan Paul, 1975), p. 22.
3 Blumer, op. cit., p. 188.
4 See Wayne Doyle et al., *The Birth, Nurturance, and Transformation of an Educational Reform* (Portland, Oreg.: Northwest Regional Educational Laboratory, 1976).
5 Seymour B. Sarason, *The Culture of the School and the Problem of Change* (Boston: Allyn & Bacon, 1971), p. 48.
6 The best example of the methodology involved is found in James Spradley, 'Adaptive Strategies of Urban Nomads,' in James P. Spradley (ed.), *Culture and Cognition: Rules, Maps and Plans* (San Francisco: Chandler, 1972), pp. 235–62. See also Spradley, *The Ethnographic Interview* (New York: Holt, Rinehart, & Winston, 1980).
7 Willard Waller, *The Sociology of Teaching* (New York: John Wiley, 1965), Jules Henry, *Culture Against Man* (New York: Random House, 1963), Philip Cusick, *Inside High School* (New York: Holt, Rinehart, & Winston, 1972), Paul Willis, *Learning to Labour* (Westmead: Saxon House, 1977).

Name index

Subject index

Entries in italics refer to figures